LET THEM EAT JUNK

Let Them Eat Junk

How Capitalism Creates Hunger and Obesity

Robert Albritton

PLUTO PRESS
www.plutobooks.com

First published 2009 by Pluto Press
345 Archway Road, London N6 5AA and
175 5th Avenue, New York, NY 10010

Distributed in the United States of America exclusively by
Palgrave Macmillan, a division of St. Martin's Press LLC,
175 Fifth Avenue, New York, NY 10010.

www.plutobooks.com

British Library Cataloguing in Publication Data
A catalogue record for this book is available from the British Library

ISBN 978 0 7453 2807 2 Hardback
ISBN 978 0 7453 2806 5 Paperback

Library of Congress Cataloging in Publication Data applied for

This book is printed on paper suitable for recycling and made from fully managed and
sustained forest sources. Logging, pulping and manufacturing processes are expected to
conform to the environmental standards of the country of origin. The paper may contain up
to 70% post consumer waste.

10 9 8 7 6 5 4 3 2 1

Designed and produced for Pluto Press by
Curran Publishing Services, Norwich
Printed and bound in the European Union by
CPI Antony Rowe, Chippenham and Eastbourne, England

Contents

Preface

On December 17, 2007 the United Nations Food and Agricultural Organization (FAO) announced at a press conference in Rome that 37 countries were in a food crisis requiring "urgent steps to protect the poor from soaring food prices."[1] One of the leading international business magazines, the *Economist*, published only minimal coverage of this crisis until its April 19, 2008 issue (four months later). Printed on the cover of this issue were the words "The Silent Tsunami: the food crisis and how to solve it."[2] Prior to this coverage, "a perfect storm" was the preferred metaphor of the business press. The "silent tsunami" metaphor appeared after food uprisings (silent?) had occurred in over 30 countries with millions of people around the world facing hunger and starvation.

Metaphors such as "storm" and "tsunami" are used to frame the food crisis for us, and suggest that we respond as we would to a more or less unpredictable natural event. "Perfect storm" is particularly appealing to the business press, because it implies a large number of causes, which suddenly and totally unpredictably come together in a way that multiplies the force of each into a very rare gigantic storm. Similarly, these metaphors suggest a response of humanitarian aid to the victims of a natural disaster, for which no one can be held responsible.

The starvation "tsunami" is not the fault of particular individuals, corporations or governments, nor is it an act of nature, but rather, the fundamental deep causes of the current global food crisis stem from the capitalist agricultural/food system that developed primarily in the United States after World War II and has now spread to varying degrees around the world. I shall make the case that the most important causes can be traced to the dynamics of capitalism, and that the long-term solutions lie in altering those dynamics.

There is a widespread assumption in the world that capitalism and democracy are mutually supporting. One aim of this book is to expose the shallowness of this assumption. Capitalism is only supportive of democracy to a limited extent, for democracy requires a high level of equality, while capitalism generates inequality. To an extent capitalism has supported individual rights, which can be important dimensions of democracy; however, if inequality leaves large numbers in dire need, these rights can be weakened to the point of being almost meaningless. Thus free speech is terribly important, but it can be undermined when inequality creates a situation where de facto it is almost entirely the voices of small elites that are heard. For this reason, the emphasis on individual rights needs to be balanced by an emphasis on social rights and responsibilities that arise from a sense of social connectedness and generosity.

In our current world, capitalism has generated such extreme and indefensible inequality that claims made by governments to be democratic increasingly ring hollow. For example, a global food system that has the means to feed everyone in the world, instead leaves half the people in the world struggling with health-destroying malnutrition (25 percent are underfed and 25 percent are overfed).[3] If, as many have asserted, we have the arable land and technical capacity to provide a diet of high quality for every woman, man and child in the world, then in principle there is no excuse for the current global famine.[4] Further, if the food crisis is something that continues to happen because we lack the will to make the changes that would prevent it, then I shall argue that far from being a "perfect storm" before which we are helpless, it is much more like a "massacre" that we allow to happen.

I don't want to give the impression that this book is only about the current global famine. Rather it is about the irrationalities and contradictions in the capitalistic management of agriculture and food provision, of which the current global famine is one of many disturbing manifestations. Other manifestations include:

- a petroleum-intensive food system in an age of global warming and petroleum tipping points

- the extensive use of arable land for producing ethanol and other non-food crops rather than food
- the low incomes for most workers and farmers throughout the food chains
- the pollution of land, air and water
- the rapid depletion of fresh water sources
- the widespread marketing of junk food
- the "obesity epidemic" largely fuelled by junk foods
- deforestation which is undermining the future of life on earth
- the enormous dangers posed by genetically modified foods (GMOs)
- the cruel treatment of animals in massive confined animal feeding operations (CAFOs)
- the corruption of public life by gigantic food and/or agricultural corporations
- last but not least, food of insufficient quantity or poor quality for at least 3 billion people.[5]

While over 1 billion people around the world face daily hunger, the Canadian government announced a plan to pay hog farmers up to C$50 million[6] to destroy as many as 150,000 breeding swine in order to reduce the glut of pork on the market, which had caused prices to plunge 20 percent in the past year. Can we really afford a food regime that destroys food in one part of the world in order to keep prices up, while high prices in other parts of the world are producing hunger and starvation? Does it make sense to leave a basic necessity like food to capricious market prices that make food affordable at one place and time and not affordable in the next?

Whether or not we can afford our current food regime, we are stuck with it for the time being. Indeed the food regime is embedded in an economic system that has enormous inertia, such that the dominant corporate powers in the world and the governments that largely do their bidding, can at most be expected to go through the motions of showing concern and taking small steps to deal with urgent problems that require much larger steps. For example, although we cannot predict with any accuracy the precise unfolding of global warming, to play it safe, a rational government would act as though we have ten years to turn things around substantially, since this is the time line suggested by over 200 top scientists studying the problem.[7] Instead, we witness the "Group of Eight" at their July 2008 meeting in Hokkaido, Japan committing to decrease greenhouse gas emissions 50 percent by 2050. This could easily mean that for now we need do little. We can leave it to the next generation. After all by 2050, most of the currently active politicians will be dead. Indeed, it is extremely likely that even if the Group of Eight goal is achieved by 2050, it will be too little, too late.

There are movements for change all over the world – some small and some large – trying to alter the food system, and the economic system that shapes it, into one that is more sustainable, healthful and just. Some will partially or even wholly succeed, even though they may be acting against the central imperatives of our capitalist system. In other words, these movements are often acting against an extremely resistant system, and the larger the changes required, the larger and more organized movements will need to be in order to succeed. It is important to be realistic about the difficulties in making significant changes, but realism should also not become a reason for inaction or hopelessness,[8] for we live in a world where transformations have become both a real possibility and a desperate need.

It is my view that the general long-term goal is to increase democracy by finding ways to make economic and political institutions more accountable to the public. The two most important economic institutions requiring democratization are corporations and markets. This claim will surprise those who think that they are already democratic. But how can corporations be considered democratic when their inner workings are not open to the public and when their aim is to maximize short-term profits for a small elite of mostly wealthy stockholders? And how can markets be considered democratic when immense social costs are excluded from market prices and are simply thrown into the black box of "externalities"? In order to be held democratically accountable, corporations need to become transparent in all their dealings – a transparency that will only become possible when corporations are no longer defined in law as "private" legal persons. Markets can be made more democratic and responsive through public interventions that bring market prices more into line with real social costs and benefits from the point of view of the long-term welfare of humankind as a whole, and through a redistribution of wealth that brings demand closer to social need. At the same time, if we are to deal effectively with truly global problems, we need to consider ways of creating more accountable and authoritative political institutions at all levels, but particularly at a global level. Currently, our global policy-making institutions are woefully inadequate when it comes to addressing the global problems that we face. Arguably competitive nation-states have largely become obstacles rather than vehicles for dealing with global problems.

We live in an age of fear, of powerful interests that spread misinformation, and of forms of consumerism that deflect the citizenry away from politics. The prevailing fear, mis-information and anti-political attitudes have inclined many to write and speak with enormous caution. Of course, when making truth-claims, a certain caution is prudent and wise. Yet when we are arguing for a point of view, as I am, we need to be as clear and forceful as possible. It is through the clash of well-argued points of view that we arrive at a degree of reason. Rational action depends on this. We must not let ourselves be swept away by "silent tsunamis" that in reality are neither silent nor tsunamis.

Robert Albritton
September 2008

PART I

INTRODUCTION

1 INTRODUCTION

... the very basis for life on earth is declining at an alarming rate.[1]

... the entire spirit of capitalist production, which is oriented towards the most immediate profit, stands in contradiction to agriculture, which has to concern itself with the whole gamut of permanent conditions of life required by the chain of human generations.[2]

Around the world, farmers and farm workers are dying, with the connivance of elected officials, and at the whim of the market. Through processed food, consumers are engorged and intoxicated. The agribusiness's food and marketing have contributed to record levels of diet-related disease, harming us today and planting a time-bomb in the bodies of children around the world .... Most of this happens with consumers ignorant of the suffering that precedes every mouthful of food.[3]

On being told that her people had no bread, Marie Antoinette (1755–1793), the soon-to-be beheaded Queen of France, purportedly remarked, "Let them eat cake." Such a callous indifference to the hunger of masses of people speaks volumes about why the French Revolution occurred. Today, the place of Marie Antoinette is taken by giant food corporations and the governments they influence, who, having learned from Marie Antoinette, would never say "Let them eat junk," but who, in the face of massive global malnourishment (one half of the global population is overfed, underfed or badly fed), simply continue to aggressively spread their radically unsustainable systems of agricultural production around the world, topped off as it were with "junk food" high in additives, sugars, fats and salts but low in nutrients. While this junk food is often relatively cheap, even its prices are rising with the diversion of large amounts of corn and soy into ethanol production, particularly since the US government has made the decision to feed the bottomless appetites of US sports utility vehicles (SUVs) rather than the hungry people of the world.[4]

GENERAL INTRODUCTION

Today we have a truly disturbing situation, with parts of the world having so much food they do not know what to do with it, while nearly half the people in the world suffer malnutrition.[5] Approximately 1 billion people suffer almost continual and acute hunger globally.[6] What is most disturbing, however, is that we are on the brink of a far more massive global starvation because of skyrocketing food prices around the world. And this is only the beginning. Imagine what such rising food prices mean to the 40 percent of the world's population who try to survive on $2 or less per day.[7]

"Let them eat junk" captures some of the indifference to global hunger, and it also highlights the existence of "junk foods" which emerged most dramatically after World War II, as a product of the capitalist food regime. "Junk food" is, of course, a colloquialism, but it is one that can be given a very precise meaning. It is food that is extremely high in sugars, fats and salts, or what are often called "empty calories". Of course, the "junkiness" of foods is a matter of degree. Some soft drinks contain only calories from sugar and no other nutrients (the epitome of "empty calories"), whereas a double bacon cheeseburger deluxe, though containing lots of saturated fats, cholesterol, salt and calories, would typically also contain a considerable array of nutrients. Thus if the cheeseburger is classified as junk food, it is not because it contains no nutrients, rather it is because the nutrients are overshadowed by the large number of unhealthy fat calories and high levels of salt. As a result, there is a grey area where people will disagree about whether a particular food item should be classified as "junk" or not, and no doubt it would be possible to construct a "junkiness index". In any case, the basic point is that eating too much junk food or food high on the junkiness index can make us obese, and because junk food lacks the nutrients that humans need, a diet of junk food can make us more vulnerable to disease.

"Junk" in its most common meaning refers to things that are worthless and should be thrown away. In the case of junk food, if the choice is between eating it frequently or throwing it away, the latter seems preferable assuming one has other sources of food. The problem is that globally close to 1 billion people do not have enough food of any kind to eat. They suffer the pangs of hunger much of the time. While hungry people are spread across the globe in both rich and poor countries, it is in the countries that have suffered the worst effects of colonialism that hunger is most often the greatest. The phrase "Let them eat junk" would be most cruel with regard to people who are hungry and starving much of the time. It is also cruel towards the working classes of advanced capitalist countries, who are lured by advertising, cheapness, convenience and the quasi-addictive quality of much junk food, to eat without consuming nutritious food.[8] An emptiness of nutrients hollows out the health prospects of the working class. And in the case of food production, field workers and poor farmers in the United States are often reduced to life at the tipping point of the barest survival. In 2005 there were 35.1 million hungry people in the United States,[9] and it is predicted that largely because of diet, children born in the United States today will on average live five fewer years than their parents.[10]

"*Après moi le deluge!* is the watchword of every capitalist and of every capitalist nation."[11] When Marx first wrote this sometime in the 1860s, he had no idea that his rhetorical flourish might some day become all too accurate. For Americans live in an age when governing bodies at all levels, ever-pressured by corporations to allow them to maximize short-term profits, are severely constrained in their policy options. Politicians are so tuned to the needs of corporations that they seem unable to act in any decisive ways in the face of the truly catastrophic consequences of global warming just around the corner of the future. We have known about global warming for over 20 years, and at least in the United States, corporations have so far largely paralyzed government into the most limited of responses. With every year that passes scientists are discovering that the indices that measure the rate of global warming are increasing at a faster rate than previously thought, and yet, given the enormity of the problem, little is being done in the United States and many other countries to effectively counter it.[12]

David Pimentel, an agricultural researcher at Cornell University, has estimated that if the whole world adopted the American agricultural/food system, all known sources of fossil fuel would be exhausted in seven years.[13] In other words, the mechanization, chemicalization, global sourcing and high degree of processing of the American food regime has made it very dependent on petrochemicals. This poses four challenging problems for the future:

- As we run out of oil, its cost will soar and with it the price of food.
- The world's agricultural/food system contributes approximately 33 percent to carbon dioxide emissions and 14 percent to non-carbon dioxide greenhouse gas emissions (methane and nitrous oxide).[14]
- If we do not stem the tide of climate change, agriculture itself will be adversely affected to the point that it may become very difficult to provide a good diet for the world.[15]
- If we use agrarian land to grow ethanol crops, both global warming and global starvation will be seriously exacerbated.[16]

Junk food epitomizes the current phase of capitalism which utilizes enormous amounts of energy without advancing the human flourishing of the vast majority of people in the world.[17] The production of junk food takes large amounts of energy, but the energy that humans get from junk food is poor in nutrients relative to other foods like whole grains, fruits and vegetables. It is for this reason that junk food is said to be food that is high in "empty calories". In a parallel fashion, we can say that "junk" capitalism is the empty expenditure of huge amounts of energy for things like permanent war, commodities that undermine human and environmental health, labour processes that damage and exploit workers, security that increases insecurity, or in other words, an expenditure of energy that is relatively empty when it comes to advancing human flourishing.

Thus the criticisms that I shall make of a food regime that so prominently produces, circulates and markets junk food, will in many respects epitomize the irrationalities of late capitalism as a whole. Our increasingly globalized capitalist economy is using more and more energy to run faster and faster, while actually losing ground when it comes to advancing human well-being. In this book, I shall argue that the principal reason for this is that the short-term profit orientation that is central to capitalism cannot deal effectively with the world historic problems that we face. We need to slow down the mindless frenzy of capital accumulation, and we need to think deeply and act radically. Minor reforms of business-as-usual are better than nothing, but in the long run will not solve the problems we face. Indeed, we may not have a "long run" left to solve problems like global warming and global hunger.

When I refer to the food system or food regime, I mean to include the whole cluster of activities and processes in provisioning us with food, from growing crops to sitting down for dinner. If this cluster of processes is referred to as the "food regime", then arguably it is this regime that is the most basic to the advancement of global human flourishing. A basic condition of all human flourishing is that individuals be able to access food of good quality and sufficient quantity, produced in ways that minimally do not diminish the ecology of the earth, and ideally might even increase its environmental integrity for the sake of future generations. In this sense, our very identities and our life possibilities are rooted in what we eat and drink. Further, the most basic divisions of labour in social life have arisen from either human reproduction or the provisioning of food, and women have typically played a central role in both. It is no accident that the word "companion" originally referred to a person with whom one shared bread (com = with, pane = bread). The provisioning of food, then, is a basic constructor of both differentiations and integrations amongst social relations. Recent scientific research has demonstrated how good nutrition is *absolutely fundamental* to human health, and how sustainable agricultural practices are *absolutely fundamental* to environmental health.[18]

The provisioning of food, then, is the fundamental connector between social relations and the earth, where humans acting through social relations utilize the forces of nature in an attempt to provision themselves better and with less effort. The key here is learning how to utilize the forces of nature in ways that are sustainable or ecologically benign, for when we carefully examine the past, we find that the unsustainability of a civilization's system of food provision often played a key role in its decline.

The processes that make up the food provisioning system may involve hunting, gathering, agriculture, aquaculture, fishing or animal husbandry. They all utilize or extract from either the land or water that covers the earth's surface, and in doing so have at least the potential to damage them, up to and including damage from which it may be very difficult to recover (for example desertification or the destruction of fish stocks). Except for wild animals and fish, nearly all our food depends on agriculture. Agriculture also includes at least some very important non-food crops such as cotton and tobacco. They cannot be completely ignored in a book on food, because they utilize fertile land that could in principle be made available for producing food. Agriculture depends on soil fertility, the weather, the availability of water, the availability of seeds, the availability of labour, and sometimes on various mechanical and/or chemical inputs. While agriculture provides most of the feed for meat production, the meat industry has enough of its own particular social costs to warrant separate treatment. Similarly, the beverage industry requires separate treatment though many of its inputs also come from agriculture.[19]

Besides agriculture, food provision depends on transportation, storage, processing, packaging, marketing, advertising, inspection, retailing, cooking and serving. At every step there are material and energy inputs as well as labour inputs. We shall see later that despite the fundamental importance of food provisioning to human flourishing, workers in this sector tend to be among the lowest paid and the most poorly treated.[20] They also disproportionately and not accidentally tend to be women, and in some cases children.

An important argument of this book is that capitalism has never effectively managed food provision, and this is because capital's concern for sheer quantity in the form of profits causes it to neglect the concern for qualitative dimensions of life that are so important to food provision. I shall point out that much food provision in

American history was from family farms, in other words from non-capitalist units of production.[21] Indeed, arguably it was the relatively non-capitalist character of food provision that made it as effective as it was.[22] Since World War II, the American agrarian sector has become more and more capitalist, and, at the same time the long-term social and environmental costs associated with food provision have shot up alarmingly. Paradoxically, government intervention in the agrarian sector has played an important role in speeding up its conversion to capitalist relations of production with their increasingly destructive spin-offs. I say "paradoxically" because strictly speaking government intervention is inconsistent with current neo-liberal ideals of "free enterprise".

We have increasingly good knowledge about what is good for human health and environmental health, and yet there is a huge gap between our knowledge and policy, precisely because policy change is tightly constrained by the interests of giant corporations. Further, while capitalism has never effectively advanced distributive justice, we have arrived at a point in history when inequality has reached truly horrendous proportions.[23] While many people are aware of this, it seems to take enormous effort to make even small gains against capital's overriding dynamic which tends to increase inequality.[24] It seems that all the dominant pressures that are currently pushing capitalism result in making the rich much richer and the poor poorer, both relatively and in many cases absolutely.[25]

Often when social costs are seen as particularly high, popular movements fight for legislation which will in some ways constrain or limit the damages associated with commodities or services seen to be causal factors of the damages. Typically the corporations that produce those commodities fight back. The paradigm case that provides a model for all corporations under this sort of attack is the cigarette industry.[26] According to Allan Brandt, professor in the Department of the History of Science at Harvard University, the US tobacco corporations were so powerful and skilful that they managed to compromise the judiciary, Congress, the media and even science in order to engineer the most effective damage control operations ever seen.[27] While this industry managed to hold off efforts to control it for many years, eventually a variety of campaigns and controls managed to reduce the rate of cigarette smoking by over 50 percent in the United States. And yet the marketing efforts of this industry are alive and well as it recruits up to 100,000 new smokers a day (mostly youth and mostly in developing countries where controls are weak).[28] Indeed, the behaviour of tobacco corporations is rational from the point of view of capitalism. All they are doing is following the basic imperative of capitalism to maximize profits.

I hope to demonstrate that our current capitalist food regime generates unacceptable social costs, the containment of which will require the development of much greater democratic controls over corporations and markets. In order to be as convincing as possible, I shall try to avoid the reductionism that is all too common when social scientists try to apply abstract theory directly to history. In my approach I shall pursue the difficult goal of developing connections between the abstract and concrete, understood as three distinct levels of theory that are interrelated.

At the most abstract level of analysis I shall draw primarily from Marx. This name may set off some reader's alarm bells because it has been demonized to such an extent that anyone interested in an academic career had best not focus much attention on his writings unless it is to criticize them. Marx's name has been associated with the former Soviet Union even though he had very little to say about communism other than to insist that any regime deserving to be called "communist" would have to be far more democratic than any capitalist liberal-democracy.[29] Marx himself felt that his most important theoretical contribution was the three volumes of *Capital*. In other words, while he had little to say about communism, he had a great deal to say about how capitalism works. Arguably, his writings on capital shed more light on the basic workings of capitalism than any other before or since.[30]

I have devoted much of my academic career to understanding his theory of capital's basic operating principles in terms that shed light on concrete history without trying to force that history into ill-fitting and rigid conceptual boxes.[31] Following this line of thought, I realized that even to write about consumption in general in the modern world would likely leave me at a level of generality that I would find unsatisfying. It was then that I decided to focus on one kind of consumption, food. At the same time, I was aware, partly from studying Marx, that I could not understand the consumption of food without also understanding its production, and understanding these two required situating them in the larger capitalist system of which they are a part.

The more I thought about it, the more I realized how important the focus on food is:

- Food is the basic necessity of all human life, and not only is food of the right qualities and quantities the basis of physical and mental health, but also health is a key element in the formation of identities.
- The provisioning of food brings human biology into close contact with the biology of the earth such that any system of food provisioning that undermines what should be a mutually supportive relationship between the environment and food provisioning is not sustainable.
- Any system of food provisioning that has the capability of providing all members of society with the nutrients essential to health, but leaves large numbers of people severely lacking in those nutrients, cannot be said to meet the basic criteria of any reasonable theory of distributive justice.
- Marx's basic framework for understanding capitalism, developed with connections to recent history, can help us understand why capitalism cannot effectively manage the agricultural/food system, and why it was not until after World War II that the American food system became substantially capitalist.

A FRAMEWORK FOR UNDERSTANDING CAPITALISM

My reading of Marx draws heavily on the notion of three levels of analysis. The most abstract level reveals capital's basic operating principles. Mid-range theory studies the way in which these principles are manifested most characteristically or typically in different phases of capitalist development. Historical analysis studies capitalism's actual historical processes of change.

At the most abstract level (Chapter 2), rather than attempting any general overview of Marx's theory of "the laws of political economy in their purity",[32] I shall focus on the question: given the basic structure of capital, how would it manage agriculture?[33] Above all I hope to present arguments supporting Marx's claim that "the capitalist system runs counter to a rational agriculture".[34] In other words, I shall argue that capitalism has never effectively managed agriculture because its basic operating principles do not permit it to.

According to Marx, the way capitalism works is basically very simple. In order to carry on a production process, a capitalist must buy all the necessary inputs including things like raw materials, machinery and labour power as commodities in markets. The basic aim of the capitalist is to make a profit by combining these inputs in a production process, the result of which is a new commodity that can be sold for more than the cost of all the inputs. The difference between the input costs and selling price of the produced commodity is the capitalist's profit. Competition insures that capitalists always strive to maximize their profits, such that capital will always gravitate from the less profitable to the more profitable commodities.

The use of the metaphor "invisible hand" in connection with capitalist markets implies that capitalism has its own inner logic. In other words, it has a life of its own that is not concerned with human flourishing, democracy or social justice, but instead is concerned with profits, which may or may not advance ethical norms as spin-offs.

Even though perfected capitalism at the most abstract level of analysis never exists in history, it is important to think about it for a number of reasons:

- While all actually existing capitalist societies are only more or less capitalist, it is important to extrapolate from these cases to reach a theory of the most capitalist society. By clarifying capital's defining features, this theory offers us a clear and precise meaning of "capitalism", such that we can utilize its criteria of identity to sort out the extent to which various societies or various practices are or are not capitalist.

- By understanding capitalism in an abstract context in which, by passing through periodic crises, it can reproduce itself and expand without significant state intervention, we can more clearly understand why in certain circumstances it may need significant state supports.

- By considering a situation where commodification[35] is complete, we can begin to think clearly about the tenuousness of such commodification. "Commodification" refers to the processes whereby products become products of capitalist production processes in order to yield profits by being exchanged for money in capitalist markets. A classic case is the enclosure of commons in England, which increasingly turned the land and labour-power into commodities. Marx makes it particularly clear that the commodification of labour-power, land and money is problematic for capital, such that in any actual historical context state supports would be required.[36]

- While capital has an inner logic, that logic is attenuated at more concrete levels of analysis precisely because it is basically a commodity logic, and where commodification is less than complete, the inner logic becomes less logic-like in its operation.[37]

- By studying capital in the abstract and in general, we can clarify its basic historical directionalities. Since these direction-alities are general, they cannot predict particular historical outcomes; however, they may be useful in helping us to under-stand historical trends. For instance, Marx shows why there is a general tendency for the dominant units of capital to get larger and larger, but by itself this tendency could not predict the rapid merger movement that occurred in the late 19th century or the financial specificities of the current globalization.[38]

Similarly, the abstract theory shows structurally why capital and labour are at odds, but it cannot predict the form that class struggles may take in different contexts. The same can be said about the tendency towards periodic crises.[39]

Chapter 3 takes what we have learned about capital's deep struc-tural dynamics and rethinks those dynamics at the level of mid-range theory where they are partially decommodified and politically supported. My focus is on the type of capital accumulation that is characteristic of post-World War II capitalism. At a mid-range level of analysis, the most important considerations are the dominant form of capital and accompanying technologies, the dominant types of industries or commodities, the characteristic types of state policy and ideology, the international dimensions of capital accumulation and the dominant types of class struggle. Thus it becomes important to think of the ways that the economic and the political intermingle and support each other. It is generally agreed that post-World War II capitalism manifested its most classic forms and "golden age" in the United States from approximately 1946 to 1970, and therefore it is from this spatial and temporal site that I extract the patterns of capital accumulation most characteristic of this phase. While the United States is the most characteristic capital accumulator in this phase of history, at the level of mid-range theory it is important to include the increasing global reach of capitalism.

Mid-range theory puts flesh on the bare bones of the theory of capital's deep structures. It allows us to examine capital's typical range of motions as it acts through phase-specific types of institutions that both constrain and facilitate those motions. Further, middle-level theory is important in order to situate the current food regime within the dominant type of post World War II capital accumulation as a whole. By understanding the dominant type of capital accumulation after World War II, we can better understand the unfolding of history. In particular, by understanding capital accumulation's dynamics when it is operating at its most successful (the so-called "golden age": 1946–70), we can better understand its problems when it evolves away from these dynamics.

The third level of analysis is the level of historical analysis (the focus of Chapters 4–9), and it is shaped and oriented by the two more abstract levels. At this level my focus will be on the evolution of the food regime over the past 20 years. While its primary centre is located in the United States, it has developed global tentacles. Also it is worth mentioning that some of the more advanced social democracies in Europe have found ways to ameliorate some of the worst aspects of the current food regime within the confines of their own countries. However, they have not been able to alter the main global thrusts of this food regime with its radically unjust way of distributing food globally.

Centred mainly in the United States, the existing food regime is becoming increasingly global, though significant local variations exist. My focus will mainly be on its recent developments in the United States and their spread outward mainly to developing countries. At the same time, I shall be aware of the colonial roots that have so influenced the provisioning of many tropical commodities like bananas, tea, coffee, cocoa, tobacco and sugar.

Chapters 4–9 develop a historical analysis of the current food regime. Chapter 4 focuses on how this regime impacts on the health of food consumers in both the United States and the developing world. Chapter 5 deals with the health and welfare of agricultural field workers and farmers in both the United States and developing countries. Chapter 6 examines the environmental impacts of the existing food regime. Chapter 7 analyses consumer choice in the context of aggressive marketing and advertising by food corporations in the United States. Chapter 8 focuses on how the immense power of giant corporations is undermining the ideals of American liberal-democracy. And Chapter 9 presents a brief overview of the types of changes that we might consider in order to deal with the problems outlined in the book.

We must find ways to make corporations more democratically accountable, and to include in their calculations not only short-term profits but also social costs and benefits. For example, in capitalism as it exists, a corporation may contribute to respiratory illness by polluting the air, but it would be irrational for it to install expensive anti-pollution devices if by doing so, its profits would be reduced. Normally under capitalism, it is the taxpayers and consumers who will pay the tab for increased health care costs stemming from air pollution. This is an example of how capitalism privatizes profits and socializes costs. The capitalist imperative to privatize profits and socialize costs becomes particularly problematic when economic activity is generating enormous social costs by running up against the limits of human and environmental health and when it is continually deepening a horrendous inequality.

And the options are not well captured by simply posing them as "markets versus planning". The large corporations that we see today are among some of the largest and most centrally planned economic units to ever exist, and as a consequence of their status as private property and legal persons, the public has only very limited and indirect ways of holding corporations publicly accountable. By law, corporations are supposed to maximize profits for stockholders, but this is a very narrow mission for such a powerful institution as the modern corporation. Further, not only is most corporate decision making behind closed doors, but it is relatively authoritarian in the sense that it is mostly top-down, being finalized by small circles of top management. Is it rational for small coteries of private individuals to have so much power over the fate of humanity? I think not.

Another major problem is a belief that markets are best not interfered with unless the interference increases corporate profits. The American government interferes in the ethanol market by giving corporations large subsidies to produce ethanol, and it institutes protective tariffs that essentially subsidize the giant corporations of the American sugar industry, while there is little or no interference in vegetable markets that would support smaller family farms or organic farmers. Typically, market intervention by government into food provisioning markets contributes to the profits of large food corporations. Interference with markets for other reasons, such as trying to alleviate unjust, unhealthy, or unecological outcomes, is generally avoided, particularly when, as a result, profits might suffer.

Most mainstream economists believe that by their own impulses markets can rationally price commodities, but when enormous social and environmental costs are not included in market prices, they can scarcely be thought of as rational. It follows that market prices need to be made more representative of real social costs and benefits. The "carbon tax" is one example where this is being advocated. A "sustainability tax" has also been advocated. Such taxes, however, can only be progressive from the point of view of human flourishing, if they are combined with redistributive measures that make the necessities of life more affordable and not less to those with lower incomes. We can make markets more democratically accountable by treating them instrumentally, and this means being willing to intervene, whenever by doing so human or environmental flourishing are advanced.

Because markets are always embedded in and shaped by power relations, their outcomes are always likely to favour the powerful. Today the mainstream speaks of "market failures", as though for the most part markets succeed. But what is the measure of their success? It surely cannot be distributive justice unless radical inequality can be made consistent with justice. Nor can it be environmental sustainability or human health. Thus I find it a little ironic that the Stern Report should state that "Climate change is the greatest market failure the world has ever seen."[40] In this case, a "market failure" may make the earth radically less inhabitable. One might also argue that other "market failures" are capitalism's continual exploitation and immiseration of workers around the world, or the health disaster stemming from its failure to provide adequate food to half the world's population. Thinking of these problems as simply "market failures" does not really help us to develop the strategies required to successfully deal with them. Indeed, they are all entirely predictable given the deep structures of capitalism.

PART II

UNDERSTANDING CAPITALISM

2 THE MANAGEMENT OF AGRICULTURE AND FOOD BY CAPITAL'S DEEP STRUCTURES

The moral of the tale ... is that the capitalist system runs counter to a rational agriculture, or that a rational agriculture is incompatible with the capitalist system (even if the latter promotes technical development in agriculture) and needs either small farmers working for themselves or the control of the associated producers.[1]

Large-scale industry and industrially pursued large-scale agriculture have the same effect. If they are originally distinguished by the fact that the former lays waste and ruins labour-power and thus the natural power of man, whereas the latter does the same to the natural power of the soil, they link up in the later course of development, since the industrial system applied to agriculture also enervates the workers there, while industry and trade for their part provide agriculture with the means of exhausting the soil.[2]

As far as we are concerned, the farmer produces wheat, etc. just as the manufacturer produces yarn or machines. The assumption that the capitalist mode of production has taken control of agriculture implies also that it dominates all spheres of production and bourgeois society, so that its preconditions, such as the free competition of capitals, their transferability from one sphere of production to another,

[18]

and equal level of average profit, etc. are also present in their full development.[3]

My purpose in this chapter is to demonstrate why it is that precisely when capitalism is operating in accord with its own most rational inner principles or deep structures, it cannot manage the agricultural/food system in rational ways. Or, as Marx puts it above, "a rational agriculture is incompatible with the capitalist system". It is precisely for this reason that this sector of economic life has always been an arena of political struggle and state intervention, one that until recently has consisted of largely non-capitalist or quasi-capitalist production.[4] If we consider self-employed production, such as family farms, to be non-capitalist, then until the post-World War II period the lion's share of American food was produced by non-capitalist family farms, and even today in the age of capitalist "factory farms" most farmers in the world still operate small or medium-scale family farms.[5]

Mainstream economists sometimes argue that failures in food provisioning stem from not enough capitalism, in the sense that the failures stem from meddling with free markets, and that almost all problems associated with food provisioning can be solved by freer markets. In contrast, based on Marx's unsurpassed analysis of capital's deep structures, I intend to demonstrate that capitalism itself, and not some autonomous misconceived state policy (although this could contribute in particular contexts), is at the root of the food provisioning problems that we face. I shall argue that not only will capitalism always resist the sorts of reforms that are needed to build a more rational food system, but also while a reformed capitalism may be a worthwhile short-term goal, in the long-run we need changes that go far beyond anything manageable purely through competitive markets and privately owned units of capital. I am not suggesting doing away with markets and corporations, but rather with making them democratically accountable in ways that some might consider post-capitalist.

Further, given that food is a basic necessity and that its production brings us into close contact with the earth, failures in this sector may impact negatively on both human health and environmental health. If it can be shown that failures of capitalism in arenas so vital to human well-being have necessitated frequent and sustained state intervention, and that even with this intervention significant failures remain, then the very rationality of capitalism must be doubted. Following Marx, it is necessary, then, to distinguish between "capitalist rationality", which is not very rational, and "rationality" per se. The rational capitalist will always act to maximize short-term profits, but an agriculture organized in accord with such an imperative may be radically unjust and may undermine both human and environmental health. Despite over two centuries of popular struggles aimed at alleviating some of the most damaging fall-out from capitalistic attempts to integrate the agricultural/food system into its short-term profit orientation, capital's continuing failures in this sector strongly suggest that capitalist "rationality" in some fundamental ways must be shot through with irrationality. For a food system that can produce enough food to provide a good diet to everyone in the world, but instead leaves at least half of the people in the world suffering from malnutrition, cannot be considered rational.[6]

Its search for profits makes capital indifferent to the qualitative aspects of life unless paying attention to them can generate quick profits. These qualitative aspects of life can include anything from environmental health to the quality of life of workers. For capital, qualitative considerations are always subordinate to quantitative ones. Historically capital has never shown much concern for the health and safety of workers unless forced to do so by state legislation. Similarly, it has not shown concern for polluting or degrading the environment unless forced to do so by state legislation. In short, all values except profit are second-order values to be subsumed to profit in cases where they conflict with it. For the purposes of this book, the main focus of criticism of capitalism is its neglect of the qualitative dimension of how we relate to each other and to the earth in order to provision ourselves with food.

According to Marx's theory of the commodity, a capitalistic commodity in its purest form must have clear and definite boundaries, giving the owner absolute control, and thereby implying the absolute exclusion of the non-owner.[7] "Good fences make good neighbours" can be translated into "good fences are required by capitalists". What is central to capitalism is that well-defined pieces of private property constituting the means of production come to be fully controlled by capitalists, thus excluding workers from them. In its very constitution private property always implies a power relation between an owner and non-owner, and in the case of pure capitalism all means of production are private property owned exclusively by capitalists. The exclusion of workers from the means of production creates a structural power relation, which in principle, forces a worker in pure capitalism to accept the working conditions and wages set by the competitive labour market.

Under the category "land", Marx includes any natural resource that can be turned into private property and thereby monopolized by its owner (oil, minerals, real estate, water and so on). The fundamental precondition for the commodification of land is the existence of private property which gives certain individuals or groups exclusive control over bits of nature. In the case of Britain, with the onset of capitalism, the commons became increasingly commodified, and this meant that feudal landlords took over land that previously had been held in common, put fences around it, and declared it to be their private property.[8] Having pushed the "common" people off the land, landlords could now charge rent for the use of their lands and could in principle sell their land. I say "in principle" because through the practice of "strict settlement", landlords tried to preserve their estates, which were the very basis of their political power.[9]

Unlike nearly all other economists, Marx does not simply assume complete commodification as a given. For example, he lets us see the commodification of land as an historical process in which lands held in common are gradually taken over and enclosed by a powerful landlord class – often resorting to brutal expulsions of the commoners.[10] By reminding us of this history, Marx also demonstrates the close connection between the commodification of land and the commodification of labour-power, for once peasants are denied access to the commons, they tend to have increasingly only their labour-power to sell to capital for a wage. Instead of simply assuming complete commodification of the land as some sort of magical *fait accompli*, or assuming a fully formed labour market, Marx sees them accurately as the result of a brutally violent and exclusionary historical process.[11]

The profit orientation of capital implies that capital should be, in principle, always ready to move from producing that which is less profitable to that which is more profitable. Legal constraints aside, capital will produce opium rather than rice, if opium is more profitable. This opportunistic readiness to shift production from one use-value to another purely in response to the rate of profit is referred to by Marx as "indifference to use-value".[12] "Use-value" refers to the material properties of a commodity that make it qualitatively different from other commodities and which give it its particular uses. For example, the flammable quality (use-value) of gasoline makes it useful in driving internal combustion engines. The indifference to use-value that Marx refers to is of fundamental importance to my argument concerning the ineffectiveness of capital when it comes to managing agriculture and food, precisely because the short-term profit orientation of capital must be insensitive and indifferent to the enormous long-term use-value considerations that are required for the production of food. Assuming that they do not impinge on profits, as they often don't, considerations of long-term human and environmental health and of social justice will be ignored.

A rational capitalist's loyalty cannot be to the material or ideological qualities of a thing (that is, use-value), but must always be to profit as pure quantity. For example, a truly "rational" capitalist, no matter how religious, would shift production from bibles to pornography purely in response to profit signals. The penalty for breaching this loyalty to pure profit would be ultimately to lose out to the competition and to cease being a capitalist. In terms of food, a "rational" capitalist will produce unhealthy food if it is more profitable than healthy food, and will utilize polluting and toxic chemical inputs as long as profits are increased by doing so. Similarly "rational" capitalist farmers will pay the lowest possible wages to field workers in order to maximize profits, and if this means hiring illegal immigrants, this will be the direction taken as long as they can get away with it.

Because most crops are annual and because capitalist farmers develop expertise and buy machinery for a limited range of production, it may be difficult to switch commodities or to switch into or out of farming in response to profit criteria in the short run. For example, while it may be relatively easy to shift from the production of corn to soybeans (although one would have to wait for the next growing season), it is not easy to shift from grain production to vegetable production, or from milk production to tobacco production. This is made even more difficult by the fact that nearly all farmers in the world carry large debts and would have difficulty raising the funds to make such a switch. And while non-capitalist family farmers would likely be extremely reluctant to leave the land they live on – sometimes for generations – in contrast, rational capitalist farmers would not hesitate to immediately shift their capital into or out of farming in response to pure profit criteria, or to shift from growing corn for food to growing corn for ethanol even if people are starving for lack of food. Indeed, as the supply of corn diminishes because a portion of the crop is being used for ethanol, corn prices will be pushed up, inviting farmers to shift from producing other food crops to corn, reducing the supply of other food crops, thus pushing their prices up as well.[13]

In this chapter on "pure capitalism" or on "capitalism in the abstract and in general", I shall group my arguments under seven main headings:

- capital's profit orientation
- capital, time and speed
- capital, space and homogenization
- capital and workers
- capital and underconsumption
- capital, oligopoly and globalization
- capital and subjectivity.

A brief summary of the main points will introduce this section.

First, capital's privileging of short-term profits over all other considerations leads to an indifference to preserving the long-term quality of land, lakes, rivers and oceans. Profits may dictate deforestation, land degradation, and the pollution of bodies of water. Long-term conservation for the sake of future generations requires a relationship of stewardship, a relationship diametrically opposed to short-term profit maximization by private corporations only concerned for their own immediate gain. In principle, the imperatives of profit could drive capital to cut down all forests; cover arable land with suburbs; convert arable land to growing tobacco and other addictive drugs; empty bodies of water of fish; pollute land, water, and air; or divert food crops to ethanol production even when large numbers of people do not have enough food. The exposure of agriculture to the vagaries of nature and the inelasticity of both supply and demand with regard to food, make food particularly resistant to effective market regulation. As a result the price of food can easily spike, exposing billions of people to famine and starvation. Finally, capitalism's tendency to privatize profits and socialize costs can shift nearly all of the costs associated with toxic environments, hunger and unhealthy food to taxpayers, while capital continues to profit at taxpayers' expense.

Second, and as a consequence of capital's profit orientation, the focus on increased speed can make agriculture highly dependent on "mined" energy inputs. Energy inputs tend to increase geometrically with increased speed, such that at some point, further increases in speed become uneconomic as the curve approaches the vertical. Speed may also impinge on nature's rhythms to such an extent that agriculture becomes environmentally destructive. The need for speed can rush chemicals into the food regime without adequate testing for toxicity. The sociality and conviviality of eating together can be undermined, and the apparent solution of "fast foods" may also undermine health.

Third, the application of mass production and mass consumption techniques to food can be spatially homogenizing. As a result biologically diverse tropical forests can be turned into monocultures, or suburban boulevards can be lined with strip malls populated in part with fast food restaurants, thus adding to a homogenized built environment. Also, because such mass production requires a global reach in order to be successful, the world is sourced for the cheapest material and labour inputs. Mass production needs mass consumption, and therefore fast food restaurants also expand around the world, enticing all (and particularly children) to become habitual consumers of junk food.

Fourth, the less capital can pay workers for a given amount of work, the more it can profit. And since food is a basic necessity that enters into all wage baskets, the cheaper the food, the less workers in general need to be paid in order to still have a living wage. Even though most agricultural field work is physically demanding, dangerous and seasonal, workers in this sector tend to be the lowest paid and often the most vulnerable. The reasons for this are complex, having to do with the needs of capital and the history of capitalism as it has intersected with class, race, gender and colonialism.

Fifth, capital is caught up in a general contradiction. It can increase profits by paying workers less, but if the pay of workers is too low, they will not be able to purchase the commodities that capital would mass produce, thus creating a problem of underconsumption. If food workers are a minority, however, by cheapening food, their low pay can free up the wages of other workers (food becomes a smaller portion of the wage basket) to buy commodities other than food. Finally, capitalist crises also demonstrate the extent to which capitalism is destructive of family farming. In a crisis, capitalists cut back production and lay off workers until the slump is over, but family farmers increase production in order to survive the lower prices. However, with many such farmers doing this, prices will go yet lower until massive numbers of family farmers go bankrupt and leave the farm. It does not necessarily take a crisis for this to happen; it can occur simply with falling prices for agricultural commodities or rising prices for agricultural inputs.

Sixth, capitalism in general has a strong tendency to form larger and larger units, but this has always come up against the qualitative natural obstacles of farming which make it so difficult and make profits so unpredictable. With the exception of some colonial plantation commodities, capital has tended to centralize less at the level of farming itself and more at the level of supplying inputs to farmers, or transporting, processing and retailing their outputs. Even to the extent that family farms survive, the larger ones tend to become part of a putting-out system in which capital supplies the inputs and contracts for the outputs, thereby subsuming the farmer totally to the circuit of capital. In this way capital leaves the truly difficult "dirty work" of farming to farmers, while it rakes in the profits. The degree of concentration in supplying seeds and mechanical and chemical inputs is great, as it also is in marketing processed foods, meat, soft drinks and fast food. The result is an enormous concentration of power in unaccountable corporations (insofar as they are not regulated) whose activities impact enormously on human health and the health of the environment.

Seventh, by placing private property and profit at the centre of economic life, capitalism promotes possessive individualism. While a degree of individualism is a good thing, it needs to be balanced with forms of sociality and a sense of community. Capitalism encourages individuals and groups of private individuals to ruthlessly expand their economic power and profits without regard to the long-term consequences for society as a whole or for the globe. It is not only that this one-sided individualism blocks the development of strong human impulses towards generosity, but also it fosters "*après moi le deluge*" attitudes. This is not to be blamed so much on individuals as on the capitalist system, which has its own intrinsic imperatives that drive people in this direction. With this brief summary, I turn next to expand on these points.

CAPITAL'S PROFIT ORIENTATION

Considered most fundamentally, units of capital compete in order to maximize short-term profits. The strength of capital's profit orientation can scarcely be overemphasized. In emphasizing profit, I am not being cynical. In a very real sense profit is the be-all and end-all of capitalism. For example, if building a safe factory cost more than an unsafe one, then a rational capitalist will cut costs and increase profits by building an unsafe one unless there is legislation or some other outside force preventing it.

Capital prefers a situation where it can focus entirely on quantitative calculations of past and likely future profits. These calculations are easiest to make when all inputs and outputs of the prospective production process are fully commodified so that their prices are determined entirely by market forces, which in pure capitalism would tend towards equilibrium as a result of competition. In such a situation the only qualitative considerations would be those directly related to profit. For example, a rational capitalist, would pay workers more only if by doing so their productivity increased more than the added cost of higher wages. Or a corporation will be "socially responsible" only to the extent that this will increase profits. For example, a cigarette company may aggressively market cigarettes to the youth in developing countries where there are few if any constraints, thus addicting a whole new generation of smokers. At the same time, in the United States where public pressures have built to reduce smoking, a cigarette company may try to appear to be "socially responsible" by featuring ads on television offering support to people who want to quit smoking. Ironically, it may even help to sell cigarettes to get the word "cigarette" on prime-time television, even in the context of helping people to quit. A rational capitalist will take into account qualitative factors like "social responsibility" if by doing so they believe that profits will either stay the same or increase. For example, by at least appearing to be socially responsible, a corporation may decrease the likelihood of profit-reducing state regulation. And this implies that the qualitative dimensions of economic activity be translated into at least a quantitative range that can enter profit calculations.

If a capitalist can increase profits by producing commodities of poor quality that will not last long, then they will do so.[14] Qualitative considerations outside of profit considerations do not enter in. Historically capitalists have shown no interest in the health of their workers or their general quality of life, unless forced to do so by the mobilization of workers, or by legislation, or by profit considerations (healthy workers will presumably be more productive, but this may not be a consideration where replacement workers are plentiful). Similarly, it has only been legislation or mass mobilizations that have constrained capitalist factories from polluting the environment, since in most cases to clean up or prevent effluents cuts into profits.

Capital's single-minded profit orientation, which is always focused on maximizing selling price over costs (profit), has never fitted well with the provisioning of food. This is because qualitative issues loom so large with food. Food can be priced, but there is no guarantee that at a given price the majority of people can afford a varied and healthful diet. Land can be given a price, but if it is more profitable in the short run to build suburbs on the most fertile land, then this is what will be done. Capitalist farmers can farm, but there is no guarantee that the price they receive for their crop will enable them to continue to farm. Or they can use massive amounts of chemical fertilizers and pesticides in order to increase short-term profits, while the long-term effect is to degrade the land and pollute the environment. Or they can make short-term profits by cutting down rain forests even though the land so exposed may not be very fertile, and the contribution to global warming may be enormous.

In its purest form, capital is absolutely indifferent to use-value in and of itself, and this frees up capital to focus single-mindedly on profit. This extremely "tough-minded survival of the fittest" orientation of capital treats the social and environmental costs and benefits of profit-making as "externalities" (outside the market). Of course, externalities (global warming, health, safety, pollution, desertification/degradation of land, exhaustion of non-renewable resources, species extinction, hunger) may have enormous effects on the quality of life and quality of the environment. This raises enormous problems for consumers, who have had to devise political controls to protect themselves against the power of capital to produce commodities that are harmful or that have negative externalities (short or long-term harmful consequences to social life or nature). In *Capital,* for example, Marx documents measures taken against the adulteration of bread (the use of sawdust and other fillers) in nineteenth-century England.[15] The battle for safe and nutritious food today against profit-mongering capital has reached epic proportions. (See Chapters 4–6.) In the end, the escalating costs of these "externalities" nearly always get paid for by taxpayers and consumers, or by future generations and not by the corporations that created the social costs.

Arguably the history of capitalism has been primarily the history of struggle against capital's indifference to use-value and to the associated qualitative dimensions of life. For example, workers have had to fight for the right to organize trade unions, for shorter work days, better working conditions; and consumers have had to fight against pollution, false advertising and commodities of poor quality. Imagine a world in which capitalists were motivated to create beautiful workplaces, to organize work to be as pleasurable and as safe as possible, and to enable workers to participate as democratically as possible in decision making. Though desirable, such a world is far from our existing capitalist economy. Given the immense power of capital in a system in which it is dominant, struggles against its indifference usually require extended and large mobilizations in order to be effective, and these struggles always face the possibility that reactions on the part of capital will result in draconian and violent repression.[16] Furthermore, when gains are made, they always face the possibility of partial or complete reversal at a later date.[17]

Ultimately indifference to use-value implies indifference to all human values that do not enter directly into profit making. From the point of view of pure capitalism, if covering up the truth is profitable, then let the obfuscation begin. If oppressing and exploiting people is profitable, and is required to beat out the competition, then the more exploitation the better. If building ugly, unsafe and polluting factories is more profitable than building beautiful, safe and non-polluting ones, then let ugliness and pollution reign. In short, without constraint from the outside by the state or by popular movements, all other human values will be sacrificed to profit when it is necessary to make a choice between the two.

The impact of capital's indifference to use-value cannot be emphasized enough when it comes to the capitalistic provision of food. For example, modern factory farms will use whatever means they can get away with, no matter how damaging to human, animal and environmental health, in order to maximize short-term profits. It is only state legislation that protects society from some of the more damaging consequences of such indifference. And in parts of the world where countries are poor and legal systems are weak, not only is capital inclined towards the most brutal exploitation of labour and severe damage to the environment, it also forces non-capitalist or quasi-capitalist small producers to engage in practices such as child slavery or deforestation in order to survive economically. In short, capital is indifferent to the social and ecological costs of both the production process and the final consumption of food commodities, whose purpose is presumably to give our lives meaning and to nourish our bodies and souls.

Food provisioning is linked so directly to our health and the health of the earth now and for all future generations, and it is so directly related to the unprecedented challenges of global warming, that to trust its production and distribution to short-term and unstable market prices and profits would appear to be particularly irrational in the current context.

CAPITAL, TIME AND SPEED

Increasing the speed of production and consumption is an important means for capitalists to increase profits.[18] If the speed of an assembly line can be doubled, profits will increase. Doubling the speed of the line means that each worker does twice as much work per unit time. Marx called this "intensification", and since we spend a lot of our waking hours producing or consuming, speeding these up will tend to increase the pace of life generally.[19] Indeed, it is completely accurate to say that for capital "time is money" (or profit), and the drive to increase profits will tend to intensify labour per unit of time, and expand the units of labour time to fill up as much of the day and night as possible. Since sleep is unproductive of profit, from the point of view of capital, it is a waste of time and should be reduced to a minimum.[20] The same can be said for home cooking and eating in general. It is natural, then, for capital to intensify, speed up and extend the production of profit to the limit of human endurance. A good capitalist worker should not go to bed until absolutely exhausted, for every minute of lost productivity is profits lost forever.

In some cases, capital can keep its means of production working 24 hours a day (agrarian field labour is usually limited to daylight hours), and it can increase the intensity of its work and speed of its machines. When workers cannot be made to work any faster, it may be possible to replace them with robots that can. Since every minute of production time that is lost is lost forever, the linear sequential counting of time becomes central to capitalist economic logic. Linear sequential time is so directly tied to maximizing profits that the stop watch became the key tool of the "Taylorist" efficiency experts and their "time and motion studies" which first emerged in the American steel industry around the turn of the last century.[21]

Time discipline becomes crucial as evidenced in the early years of the industrial revolution in England, when children as young as six years old could be beaten for being five minutes late to work.[22] It is not inaccurate to claim that the cardinal sin of capitalism is idleness – idle hands and idle machines are capitalism's hell. The human needs for rest, recreation and sleep are constraints on capital's need to increase profits; so too are human bodies which can get sick, injured, wear out or die. For capital would not only like to be immortal, but forever profitable and yet more profitable. In short, capital would like to be an ever-expanding perpetual motion machine.

When we look at the history of capitalism, we find that where there are no legal constraints and where workers are plentiful, capital is prodigal in using them up. Working days of 15–16 hours with only a half-hour break were common once gas lighting made it possible for factories to operate at night.[23] Referring to the nineteenth-century lace trade, Marx quotes the comments of county magistrate Mr Broughton Charlton at a meeting held on January 14, 1860:

> Children of nine or ten years are dragged from their squalid beds at two, three, four o'clock in the morning and compelled to work for a bare subsistence until ten, eleven, or twelve at night, their limbs wearing away, their frames dwindling, their faces whitening, and their humanity absolutely sinking into a stone-like torpor, utterly horrible to contemplate.[24]

It is clear that even as late as 1860 in England, there were sectors of industry not regulated by the Factory Acts. The Factory Act of 1833, the first legislation to set limits on such extreme exploitation of the human body, set the ordinary working day from 5:30 am to 8:30 pm, a mere 15 hours.[25] While after over two centuries of struggle some groups of workers have fought for and won limits on the length of the work day and on the intensification of work (essentially "speed-up"), where capital can get away with it, it will often to this day push the length and speed of work up to and even beyond the limits of human endurance.[26]

In recent years we use the term "quality time" to refer to time saved for giving undivided attention to something or someone in which counting the minutes takes a back seat to our attentiveness. In other words, the qualitative aspect of time comes to the fore. But capital's efforts to get more and more productivity out of units of time has speeded up of the pace of life, such that "quality time" becomes a highly valued piece of time for friendship and love squeezed out of a life on the run. Indeed, the expression "quality time" is particularly appropriate in the context of capitalism, where time has become so purely quantitative. It can be viewed as the "last stand" of the quality of life increasingly engulfed by the purely quantitative drives of profit making. The general tendency of capitalism to subsume quality to quantity in this case means that a person's very "life time" is sacrificed to capital's drive to absorb as much as possible all life energy into profit making. And when we look at capitalism historically, we see that unless pressured from the outside, life time that is too young, too sick, too disabled or too old to be productive is either ignored or considered as an unwelcome burden.

Because time is money, there is enormous pressure to quickly approve new commodities such as chemical products so that corporations that have devoted resources to developing them can begin to profit right away. It is not surprising, then, that increasingly we are questioning whether the chemicals utilized in the food chain have been adequately tested for toxicity. The pressures of time and profit making are simply too great, and corporations typically do not need to concern themselves with long-term damage to human or environmental health, costs which are typically socialized and paid for by taxpayers, or the injured individuals themselves.

When speed becomes all important to profit making as it seems increasingly to be, then fast foods come to epitomize the existing food regime. Not only are these foods manufactured with minimal gestures towards the environmental damage that they do, but also their cheapness, semi-addictive qualities and their being pushed by aggressive mass marketing have made them a major contributing factor to the current "obesity epidemic". Those fast foods that are junk foods (in terms of calorie/nutrient ratios or salt content) are enormously profitable, are cheap, and are convenient for lives on the run. At the same time, their apparent cheapness is gained at very high social costs – both because many workers in the fast food chain receive wages that place them below the poverty line, and because in their production and consumption both human and environmental health are all too often compromised.

Until recently, agriculture has been so tied in to the seasons, and to local soil, weather and insect variations, that it offered capital little opportunity for speed up. As I shall argue at greater length later in the book, it is only with the extensive development of mechanization, chemicalization and bioscience after World War II, that capitalism penetrated agriculture in the United States, and utilized these technologies to actually speed up agriculture, animal husbandry and the food regime as a whole.

CAPITAL, SPACE AND HOMOGENIZATION

Capital is happy when it is expanding, and it is happiest when it is expanding the most rapidly. Depending upon the type of capital and its size, expansion may or may not involve significant spatial expansion, although the frequency of many directional spatial expansions makes Frank Norris's image of a rapidly growing octopus realistic.[27] More often than not spatial expansion also implies, at least to some degree, the homogenization of natural and built landscapes. Capital homogenizes natural landscapes by destroying species diversity, by desertification, by pollution, by monoculture, by harvesting "exotic animals", by strip mining, by strip malls, by diverting rivers, by urbanization and suburbanization, by over-fishing in the oceans, by building dams, by paving over the landscape, by clear-cutting forests or by any smoothing or homogenizing of the landscape that would speed up the turnover of capital's circuits and thus profits. In general space is homogenized by capital when its diversity gets in the way of capital mobility, when mass production and consumption require standardization, and when the built environment is standardized by capitalist commercialization and profit fixation.

The material, qualitative or use-value characteristics of space can be quite resistant to being totally subsumed to short-term profit maximization. A major result of this is that capital has always developed unevenly spatially. Yes, it has always had an expansive and globalizing thrust, but this has run up against oceans and untamed land masses, the limits of technology, political policies stemming from semi-sovereign nation-states, and social formations that are to varying degrees resistant or hostile to capitalism. Indeed capital has only managed to gain as much global hegemony as it has by often compromising its own inner principles, as, for example, when popular movements have forced upon it concerns for quality of life which it would otherwise ignore.

Mass production is greatly facilitated by standardized and

homogenized inputs which can be easily manipulated by machines to produce standardized commodities. Indeed homogenization in general plays a major role in speed-up. While mass production is an important economic advance for producing many commodities, it does not always work well with food. For example, tomatoes that are bred to all grow to the same size at the same time can be machine picked when hard and green, and later turned red by being gassed. However, this is done with loss of both nutrients and flavour, and it is only the consumer that suffers these losses. Standard seeds, chemical fertilizers and pesticides can combine to produce highly profitable monocultures that may run roughshod over local variations which would require sensitive care without these technologies. One of the amazing gifts of nature is its diversity, and forcing it into standardized boxes or forcing it to produce at a faster pace than its own rhythms can be ecologically destructive.

The built environment tends to be homogenized when corporations of ever-increasing size construct it such that industrial parks, strip malls, cities and suburbs everywhere become increasingly indistinguishable. Like "quality time" we can speak of "quality space" as referring to the ever-rarer places of qualitative diversity and uniqueness, which tourists flock to precisely because of the rarity of the qualitatively beautiful in the built environment of recent capitalism. Similarly nature has been so sourced for raw materials and so polluted, or in short so stressed by every increasing rate of turnover and expansion of capital, that tourists will often pay top dollar for a taste of the qualitative in relatively pristine natural places (no place is truly pristine any more). Given that usually it is the very rich who can afford to go to pristine places, to the extent that space becomes homogenized, capital may profit from more accessible artificially constructed heterogeneities (for example Las Vegas or Disneyland).

Considered spatially, arable land is limited in supply, and land often cannot be capitalistically produced or made fertile in response to a sudden increase in demand. It is possible that the most fertile land may succumb to the higher profits associated with suburban sprawl. Or marginal or arid land that should not be used for agriculture may be so utilized, resulting in the profligate use of fresh water for irrigation and chemical fertilizers to boost fertility. The most damaging capitalist response to land shortages is deforestation, which, in the case of tropical rain forests, is the single largest contributor to global warming. Global warming, in turn, generates extreme weather and rising oceans, both of which will impact negatively on agriculture. In the current global agricultural system, it appears that land is being lost to deforestation in order to raise beef cattle for the fast food industry, and that tropical forests are being lost to the production of tobacco crops.[28]

On top of differences in soil fertility, agriculture is subject to natural forces such as weather, blight or insect infestations. These potential qualitative disruptors may interfere with even the best capitalistically rational quantitative calculations. Capitalism depends for its rationality on being able to move from less profitable to more profitable investments, and this in turn depends upon some stability in profits over time. It is true that in some agricultural sectors in some parts of the world, where water is supplied by irrigation, fertility of the land by chemicals, and crop protection by chemical insecticides, herbicides and fungicides, capitalism has reduced at least some of the unpredictability stemming from natural forces. But this predictability, which is so crucial to capitalist rationality, has been bought at a price that, in the long term, could be immense. For not only are supplies of water and petrochemicals likely to shrink radically in the future, global warming is likely to cause both weather variability and higher temperatures which will both lower agricultural yields and make them increasingly unpredictable. It is possible that temperature increases will rule out agriculture altogether in many parts of the world where it is now carried out (the major grain crops will not grow at temperatures above 40 degrees Celsius).[29] As a result, the unpredictability of profits in the agrarian sector could render it unsuitable for capitalism (or even for old-fashioned family farming embedded in capitalism) without some sort of guaranteed income for farmers.

The earth's surface is too qualitatively diverse to be totally subsumed to the quantitative orientation of capital expansion:

- Only some land is useful for producing food, and even that land varies enormously in its fertility or productivity.
- Alternative long-term uses of land are too important to be

decided by short-term profit considerations. Short-term profit would dictate, for example, that we cut down all forests. But this is clearly irrational for many reasons, and perhaps most importantly because the disruption of water cycles and global warming would result in massive desertification which could in the long run make the earth almost uninhabitable.

- Capitalism in its purest logic is diametrically opposed to the long-term democratic planning required by a stewardship of the land which would ask of each generation that they pass on the land to the next generation in at least as good shape as it was passed on to them.

Time and space, treated as purely linear-sequential quantitative inputs and outputs of capitalistic mass production techniques, have proven to be particularly resistant obstacles in the way of capitalist agriculture's drive to increase profit rates. Crops are limited not only by seasonal growing times, but also by climate, soil conditions, pests, weeds and diseases. Similarly meat production is limited by the time it takes for animals to grow sufficiently to be slaughtered. Furthermore many kinds of food will spoil if too much time passes between their production and consumption. Without preservative technologies and cheap high-speed transportation, foods that spoil easily like fresh meat, milk, fruits and vegetables are necessarily limited spatially and temporally in their marketability. Indeed, in the United States it was only in the second half of the twentieth century, with the mechanization and chemicalization of agriculture coupled with advances in the technologies of transportation and food preservation, that capitalism was increasingly able to replace the family farm with mass-producing factory farming. But it is precisely the technologies that have enabled capitalism to largely replace or subsume self-employed farmers that also make capitalist agriculture radically damaging to human and environmental health. The use of chemical fertilizers and pesticides, massive increases in irrigation, ever-larger agricultural machinery (it compacts the soil), GM (genetically modified) seeds, new preservation techniques, and faster transportation systems have fostered larger farms and increased crop yields, but the long-term human and environmental costs of these innovations are unsustainable.

In the case of cotton spinning, enormous productivity gains were achieved in a very few years: factory spinning became 300 times more productive than spinning by hand. However, productivity gains like this in agriculture have been hard to come by. Getting cattle to grow faster by administering growth hormones and antibiotics, and by feeding them mostly corn in giant feedlots, rapidly runs up against the limits of the animal's health, human health and environmental health. Similarly, engineering tomatoes so that they become tough enough to machine pick and gain precious days of shelf life runs up against the limits of taste and nutritional value. Thus, speeding up the circuits of capital and reducing spoilage poses greater challenges with many types of food production, precisely because qualitative factors get in the way of the sheer expansion of quantity that is central to capitalism.

Capitalism works best with commodities that do not spoil and can therefore sit on the shelves for whatever amount of time is needed for supply and demand to adjust. With commodities that spoil quickly, distant markets become more and more impractical, and as well, supply and demand often do not have the time to adjust to each other without either sudden price spikes or massive spoilage. And although refrigeration technology has extended the half-life of such commodities as milk, eggs and meat, these technologies use a lot of energy and can only extend the best-before date by a limited amount. Thus producers in these sectors are subject to excessively large market fluctuations, and the product is subject to spoilage and total loss of value.

CAPITAL AND WORKERS

Earlier I used the phrase "degrees of commodification". The labour market in pure capitalism can serve as an example of what I mean by this. A completely commodified labour market would be managed completely by the wage rate, which in turn is a result of the supply of and demand for workers. A large supply of workers relative to demand will lead to lower and lower wage rates. If this situation continues, wages will eventually fall below bare physical subsistence and workers will die off, until their supply shrinks enough to once again push wages to a level at or above subsistence. This is how a totally commodified labour market would operate.

Early on in the history of capitalism, however, it was realized that capitalism passes through cycles, and that workers who die off now may be needed in the future when capital is more expansive. As a result, various kinds of state legislation were developed in order to keep workers alive through the downturns so that they might be exploited in future expansive phases. These measures might involve various combinations of state intervention to dole out work, money, commodities – or retraining to workers whose wages were below subsistence or who were unemployed. "Safety nets" were further expanded to include state-supported retirement benefits, health benefits or education benefits. Further, workers organized unions and political parties and achieved various types of constraints on their being reduced to simply one more commodity input into a capitalist production process.

All of the above interferences in the labour market could be considered steps that to some degree brought about the decommodification of labour power. The point is that any market may be interfered with, and that interference may serve to further decommodify the market or to recommodify a market that is already partially decommodified.[30] In other words, where commodification is complete, markets operate without state intervention, and instead they are self-regulating. It is fair to say that while complete commodification may be assumed at the level of abstract theory for the sake of clarity and precision, at the level of historical analysis, the commodification of labour-power would never be complete, because workers always combine to constrain the brutality of the labour market, and because the state often steps in to place limits on some of the more extreme kinds of exploitation.

Like land, the commodification of labour-power is tricky because labour-power cannot be capitalistically produced in response to capital's expansive dynamic. Yet this commodification is the *sine qua non* of capitalism, since without it there could be no systematic basis for profit making that did not rely on either force or systematic unequal exchange. (Presumably no one would voluntarily and knowingly enter into an exchange where something of greater value is exchanged for something of lesser value.) As already mentioned, historically the commodification of labour power is brought about by the separation of workers from the means of production, primarily land, and the continued commodification of labour-power depends upon some means of maintaining an industrial reserve army so that when capital needs more hands, they can be hired. "Hands" is an appropriate metaphor because capital is indifferent to the distinct qualities of the worker as a person, but rather simply hires the quantity of hands that it requires at the lowest possible pay ("subsistence" in pure capitalism). Machines need hands to operate them, and as Marx puts it so appropriately, in pure capitalism workers are simply "appendages" of machines.[31]

In the closed system of pure capitalism, capital cannot be so indifferent to the depletion of the ranks of the industrial reserve army of labour, because when labour becomes scarce, labour-power has the possibility of bidding up wages, and should the scarcity persist, labour's new-found power could threaten the very commodification of labour-power itself. For this reason, as we shall see, in pure capitalism a radical reduction in the size of the pool of unemployed is a sure sign that a crisis, which will drastically expand the industrial reserve army, is on the way.[32] In history, capital does everything in its power to insure that prolonged and widespread labour shortages never occur. Indeed, next to the separation of workers from the means of production, the existence of an industrial reserve army of unemployed workers is the most crucial condition for the commodification of labour-power.[33]

In the theory of capital's deep structures, Marx assumes that labour is homogeneous, and most basic to this assumption is that labour is unskilled so that the substitution of one worker for another makes no economically significant difference.[34] Commodification implies that labour-power is mobile, such that wage labour will move about until wages for unskilled labour and working conditions are more or less equalized. The complete commodification of labour-power that is assumed in pure capitalism may make workers mobile, but would also in practice place workers in a situation of extreme insecurity. The job that is necessary for survival can disappear at any moment at the whim of the capitalist, leaving a worker without means of support. Further, the periodic crises that are a necessary part of capital's inner logic expose even the most hard-working and disciplined workers to unemployment.[35] These are two of the crucial reasons why in history workers have always struggled to gain at least a modicum of job security through either trade unions or state legislation. In other words, they have fought to achieve at least a limited decommodification of labour-power, while capital has always fought to recommodify labour-power by atomizing, disorganizing or demoralizing the working class. From the point of view of capital, profits can be most single-mindedly pursued when labour-power is as docile and passive as any other commodity input into the production process.

Capitalist agriculture has always had difficulties with the commodification of labour-power that capitalism needs, because of the seasonal requirements for agricultural labour and the back-breaking nature of so much harvesting labour. This is no doubt one of the stronger reasons that the family farm persisted for so long in the United States. Given the typical low pay and sporadic employment in the agricultural sector, capitalist farmers often have had to rely on vulnerable workers (children, women, "guest" workers, illegal immigrants, immigrants and low-status minorities not protected by unions). In the United States today much of the work on capitalist farms is carried out by vulnerable immigrant labourers, who work very hard for little pay.[36] Further, there is a long history of forced labour attached to colonial agriculture, which to some degree has lasted to this day.[37]

Up until the twentieth century, workers spent as much as 75 percent of their income on food. In order to keep wages down, it was important that food be relatively cheap, and no doubt this was an important reason that agricultural workers always received lower wages than industrial workers, even though they were only seasonally employed. Gender considerations also enter since historically women have received lower pay, and it is they who often did much of the food-related work. Starting with Irish immigrants in England as early as the 18th century, it was common to hire desperately poor immigrant workers to work in the fields. In recent years in the United States, cheap immigrant labour, women's labour or youth labour is still used at many steps in the food chain, and not only are wages in the food sector on average much lower than most other sectors, a system of state subsidies stimulates the continual overproduction of food, which until recently assured low food prices. But since food has become a much smaller portion of the wage basket, cheap food has functioned to free up income to be spent on other commodities, which, as we shall see in the next chapter, was crucial to capital accumulation after World War II.

To summarize, because the labour needs of agriculture are seasonal, because the work is extraordinarily demanding, and because cheap food is so important to capitalism, particular difficulties are raised for the commodification of labour power, making agriculture unusually dependent upon marginal or vulnerable workers. The historical dependence of most colonial crops (tobacco, tea, bananas, cotton and sugar) upon forced, quasi-forced or vulnerable labour doing back-breaking work for little or no income continues to this day in many developing countries and even in many of the fields in California and other states in the United States.

CAPITAL AND UNDERCONSUMPTION

Capital would in principle like to continually expand its profits, and in the food sector, one way of doing this is to get people to eat more. It has often been thought that this is limited by the fact that when someone is full, they will stop eating. Unfortunately the food industry has found ways of defeating what might at first seem to be a natural limitation. While there are various ways of doing this, one way is to get people to eat a lot of snacks. Snacks have the highest profit margin, and now there are people who snack nearly all the time, being limited only by waking hours. In the United States 50 percent of all eating occasions consist of snacking.[38] This means higher profits for food corporations and larger waistlines for consumers, whose obesity is likely to make their lives more disease-prone and shorter. The food industry has dealt with the problem of underconsumption by contributing to overconsumption.

One way capital can maximize profits is to get as much work as possible from each worker while paying the lowest possible wage. I say "lowest possible" because there is a major constraint in pure capitalism: workers need to subsist. What they can want is sharply constrained by the size of their income, their most basic needs, and the cost of the commodities required to meet these needs. As a result we have a sharp contradiction between capital, which would like to expand production indefinitely in order to expand profits indefinitely, and a working class whose capacity to buy this ever-expanding commodity product is sharply constrained. This would seem to be a classic case of limits set by underconsumption. There would seem to be no way out of this contradiction in a purely capitalist society where everyone is either a capitalist, a landlord or a worker, and where the capitalist and landlord classes are relatively small. However, in the next chapter, where I theorize the phase of consumerism at the level of mid-range theory, I shall show how the mode of capital accumulation characteristic of post World War II capitalism maximally developed every conceivable means of expanding consumption, through such avenues as sourcing the world for the cheapest inputs, debt expansion, marketing and advertising; hence my reference to this phase of capital accumulation as "the phase of consumerism".

As previously stated, in the case of family farms, if the price for their farm commodity falls, their natural reaction is to try to increase their yield to make up for the lower price with a larger mass, rather than leave the land. Of course the result of many farmers doing this will increase supply, thereby further lowering prices. Such a vicious cycle would only end with the complete bankruptcy of many farmers, who, once forced off the land, would be unlikely to return. This is a principal reason that family farming and capitalism are ultimately incompatible.

Because farming is so dependent on the weather, soil, insects, diseases and other natural conditions, it is difficult for farmers to know from one year to the next what their yields will be. In bad years they will need to incur debts that they can presumably pay off in good years. This makes them very dependent on credit-granting financial institutions, which may, after a run of bad years, force farmers to sell their farm to pay their debt. I believe that it may be accurate to say that very close to 100 percent of smaller family farms globally are deeply in debt. The problem here is that family farming requires long-term stability so that farmers can expect a continuing good quality of life, but the short-term market vagaries of capitalism militate against this. The ease of movement into and out of the production of particular commodities required if capitalism is to be rational is simply not so easy even in the case of fully capitalist farming, much less family farming. If supply and demand cannot easily adjust to one another, as is the case with much agricultural and food production, then pure capitalism cannot be very effective. For credit-granting institutions time is money, and allowing farmers to remain in arrears goes against the profit orientation of financial institutions.

The cheapest possible food is needed to keep wages down, since food would be a major item in the wage basket of pure capitalism. In the food sector, then, keeping costs down while increasing productivity is particularly important, but at the same time it is particularly difficult. Until recently, productivity increases have been limited by time and space constraints imposed by nature. The mechanization and chemicalization of agriculture, which has breached these constraints, has increased short-term profits while leaving behind a giant ecological and toxicological debt to be dealt with by future generations.

The other capitalistic way of keeping costs down is to utilize the cheapest possible labour, something that globalization has made more and more feasible. But the most astounding advance made by food capitalists in combating underconsumption in this sector is an historically unprecedented expansion of the quantity of food eaten. This has been achieved by many new techniques that stimulate excessive appetites and that take advantage of the quasi-addictive character of certain foods. The resulting so-called "obesity epidemic" creates an enormous health debt for future generations to deal with, a debt that may bankrupt many countries.

CAPITAL, OLIGOPOLY AND GLOBALIZATION

Although competition is assumed in the context of the theory of capital's deep structures, at this most abstract level of analysis, we can at least understand the general structural pressures that would cause capital to form larger and larger units and to expand globally. Marx emphasizes two fundamental structural reasons that explain why capital is likely to centralize over time. First, during periodic crises the stronger units of capital grow by swallowing up the weaker units. Second, the mobilization and concentration of social savings through institutions, such as banks and stock markets, that grant credit to capital, also facilitate concentration into larger units.

In order to understand something like the "merger movement" of the late nineteenth century, however, we need to move to mid-range theory and historical analysis, because many of the causal factors are phase-specific and cannot therefore be derived from capital in the abstract and in general. In England, for example, the leading capitalist power in the world until the late nineteenth century, the corporate form had been legally constrained since the burst of the South Sea Bubble in 1720, which nearly bankrupted the country.[39] Giving the limited-liability joint stock company the legal go-ahead was a prerequisite for the merger movement of the late nineteenth century. Other causal factors or conditions of existence of the merger movement would include:

- the development of financial institutions, like banks and stock markets
- the increasing movement of capital into resource extraction and heavy industry where economies of scale are important
- protective tariffs and dumping
- government spending on infrastructure and military build-ups
- the need to control a more militant work force
- the need for corporations to influence government policy
- better transportation and communication technologies
- the increasing importance of having a global reach in many industries for the cheapest resource extraction
- inter-imperialist rivalry.

Early monopolistic trading companies like the East India Company and the Royal African Company involved themselves in trading spices, sugar, tobacco, cotton, tea, opium and slaves or indentured servants, but usually avoided getting involved in actually running plantations. Out of the activities of these companies, a colonial system gradually developed into two types of neo-colonial capitalist arrangements. In one the capitalist corporation owns the land and runs the plantations, and in the other the capitalist corporation buys from primary producers, which vary in size and the degree to which they are capitalist. For example, with banana production both types exist and fade into one another, whereas with coffee and cocoa production most production is carried out by family farms.

But in either case the colonial set-up with the very large monopolistic trading companies fostered a relatively easy transition to a capitalist food regime. As a result, capitalist agriculture often developed earlier in the context of plantations of colonies and ex-colonies than in the United States, where the family farm was only subsumed to capitalism on a large scale after World War II.

With capitalism the possibility exists that large tracts of land are owned by a small number of individuals or corporations, which because of their huge holdings may only be concerned with short-term profits and not long-term stewardship of the land. For example, we see severe damage to Florida wetlands and the Everglades by large sugar corporations, which have not shown much concern for their environmental devastation except to the extent that outside pressure has been brought to bear.[40] The situation can be even worse in developing countries where weak states either lack effective environmental regulations or lack effective enforcement for regulations that do exist.

For many years the family farm reigned in US agriculture; however, particularly since World War II, concentration has occurred in every step of food production and circulation from field to table. Farms have grown in size only to be subsumed to immense corporations that supply inputs and process outputs. Size not only gives corporations control over markets with the possibility of raising prices above their competitive level, it also gives them enormous political and ideological power to influence government policy, to access educational institutions, and to fill the media and public spaces with associations between their commodity and happiness. Expensive media access is particularly important in the food sector because of the need to get young people hooked on certain types of high-tech, high-caloried foods, and in order to create an atmosphere of food cravings that continually inundate consumers with the quasi-addictive qualities of foods laced with sugar, fat and salt. Corporate size is similarly important in lobbying government, because of the extreme importance of government subsidies and trade policies in this sector. Finally, corporate size is important in the production of high-tech fast foods and junk foods because of:

- the advantages associated with standardization and mass production

- the need to source the world for low-cost inputs, because of the cost savings associated with sometimes expensive highly computerized systems of production, preservation and delivery of product globally
- the huge costs of marketing and advertising.

In general we can say that the larger the unit of capital, the better it can weather the storms of economic downturns or of competition from other large units. Oligopoly and monopoly make it relatively easy to pass on any increased costs to consumers. Further, we can say that the largest units of capital that have ever existed in the world, exist now, and that in our current globalizing capitalism, the forces that lead to the centralization of capital are many and are strong.[41]

CAPITAL AND SUBJECTIVITY

A separation between us as subjects and the objects around us is a common sense assumption of everyday life. A recent preoccupation of social science has been with how our senses of identity are formed, or in what sense and how we get constructed as subjects. Marx's *Capital* can contribute a good deal to the clarification of how capital in its basic structures helps to shape the sense of self as autonomous subject. It can also contribute to our understanding of how corporations as legal subjects take on aspects of subjectivity. Much has been written about these things. Here I shall simply make a few basic points.

Our identities and sense of self can be shaped by many things including family structures, religion, education and ideology; but what about the basic economic structures of capitalism? Under capitalism many objects in the world are someone's private property, and this subordinates them to the owner's will. From the point of view of private property, every person or subject is an island of private property connected to other islands through monetary exchange. And one's island identity depends primarily upon the size and type of market in which the island shrinks or expands, by selling off pieces of it or buying pieces to add to it. Thus the capitalist sells capitalistically produced commodities for a profit, workers sell their labour-power for a wage and landlords lease their land for rent. The more islandized or atomized a society becomes, the more each family or each individual stands alone. The end point of such subjectification is extreme possessive individualism, and it is precisely this extreme subjectification that makes competition so intense in pure capitalism, and that undermines the possibilities for individuals to band together to resist the objectification that subsumes them to self-regulating markets. And not only does such subjectification make the objectification of human agents all the more complete, it also aids capital ideologically by making it possible to equate extreme individualism with freedom. Capital does not need to take responsibility for the plight of any particular individuals, if as totally free agents they are assumed to be fully responsible for their condition. In a strange way, subjectification is a form of objectification in the context of capitalism.

As islands, capitalist subjects are also legal subjects or legal persons with the exclusive right to their island, and to add to it or subtract from it by buying, selling or contracting. This follows from the necessity that subjects in a purely capitalist society must be capable of participating in at least some capitalist market, since survival depends on being able to buy at least the basic necessities. Participants in capitalism must recognize each other as legal persons able to own private property.[42] And in the first instance private property must also have clear boundaries in order to separate "mine from thine". According to its basic and clearest form, private property implies total control by the owning self, and total exclusion of the other, unless the owning self grants access. And since each self is an island centred in private property, where the self has total control, others must always be at least a little threatening, since the self has total control on their island, but none offshore. Not only are others in continual competition over island enlargement, since this is the only means to establish status, but they may at any time trespass and even take away a piece of your property. The basic form of private property, then, creates a sharp divide between self and other, constructing the other as always a potential threat. Contrary to the view that "no man is an island", capitalism in its purest form converts every man, woman, family, corporation or government into an island.

As strange as it may seem, while capitalism is a powerful atomizing or subjectifying power, at the same time it also objectifies subjects, while capital itself takes on some properties of subjectivity. If we imagine pure capitalism where markets are entirely self-regulating in the sense that they are regulated by the movements of prices generated by forces of supply and demand, human agency can only be rational in so far as it can follow the price signals of markets. If, because of short supplies and large demand, prices and profits rise, then rational capitalists, best placed to do so, will shift production into the sector with higher profits until profits diminish to the average level as a result of increased supply. There is rational agency here, but only in so far as it is able to follow price signals. Errant behaviour is continually corrected by markets, with the ultimate sanction being bankruptcy and the possibilities of being deprived of food, clothing and shelter. While from the point of view of immediacy, human agency may seem free to buy or sell, in fact, over even relatively short time spans success and failure are dictated by the movement of commodities. This is what Marx is referring to when he considers capital to be an object with important characteristics of subjectivity. Each capitalist aims to maximize profits, and, as a society-wide aggregate of competition, capital as a whole becomes a self-expanding force, or what Marx calls "self-valorizing value". But a self that consistently pursues a goal (capital) shares this important similarity with human subjectivity. It follows that in a purely capitalist society, capital can be viewed at least metaphorically as a subject, and human agents as objects that it utilizes to maximize its aggregate expansion.

It would seem, then, that capital objectifies humans, but paradoxically this process of objectification is made more effective by a parallel process that at the same time subjectifies in the sense of atomizing. Commodities and money form a collective subject by interrelating quantitatively through markets, but at the same time they connect individuals isolated by their private property. Marx was not exaggerating when he utilized the term "cash nexus" to refer to the basic social connection of a purely capitalist society. Capital promotes an extreme subjectification of individuals (alienation or possessive individualism), in order to more effectively objectify them. Or, in other words, to the extent that capital breaks down the sense of community or solidarity amongst people, it is far easier to objectify isolated individuals without resistance.

The strange result of this subject/object inversion is that although the majority of people who produce food in the world cannot afford a good diet and are hungry much of the time, the response of pure capitalism would simply be: it's their own fault.

CONCLUSIONS

In this chapter I have outlined some of the basic structural dynamics of capitalism at the most abstract level of analysis, and have presented a number of historical illustrations of how these dynamics could play out or have played out in concrete situations. I have tried to demonstrate that even if we assume that capitalism is operating at its competitive and equilibrating best, it cannot rationally manage agriculture or food.

Given these irrationalities, it is not surprising that most agriculture at most times and places in capitalist history has not been capitalist, but has instead been carried out by self-employed families, has been feudal, or has involved forced labour to varying degrees. Furthermore, when we look at the historical record, it appears that capitalism has actually had an easier time relating to agrarian systems of forced labour than systems of self-employment. For example, capitalism managed to relate to the southern US slave economy quite effectively in the first half of the nineteenth century. In contrast, the great depression wreaked havoc with the American system of family farms, and it was only very significant state intervention carried out by President Roosevelt in the 1930s that re-established a degree of price stability at levels which enabled some farming families to survive.

After World War II, with the enormous upswing of the mechanization and chemicalization of agriculture, and with enormous state support, the American food system became increasingly capitalist at every step of food provision from field to table. In this chapter I have presented reasons why pure capitalism, at its competitive best, necessarily fails to effectively manage agriculture or feed people well through its "self-regulating markets". This is the principal reason why the agrarian sector has nearly always received significant state support. In the next chapter, I shall locate the origins of our current agricultural/food regime in the mode of capital accumulation that emerged in the United States after World War II. Although this mode of accumulation increasingly subsumed agricultural production to capitalism, and in some instances doubled or tripled crop yields, these gains were achieved at immense and ever-increasing social costs that have led many experts to refer to existing agricultural and food practices as "unsustainable".

3 THE PHASE OF CONSUMERISM AND THE US ROOTS OF THE CURRENT AGRICULTURE AND FOOD REGIMES

Hungry men listen only to those who have a piece of bread. Food is a tool. It is a weapon in the US negotiating kit.[1]

This research created hybrid seed varieties that yielded more than traditional ones. In order to work, the seeds required almost laboratory-perfect growing conditions, which demanded irrigation, fertilizers, and pesticides. These in turn depended on fossil fuels for their production.[2]

In Chapter 2 I situated food provisioning in the context of pure capitalism, and in this Chapter I shall situate it in the context of the post World War II phase of consumerism (mid-range theory). These two chapters will provide the frameworks for understanding the structures and historical development of our current food regime. I do this because I want to be as clear as possible about how the current food regime fits in with capital accumulation as seen through three levels of abstraction. It seems to me that the neo-liberal response to the crises of the 1970s, while continually flashing to the world its great successes, has actually generated fairly superficial successes which have bought time in the present at enormous costs to the future.[3] In this unfolding analysis, I want to convince the reader that capitalism is essentially bad for agriculture and food provision, and is increasingly bad. In the future we shall need extensive long-range democratic planning, cooperatives, and for the most part relatively small or mid-sized mixed organic farms that receive significant public support and are encouraged to support each other through various types of cooperative arrangement.

I call the so-called "golden age" of capitalism in the United States (roughly 1946–70) *the phase of consumerism* because mass consumption is so central to it. For instance, between 1945 and 1950 the consumption of autos and household appliances increased by 205 and 240 percent respectively.[4] Since the early 1970s this phase of capital accumulation has gradually declined into a transitional phase marked by increasing inequality, violence, social/political decay, economic stagnation, and damage to human and environmental health. It is not certain whether a new phase of capitalism (that is, a new "golden age" or new relatively stable, expansive and hegemonic mode of accumulation) will emerge out of this transition; however, it seems highly unlikely given the radical dysfunctions and contradictions of the current phase and the basic tendencies of capital's deep structures.[5]

I strongly believe that nearly all the changes that are needed to prevent the world from falling into a kind of barbarism are changes that tend to compromise or undermine capital's inner operating principles. The changes are those that would make corporations and markets more democratically accountable in ways that are inconsistent with unbridled capitalism. Indeed, it might not be appropriate to call a sufficiently democratized capitalism, capitalism at all.

While I would argue that each phase of capitalist development has its own "golden age", many theorists refer to what I would call the golden age of consumerism as the "golden age of capitalism" in general. The celebrated successes of the "golden age of capitalism" were rather superficial for three primary reasons:

- They arose in part because of a never to be repeated American hegemony resulting from a victory in World War II that did not damage the economic infrastructure of the United States.
- It is a little paradoxical to refer to the most socialist phase of American capitalism as "the golden age of capitalism". As Brandon puts it, "For the stunning paradox of the McCarthy period and the Cold War years that followed it is that this era of

flaming anti-collectivist rhetoric saw the greatest public investment, in both housing and transport that America had ever
known."[6]

- Many of the achievements were superficial in the sense that
  they were short-term gains achieved at the cost of truly staggering long-term pain, and some of the gains were reversed by
  subsequent changes in government policy.

When the golden age went into crisis in the early 1970s, the
direction taken by government policy moved the United States
increasingly away from the mildly socialist proclivities of the
golden age, which had seemed to humanize capitalism, towards an
increasingly brutal "survival of the fittest" mode of capitalism. To a
large extent the stagflation difficulties of the private sector were
resolved through a massive shift of wealth from the public to the
private sector, a shift that left health, education, infrastructure,
research and welfare seriously underfunded.

In order to understand the roots of the current agricultural/food
regime, it is necessary to trace them back first to the roots of capitalism in general (Chapter 2), and second to the golden age of
consumerism, which I shall proceed to outline in this chapter. This
requires locating the phase-specific roots of mid-range theory within
the dominant phase of capital accumulation centred in the United
States after World War II, and which presented fairly coherent and
fairly successful patterns of accumulation for 25 years.

It would be a mistake to apply the theory of capital's inner logic
directly to the explanation of history, because although it traces the
basic dynamic patterns of capitalist economic categories, the categories remain abstract and unspecified in terms of concrete historical practices. For example, we know from the most abstract level of
theory that capitalism has a tendency to speed up the movement of
inputs, of production and of outputs, but without the knowledge of
historically specific technologies, the possible forms of these
speed-ups cannot be known. So while it is useful to continually
refer back to the abstract logic to remind ourselves of capital's basic
propensities, we also need a middle level of categories that will
facilitate periodizing the history of capital accumulation in terms of
phase-specific technologies, institutions and practices. To be able to

effectively think the specificity of these contexts, we need more concretely specified economic categories as well as political and ideological categories.[7]

Of key importance to mid-range theory is the fact that historically and globally capitalism develops very unevenly. Capitalist history can be viewed as a series of predominant modes of capital accumulation typically centred in one or a few capitalist powers.[8] As one mode declines a new mode arises to replace it, and the replacement may geographically relocate the centre of capital accumulation, as when the centre shifted from England to Germany and the United States in the late nineteenth century. Each successive mode of accumulation passes through a sort of "golden age" when it is most hegemonic and successful, only to be followed by a "leaden age" when it is in decline.[9] Of course, it is always possible that a golden age will be followed not by a transition to a new phase of capital accumulation, but by a transition away from capitalism itself.

I would argue that the golden age of the phase of *mercantilism* was centred in Britain between 1700 and 1850, when capital accumulation was centred in a putting-out system most characteristically developed in the cottage spinning and weaving of woollens. The golden age of the phase of *liberalism* was centred in England from 1830 to 1860, when the most characteristic mode of capital accumulation was the factory manufacturing of cotton textiles. The golden age of the phase of *imperialism* was centred in the United States and Germany from 1890 to 1914, and capital accumulation for this phase was most characteristically manifested in the steel industry. Finally, the golden age of the phase of *consumerism* was most fully developed in the United States from 1946 to 1970, and the industry that was most characteristic of this phase of accumulation is the auto industry.

Following this schema, I would argue that the transition from the phase of *imperialism* (golden age 1890–1914) to the phase of *consumerism* (golden age 1946–70) came close at various junctures (particularly in the immediate post World War I era and after the Great Depression) to turning into a transition away from capitalism. Indeed, capitalism had to pass through fascism and another world war before it could find its way to a new relatively stable and expansive mode of accumulation.

There are many factors that contributed to the economic "take-off" in the United States after World War II. The following list includes the most important factors. One thing to consider when reading this list is the extent to which many of these factors are historically specific and cannot be reproduced now or in the future:

- Pent-up demand and lack of competition from other capitalist powers after World War II.[10]
- A gold-dollar international monetary system which to a considerable extent freed up the United States from concerns about balance of payments deficits at least until the 1960s.
- Cheap and plentiful oil and natural gas which fuelled a petrochemical revolution of new technologies and the mass consumption of consumer durables.[11]
- Oligopoly in the dominant economic sectors which increased not only the economic power but the political and ideological power of large corporations.
- Relative industrial peace made possible by a rate of growth in productivity and profits which could sustain a collective bargaining process that generally improved real wages, benefits and working conditions in the main sectors of industrial accumulation.
- A strong sense of togetherness generated by victory in World War II and maintained by the cold war.
- A welfare state which made huge investments in material and social infrastructure.
- Rapid population growth.
- Cheap land.
- Cheap food.
- Expansion of every kind of debt.
- A lack of concern for environmental issues.
- An auto industry that became the centre of economic growth, ensuring car-centred development.
- A process of suburbanization which fitted with car-centred development, that stimulated the mass consumption of consumer durables, and which created de facto racially segregated housing.[12]
- Television which opened up vast new possibilities for the commercialization of life, ideological manipulation, and to a large extent became the "opiate of the masses".[13]

Each one of these factors could be discussed at length, and they could be discussed as they interrelate and support each other in a mode of capital accumulation. For my purpose, which is to set the table for understanding the current agricultural/food system, I shall focus on the above factors as they relate to the seven dimensions that flow from capital's inner logic as outlined in the last chapter. In this chapter these dimensions are discussed more concretely in the context of the *phase of consumerism*. In other words, I explore some of the particular institutional embodiments of capital's abstract tendencies as they are manifested by the post World War II mode of accumulation most characteristically developed in the United States.[14]

The dimensions to be discussed are:

- consumerism's profit orientation: petroleum, cars, suburbs and television
- consumerism, time and speed: unchecked toxicity and life on the run
- consumerism, space and homogenization: suburbanization and monocultures
- consumerism and workers: hiding the social costs of hazardous working conditions and low wages
- consumerism and underconsumption: new forms of debt expansion and advertising
- consumerism, oligopoly and globalization: a command economy of corporations
- consumerism and subjectivity: the politics of fear.[15]

CONSUMERISM'S PROFIT ORIENTATION: PETROLEUM, CARS, SUBURBS AND TELEVISION

Petroleum and natural gas are miracle substances in their energy intensity and versatility. The golden age of capitalism in the United States would not have been possible without their inexpensive availability, for it was they that provided the energy that was converted into large increases in productivity, high profit rates and rapid economic growth. One of the main markers for the ending of the golden age was the quadrupling of the price of oil by the

Organization of Petroleum Exporting Countries (OPEC) in the early 1970s.[16] Other significant markers were the Viet Nam war, America's abandoning of its Bretton Woods commitment to exchange dollars for gold at $35 an ounce, and the abandonment of the visions of social justice arising out of President Johnson's "Great Society" programme.[17]

Petroleum and natural gas generated a chemical revolution, the outcome of which was tens of thousands of new products including pharmaceuticals, plastics, paints, preservatives, solvents, cleaners, synthetic rubber, synthetic fabrics, pesticides, fertilizers, explosives, lubricants and fuels. Indeed industrialists, who bought chemical plants from the government for a song after World War II, knew that these plants could relatively easily be converted to the production of pesticides, fertilizers and other chemical products.[18] And finally, of course, there was the marriage of cheap petroleum and the mass production of the auto-mobile, with it taking a minimum of 20 barrels of oil (in the early twenty-first century) to produce a single car.[19] During its lifetime an average car consumes 3,000 gallons of gas, 50 gallons of oil, and emits 35 tons of carbon dioxide.[20] All this was made possible initially by the cheap and declining price of petroleum and by a commodity, the car, that was so profitable and so popular that almost no one thought about the fact that oil is a non-renewable resource and that it (as in oil spills) and many of its derivatives can have long-term damaging impacts on human and environmental health. Nor was much thought given to the impact of the car on city planning, on public transportation and on air quality.[21] A study in the early 1990s estimated that the social costs (not including the costs of global warming) of driving in the United States amounted to $300 billion per year.[22]

Arguably there were no sectors of the economy where the petro-chemical industry had a greater impact than agriculture and transportation. It has been claimed that the Haber–Bosch process for fixing nitrogen was the most important invention of the twentieth century.[23] This may seem like a most surprising claim since most people have never heard of this process. But when Haber invented the process in 1909, it was the first commercially important synthesis of nitrogen out of natural gas. It could be argued that this invention was important to the petrochemical revolution, and it is certainly the case that it eventually revolutionized agriculture. For after World War II, nitrogen fertilizers started to be used by farmers to dramatically increase their yields. The use of chemical fertilizers meant that crop rotation or leaving land fallow was no longer necessary, and that lands of very marginal fertility could be used for agriculture. The impact was such that recent scholars have written metaphorically of an agriculture that used land to convert petroleum into food. The resulting food commodities, then, can be referred to as "petrofoods".[24]

Indeed, as time has passed our food has become more and more petroleum-intense, as it has taken more and more calories of petroleum to produce one calorie of food. By the beginning of the twenty-first century it took on average ten calories of fossil fuel to produce and deliver one calorie of food, excluding household storage and cooking, which also use a lot of fossil fuel.[25] The immediate revolutionary impact of new hybrid seeds combined with petroleum-based fertilizers and pesticides, and with irrigation, was an impressive increase in productivity (agricultural yields doubled between 1947 and 1979) which came to be known as the "green revolution".

The green revolution was exported to developing countries, such that the total area of pesticide-sprayed land in developing countries increased 13-fold between 1960 and 1980.[26] But as the energy inputs increased, the returns diminished, so that while between 1945 and 1994 fossil fuel input to agriculture increased four-fold in the United States, crop yields increased three-fold.[27] Returns diminished because more and more pesticides were required to wipe out increasingly resistant pests, and more chemical fertilizer was required as soils degraded.

Increased productivity within the agricultural industry (agriculture was becoming increasingly "industrialized") not only provided inexpensive food for the burgeoning baby boom population growth after World War II (it peaked at 4.3 million births in 1957[28]), but also provided food surpluses that could be exported as a means to lessen the growing balance of payment deficits in the United States, which were viewed by many as a cause for concern by the mid-1960s. Further, in the context of the cold war, self-sufficiency in food was considered a necessity, and at the same time surpluses in the form of food aid were used in some cases as an incentive to identify with the American "camp".[29]

During the golden age of capitalism (or phase of consumerism), because increases in agricultural productivity meant that fewer farmers were needed, there was a certain attrition of farmers moving off the land. This attrition, however, was limited by government support of farm incomes through policies of supply management and loans. But the pressures to use food surpluses to make up some of the balance of payment deficit, and to make food even less expensive so that workers would have more money to spend on houses and consumer durables (which were being mass produced as never before), led to Earl Butz's (Secretary of Agriculture) agricultural bill of 1973, which removed supply management, price supports and loans, in favour of subsidies based on yields (the greater the yield, the greater the subsidy). The new policy encouraged the production of more and more food even if the costs of production were greater than the selling price, because subsidies would make up the difference. Hence, the larger the farm and the greater the yields, the greater the government subsidy. These could easily amount to over 50 percent of a farmer's income in the case of large industrial farms. It was a policy that encouraged evergreater agricultural surpluses, many of which were dumped in developing countries at below costs of production.

Although the food and agriculture sector saw dramatic developments due to petroleum inputs, it was the car which was the real hallmark of the phase of consumerism.[30]And it is for this reason that this phase of capital accumulation is often referred to as "Fordism" and the auto industry as the "industry of industries".[31] The automobile is a complex commodity, the production of which requires inputs from many other industries including steel, aluminium, chromium, glass, rubber, lead, paint, plastics, electronics and synthetic textiles. Once produced, automobiles require petrol stations, garages, parking lots, insurance, police, roads, bridges and many other supporting commodities and services. The automobile, then, has so many forward and backward linkages that it has been estimated that one out of six jobs in the United States in the 1950s and 1960s depended on the auto industry.[32]

In a very real sense, what was good for General Motors was

good for the economy.[33] After all, General Motors (GM) was the largest corporation in the world, producing 60 percent of the cars in the United States in the 1950s, and in that decade the auto industry contributed as much as 20 percent to the US Gross National Product (GNP).[34] And this key industry was profitable, with average returns on American industrial assets between 1946 and 1967 standing at 6.64 percent, compared with the average for GM of 14.67 percent.[35]

The growth of automobile production and consumption was staggering, as the number of cars on American roads increased from 50 million in 1958 to 100 million by 1970.[36] Automobiles were made more affordable by cheap material inputs, by cheap oil, by increased real wages, by cheaper food, clothing and housing which freed up discretionary income, and by debt expansion. They were made more necessary by the public funding of suburbanization and more desirable by massive public funding of free roads, which gave the auto owner enormous freedom of movement. By 1973, 68 percent of Afro-American wage-earners and 95 percent of white wage-earners owned a car.[37] The expansion of credit meant that most employed people could aspire to owning an automobile, one of the most desired commodities ever invented. While cheap oil was a necessary condition to fuel the enormous economic growth of post World War II American capitalism, the automobile was truly the central driving force; hence, it is accurate to refer to the rapid economic development that occurred as "car-dependent" or "car-centred".[38]

Besides the automobile, suburbs and television, one of the most profitable commodities of the golden age was cigarettes. In the 1950s the United States produced 70 percent of the world's tobacco.[39] While research had shown a connection between smoking and cancer as early as the 1930s, Davis reports that by the early 1950s the evidence supporting such a connection was growing rapidly, and the cigarette companies responded by assuring smokers that there was no proven connection between smoking and lung cancer.[40]

The case of the tobacco industry offers an important example for understanding capitalistic agriculture, and understanding capitalist corporations in general, which use their enormous power to continue doing what they are doing despite mounting evidence of growing social and/or environmental costs. Given its centrality to human well-being and the well-being of the environment, one would think that agriculture and food provision should be at the centre of economic theory and practice. But for capitalism it is industry that is central, and agriculture is an annoyance because for so long it has resisted the application of industrial methods. It is largely because of the recent petrochemical revolution that industrial methods have finally penetrated and increasingly subsumed agriculture to capitalism as simply another industrial sector. What started out as a green revolution, which by increasing yields would provide inexpensive food of good quality for all, has turned into a brown revolution, with 25 percent of humanity lacking adequate food and another 25 percent suffering from too much food, often of the wrong kind.[41] At the same time, the increasing damage to the environment done by this food regime jeopardizes the very future of humanity.

CONSUMERISM, TIME AND SPEED: UNCHECKED TOXICITY AND LIFE ON THE RUN

Because the cold war was in part cast as an economic race to see whether the United States or USSR could achieve a higher rate of growth in GNP,[42] and because capitalism in general is so single-mindedly profit oriented, the dark sides of the petrochemical revolution and car-dependent development were pushed into a seldom noticed background.[43] Tens of thousands of chemicals were released into the environment with little or no concern for their possible long-term toxic properties. According to Davis, even as of 2007, of the 80,000 chemicals in widespread use, only about 1,000 have passed through complete toxicity tests.[44] And when concerns finally were raised, as in Rachel Carson's *Silent Spring* (1962), the corporate sectors that profited from particular chemicals would often organize propaganda campaigns to cast doubt on the science behind the claims, and would lobby government to do nothing. It was in this way that the toxicity of most chemicals remained untested, that the toxicity of some chemicals was covered up, many chemicals that were discovered to be toxic continued to be used, and known carcinogens remained uncontrolled in the environment.[45]

On top of capitalism's general addiction to speed, the cold war added yet a further impetus to the general frenzy to expand profits and economic growth with minimal attention to the long-run toxicities of new chemical products. It is also worth noting that adequate testing would have required a significant government commitment of resources to establish scientific research bodies that would be completely independent from the corporations or industrial sectors whose products they were to test. Such independence would require sufficient government funding and careful monitoring of flows of influence to ensure that researchers would not be influenced by corporate power and largesse. This was not done because the ideological context was such that it would have been viewed as too socialist and too constraining on corporate profit making. President Reagan, for example, not only cut funding for testing chemicals, but also provided enormous funding to the abortive project of research to find a "safe" cigarette.[46] When corporations have invested a lot of money to fund research on a new product, they need to get returns on their investment as soon as possible. The last thing they want is long delays and possible rejection of their commodities for being toxic or in some sense dangerous. Lost time is lost money.

So unfolded a disturbing example of how capitalism privatizes profits and socializes costs, since in this case the social costs were the premature sickness and death of millions of people. What was the rush? Why release so many untested chemicals into the environment? While the overriding general reason was the single-minded drive for profits, there were also more contextual reasons having to do with the cold war, which was not only an arms race and a space race, but also a race to see which system could grow its GNP the fastest. In this context, to take a stand criticizing business for knowingly exposing humans to toxic substances could easily be labelled as "anti-business", and anyone who was anti-business could easily be labelled as "pro-communist". Given the enormous fear of the "red menace", to be so labelled in the 1950s or 1960s could result in becoming an unemployable social outcast. Later in the 1980s President Reagan actually cut back on the little spending that there was for testing the toxicity of chemicals, and at the same time the National Cancer

Institute was chaired by Armand Hammer, CEO of Occidental Petroleum, the producer of over 100 billion tons of toxic chemicals.[47]

When President Nixon declared a "war on cancer" in 1971, thereby kicking off the single largest public expenditure ever to combat a medical problem, nearly all the money went to finding and treating cancer in individuals rather than to finding and eliminating the causes of cancer. Big profits are to be made in a largely privatized medical system that comes up with pharmaceutical, surgical, or genetic means to treat individuals with cancer. Individuals will pay a lot to a system that can save their lives. In contrast, public money spent on researching carcinogens in the environment is not likely to lead to profit and is likely to step on the toes of capital by constraining their use of chemicals and thus their profits. As a result, it is often only when enough humans get ill in a way that is easily traceable to a particular chemical that that chemical becomes adequately tested.[48] Thus it is not surprising that items in such widespread use as certain chemical food additives should only recently have been found to be possible risk factors in the development of Attention Deficient Disorder (ADD) in children.[49] It is no exaggeration to say that we live in a world where humans have become guinea pigs in which the toxic properties of substances are only recognized when enough of us get sick or die. And further, if the substance is profitable enough, it may continue to be sold even if the result will be sickness and death for millions and even billions of people.[50] For example, it has been estimated that in the twenty-first century as many as a billion people will die of tobacco-related diseases.[51]

It is not surprising, then, that little public money has been spent on finding out which chemicals are carcinogenic. Indeed, between 1952 and 1956 12 billion Kent cigarettes were sold with asbestos filters, thus actually increasing the chance of cancer in smokers who thought that they were lowering their risks by smoking a filter cigarette.[52] To focus on the causes of cancer is not only unprofitable, it might interfere with and undermine the gains made by highly profitable sectors of the economy. While capitalism has always been in a rush to make profits, it was mainly after World War II and the petrochemical revolution that this rush moved the world so fast towards deadly consequences for both human health and the health of the environment.

Speeding up the turnover of capital increases profits, but also increases the pace of life. This has taken a number of forms. By the late 1950s 20 percent of Americans moved their place of residence every year.[53] The average sleep time of Americans decreased by 20 percent in the twentieth century. Now Americans work on average 350 hours more per year than Europeans.[54] All of the above are examples illustrating the speeding-up of the pace of life.

Finally, capitalism has increasingly developed a very narrow time focus, in which the past and future are largely ignored in favour of the present. One reason for this is the short-term profit orientation of capital, which favours profit now even at the expense of enormous future costs. If defined broadly, this is what debt is. Essentially it is the preference for present pleasure at the cost of future pain. One of the truly shocking dimensions of current capital accumulation is the degree to which it is profiting by passing on enormous costs to future generations, costs that might not only sharply diminish the standard of living for many people, but might even place the human condition on earth in jeopardy. In a very real sense, we are eating the future.

CONSUMERISM, SPACE, AND HOMOGENIZATION: SUBURBANIZATION AND MONOCULTURES

The primacy of capitalist profits necessitates rushing, which in turn leads to making space and time as linear and sequential or as homogeneous as possible so that they can be maximally compressed. Car-dependent development, which speeds up the movement of each individual with a car, has impacted enormously on our use of space and time, including the provisioning of food. From field to table, car-dependent development impacted nearly all aspects of agriculture and food. A spin-off of the car was the farm tractor, which mechanized farming and brought significant economies of scale to it, thus undermining smaller family farms. (Today a high-tech combine can cost over $800,000 and is so heavy that soil compaction is an ongoing problem.)

The large internal combustion engines of trucks moved food commodities from the fields up the line to storage, further processing or final consumption. The car made it possible for day labourers to appear at the fields at harvest time without living nearby, and made the life of the farmer less isolated. Car-dependent suburbanization and road building resulted in paving over significant amounts of the most fertile farm land. For example, by 1970 one-third of the land encompassed by Los Angeles' suburban sprawl was covered with paving or concrete, amounting to 250 tons of concrete per inhabitant.[55] The car ultimately changed retailing by making supermarkets and shopping malls possible. And finally, it is impossible to imagine fast food chains without car-centred development.

The rapid growth of car ownership fed the growth of suburbs and the rapid growth of suburbs fed car ownership. And the "visible hand" of government played a significant role in each. Ironically the rabid anti-communism of the 1950s was accompanied by the US government adopting the most socialist programmes in its entire history. To put it in crystal clear terms, "quasi-socialist" policies involving huge public spending on roads, housing and education were justified by anti-socialist rhetoric.

With over 15 million veterans of World War II returning to civilian life in 1946, the government prepared the finances that would spawn the mass production of suburban single family dwellings. For veterans there was often little or no money required as down payment, and with 30-year mortgages, the monthly payments were very low. According to the Housing Act of 1954 no money down was required for veterans and 5 percent for others.[56] In 1944 only 141,800 homes were built in the United States, whereas in the 1950s an average of 1.5 million homes were built each year.[57] All these new homes not only provided employment, but invited babies to fill the rooms. The number of American children under 15 increased from 39.97 million in 1940 to 55.77 million in 1960.[58] By 1970 there were 50 million small houses, and seven out of ten households were single-family, suburban dwellings.[59] And to serve as retail centres for these suburban developments, shopping malls increased from eight in 1945 to 3,840 by 1960.[60] Between 1950 and 1970 the population living in suburbs doubled, but suburbanization led to de facto segregated housing, which perpetuated the deep and abiding racism that has so marred the history of the United States.[61]

One would think that single-family homes would foster home-cooked family meals. But the cost of the home, the car, the television and all the other consumer durables needed to stock a single-family dwelling meant increasingly that both parents (in the still predominant dual-parent family) needed to work in order to pay off the increasing private indebtedness, which went from $73 billion in the early 1950s to $196 billion in the late 1950s.[62] This created a need for convenience foods (typically more highly processed) and eventually for fast foods.[63] Beyond the old standbys like Spam and corned beef hash, an early innovation in the area of convenience foods was the TV dinner. Since these frozen dinners only needed to be heated in the oven and could easily be eaten in front of the television, they made it possible to eat without missing any television.

In agriculture the profits associated with homogenization often meant a move towards monocultures. Crop rotation, inter-planting, green manure crops and returning organic matter to the soil, all of which preserved the fertility of the soil and foiled pests, could be dispensed with in favour of chemical fertilizers and pesticides, as well as large combines for one type of crop. Farmers would generally gravitate to the breed of seed with the greatest yield, thus reducing the species of the particular type of crop. Typically these seeds would be hybrid seeds bought every year from a handful of corporations. Genetic diversity would thus be reduced, and with it the possibility of breeding new seeds to resist particular diseases or changing environmental conditions. The same thing occurred with farm animals. We are now learning that it is possible to increase yields by working with an extremely heterogeneous nature rather against it.

CONSUMERISM AND WORKERS: HIDING THE HEALTH COSTS OF HAZARDOUS WORKING CONDITIONS AND LOW WAGES

While workers with powerful unions in the oligopolistic sectors of the economy generally benefited from rising real wages during much of the golden age, the same cannot be said for much of the agrarian and food sectors. Field workers and slaughterhouse workers performed work with very high rates of health and safety problems.[64] And while unionized slaughterhouse workers typically made an average industrial wage, the typical immigrant field worker made the lowest wage of any sector. Wages in the agricultural and food sectors in general, from field workers to workers in canneries, to supermarket clerks, to waitresses, were far below average and often below the poverty line.

Food tended to be cheap because of low wages in this sector, increased yields due to fossil fuel inputs, and cheap imports largely due to very low wages in developing countries and cheap transportation costs. This meant that workers in unionized industries with increased real wages could have more discretionary income to spend on the array of commodities other than food, as needed for this consumerist phase of capitalism. And near the end of the golden age, the invention of fast junk foods combined with television advertising aimed at youth, made food yet cheaper, more addictive, more profitable and less healthful. Because such foods are the cheapest and the most available, workers and the poor are the most likely to eat them, thus undermining their long-term health prospects.

Workplace hazards, which have always been a problem with capitalism, took new forms in an economy so oblivious to the dangers of toxic chemicals. Because of the rights of private property, scientists, policy makers and the public did not have access to data on cancer rates amongst workers exposed to particular toxic substances in factories. It was all too easy to classify anything going on within a factory as a "trade secret" not available for public or scientific inspection.[65] And when damning statistics did emerge, corporations would do everything in their power to explain them away, or they would challenge anyone to prove that a particular cancer in a particular individual was caused by a particular chemical exposure in their workplace. Thus when African-American coke oven workers began to display noticeably high rates of lung cancer, steel companies would pass off the data by claiming that "negroes" were simply more prone to lung cancer than whites. This argument could not be disproved until white Mormon coke oven workers in Utah started to display the same high rates of lung cancer.[66]

CONSUMERISM AND UNDERCONSUMPTION: NEW FORMS OF DEBT EXPANSION AND ADVERTISING.

When an economy needs to continually expand as fast as possible, there must be ever new ways of enticing each consumer not only to part with their income, but also to go into debt in order to consume more and more. The unfolding of what seemed to be a consumer's paradise in the United States in the 1950s and 1960s was in part made possible by easy money. For instance, private debt in the 1950s increased from $73 billion to $196 billion.[67] Debt of every kind, from bank loans to mortgages to instalment buying at a personal level, to balance of payments deficits and debt expansion at a federal level, fuelled the rapidly expanding consumption. Debt expanded at every level from the national to the local, and from the corporate to the individual. But in due course easy money ultimately leads to hard choices, and it was the balance of payments deficits that seemed particularly threatening.

The Bretton Woods international monetary system agreed to by the great powers after World War II made the US dollar the international currency, to be stabilized by being exchangeable for gold at $35 per ounce. As previously mentioned, one consequence of this was that the United States could be less concerned about balance of payments deficits than other countries. But as the balance of payments deficits became larger and larger, by 1969 the dollars in foreign hands could buy all the gold in Fort Knox three times over. In response the US government took a number of steps to alleviate the situation, culminating in a total severing of the dollar from gold in 1973. This set of policy moves, plus the substantial increase in the price of oil imposed by OPEC, symbolize the end of the golden age of capitalism in the United States. The enlarged debt and oil price increases generated a high rate of inflation in an economy that was stagnating, and this stagflation thwarted the traditional Keynesian fiscal and monetary policies that would slow down the economy in the event of inflation.

What does all this have to do with agriculture and food? Arguably the balance of payments problem triggered some radical changes in American agricultural policy, ushered in by Earl

Butz, Secretary of Agriculture from 1971 to 1976 under Presidents Nixon and Ford. Prior to Butz's reforms the principal policy emphasis in dealing with the perennial agricultural surpluses was on various efforts to reduce supply, such as paying farmers to let some fields lie fallow. However, after Butz's reforms, farmers received subsidies for increasing their yields, and the ever-increasing surpluses were sold in international markets at whatever price necessary to sell the desired quantity, even if it was far below what would otherwise be the international price. A positive result of this policy was to improve America's balance of trade and hence balance of payments. This seemingly innocent policy change has had immense and in some cases devastating consequences, which are explored in greater depth in Chapter 5. Suffice it to say here that the policy stimulated more rapid concentration in the agrarian sector to the detriment of the family farm, increased the use of large tractors, increased the use of chemical pesticides and fertilizers, and undermined agriculture in developing countries where farmers could not compete with the subsidized low prices of US crops. Another impact was cheap food, enabling capitalists to pay lower wages to workers and to buy cheaper agricultural inputs for industry. To put it most succinctly, Butz's reforms spurred on the United States, and to a lesser extent the rest of the world, towards the development of a highly oil-dependent and concentrated agricultural/food system.

On the demand side, an important key to consumerism is getting people to want what they do not need. In clothing this is done by a fashion industry which defines what is "in" for the fashion conscious. In a sense, something like fashion occurs with food. Thousands of new and more processed products are introduced every year, and often much of the marketing and advertising is aimed at young children since they are impressionable and are easily manipulated by the blandishments of sugars, fats and salts combined in ever new and enticing ways. Television is the most effective advertising medium ever invented, and, like the car, is an extremely popular commodity that few people would want to be without.

The television market grew at an incredible rate, from only 9 percent of homes with televisions in 1950 to 90 percent by 1960, bringing a steady flow of commercial messages and entertainment into the otherwise isolated homes of suburbia.[68] Americans began to spend more and more time in front of the television, and, as a result, the average American came to devote 20 percent of their waking life to watching television and its relentless flow of commercial advertisements.[69] The largest single source of advertising revenues in the 1950s came to television from cigarette companies[70] which increased spending on television advertisements from $40 million in 1957 to $115 million in 1962.[71]

As we shall see in future chapters, television has come to play a central role in advertising highly processed foods, fast foods and junk foods – foods that tend to be very high in sugars, fats and salt relative to their nutritional value. And with strong evidence that lifetime eating habits are formed in childhood, more and more of this advertising has been aimed at children. Further, the high cost of television advertising, combined with its effectiveness in shaping consumer behaviour, has stimulated the concentration of capital in general and the food industry in particular. Corporations need to be large in order to afford sustained television advertising, and oligopoly generally facilitates passing on the costs of advertising to the consumer.

Television in the United States started out not only as highly commercial, but also as highly concentrated. The centrality of profit making has meant that television networks must always strive to accumulate the maximum possible audience for their flow of commercials. In other words, they aim to capture audiences who have money to spend now or will have in the future, primarily the white upwardly mobile middle and upper middle classes.[72] Today, the bulk of prime time television shows are produced in Los Angeles by a small number of companies, and the 100 top US advertisers pay for two-thirds of all network television. As a result television tends to homogenize the cultural environment. In the 1950s and 1960s American television was dominated by ABC, CBS and NBC, whereas today it is dominated by a small number of global media conglomerates. The great success of television advertising is one of the most powerful forces that maintain consumption at high levels in the United States, even if it means that consumers go deeply into debt.

CONSUMERISM, OLIGOPOLY AND GLOBALIZATION: A COMMAND ECONOMY OF CORPORATIONS

In the phase of consumerism, oligopoly in the dominant sectors of the economy was typical, and the global operations of most large corporations really began to take off in the declining years of the golden age.[73] Oligopoly combined with global operations has numerous advantages, including the ability to:

- have considerable influence on prices
- avoid taxes
- avoid governmental regulations
- source the world for the cheapest inputs
- open new markets globally
- undermine trade unions
- pressure governments to pass favourable legislation
- finance expensive advertising and marketing campaigns
- finance research and development.

The ability to set up competitions among governments in order to win the favour of major corporate investments gave large corporations huge advantages. For example, an aluminium corporation might make the following offer: we will build a smelter in your jurisdiction creating 3,000 jobs if you agree to low rates for electricity, low rates for water, reduced need to meet environmental regulations, freedom from paying taxes (or a tax holiday), and a government investment of $50 million to help build and equip the plant. While I have made up this example, there is nothing in it that you could not find in numerous such agreements.[74] Indeed, subsidies to corporations have now reached obscene proportions, with Tennessee announcing in 2008 that it would pay a massive subsidy of $500 million to Volkswagen in order to secure the location of an assembly plant in the state.[75]

While certain food companies like Coca-Cola were already very large at the start of the golden age, many of the enormous corporations in the food sector were just getting off the ground as the golden age was winding down in the late 1960s. The high levels of concentration in the tropical foods sector (coffee, chocolate, tea, bananas) were already in place as a sort of extension of colonialism, or what has often been called "neo-colonialism". While most tea, bananas and cane sugar are grown on large plantations, coffee and chocolate are predominately grown by small farmers. The transportation, processing and marketing of tropical commodities, where most of the profits are made, had for a long time been controlled by a small number of large corporations.

CONSUMERISM AND SUBJECTIVITY: THE POLITICS OF FEAR

I agree with Putnam's (2000: 271) claim that World War II was the most levelling event in US history, and I would add that it was also the event that most advanced a sense of community. Everyone was prepared to sacrifice, and most did sacrifice to win the war against fascism. In other words, it strongly countered the deep structural dynamics of capitalism, which as we have seen promote inequality and social atomism or alienation. World War II was a gift for capitalism, because although capitalism promotes inequality, it does not work well if inequality and alienation become too great; and yet it cannot on its own counter these very tendencies that it generates.

The possessive individualism that is generated by capitalism in general and by the new consumerism in particular, as it is associated with the auto, suburbia, television, military complex, did not bring the contented life as hoped for.[76] The new suburbs were racially segregated, and the extreme car-dependency of Los Angeles gave it the dubious fame of being the first city inundated with smog. After the war, women were unceremoniously excused from their jobs to find their "traditional" place in the home. Many women became relatively isolated in their new suburban homes, and such contrivances as Tupperware parties only temporarily filled the void. It is not surprising, then, to find that by 1978 20 percent of US women were taking valium.[77]

The car fitted perfectly with the possessive individualism characteristic of capitalism because it seemed to maximize the freedom of movement of each individual, increasing the speed each of us can move through time and space. A case could be made that the freedom and empowerment that seem to attach to the car are rather superficial in the larger scheme of things. Car ownership promotes a kind of possessive individualism which, while instilling feelings of power, at the same time undermines such power with the total futility that comes with isolation. Because more and more individuals spend more and more time alone, isolated in the steel box that is the car, it would seem that the car has probably promoted social atomism and compromised community involvement. Recent statistics reveal that 19 percent of all meals eaten by Americans are now eaten in cars, and American parents spend more time in cars than with their children.[78]

The range from relatively cheap cars to luxury cars, combined with nearly annual model changes, made the car into one of the primary status symbols in modern society, and hence an important accoutrement in support of identity formation.[79] Arguably a major reason for the car's popularity is that it placed the immense energy intensity of oil at the service of each car owner. Drivers could now get from almost any point A to point B more quickly than ever before, and right under their foot was the power of acceleration. The car seemed like the ultimate conquest of space by time, compressing the amount of time that it would take to move across space. Such a freedom of movement and such power could not help but tap deeply into the wish fulfilments of most people, making car ownership not only a necessity but also a great source of pleasure.

It is important to emphasize the degree to which capitalism promotes a kind of extreme individualism which can be undermining to social life if not countered. Capitalist ideology tends to make the individual basic, and it views collectives as simply larger individuals. Most corporate bodies are considered in law as "legal persons", but there can be considerable difference between the rights and duties accorded to corporations, for example, and those of trade unions, both of which are legal persons. Arguably in the case of business corporations, ironically, the fiction of legal personhood has meant in practice that it has been difficult to hold them socially responsible and democratically accountable.[80] The privacy that often attaches to legal personhood has meant that far from being open and transparent, the workings of corporations largely occur behind closed doors.

While the solidarity and sense of community promoted by the left and by trade unions was steadily eroded by capitalism's atomizing forces in the 1950s and 1960s, it was not until the Thatcher and Reagan regimes in the 1980s that government became extremely interventionist in its efforts to crush trade unions and the left worldwide.[81]

Governments can and usually do use their power to indoctrinate people to the extent necessary to mobilize their support for various policies. Typically much more indoctrination is required to get people to support a war, for example, than to support legislation that would increase the minimum wage by 50 cents. The very active state indoctrination associated with World War II increased even further during the cold war. This was made possible in part by more effective and extensive mass media, by an interventionist warfare/welfare state, and by an escalating politics of fear.

Notice that I intentionally place warfare before welfare in "warfare/welfare" state, for a great deal of the welfare that made the phase of consumerism a little socialist was only made possible by warfare, or the threat of warfare. It certainly did not arise from some sudden change of heart on the part of capitalists to place human need before profits, or a change of predilections amongst many Americans to stop favouring individualism and small government. It was World War II, the Korean War and the cold war that enabled successive governments to institute policies that would otherwise be an affront to the ethos of American individualism and free enterprise.

As previously argued, unless countered by other forces, the inner logic of capital generates individualism. It just so happened that two major forces created an unprecedented sense of community and sense of patriotism in this historical period. First came the collective crisis of the Great Depression, which led to the state-sponsored collective solutions of the New Deal. A significant degree of working-class solidarity emerged from the economic crises of the 1930s, but this was to a large extent absorbed into the national solidarity of World War II and the struggle against fascism. So it happened that America emerged from World War II with a sense of togetherness rivalling that achieved by the American Revolution and the founding Constitution, and this sense of solidarity was maintained by a cold war which aimed to isolate and destroy a new enemy – communism.

During World War II government spending constituted nearly half of the GNP, and though this was significantly reduced after the war, the precedent was there. With many having risked their lives to achieve victory, suddenly with the end of the war, 15 million military personnel needed to be demobilized and reintegrated into the economy. The US government responded by making large amounts of money available to subsidize education, housing and health for GIs, and to a lesser extent for others. This meant a significant expansion of the welfare state, already given a significant advance by President Franklin Delano Roosevelt.

The cold war and the fear of communism were used repeatedly to justify government spending which would probably not have passed Congress otherwise.[82] For example, between 1947 and 1970 a series of Interstate Highway Acts fostered spending at all levels of government, which is estimated to have reached $249 billion, making it the largest single public project in history up to that time. One of the justifications given for this spending (which might have been labelled as "socialist") was the need for roads so that people could exit cities in case of a nuclear attack on the United States. As the "cold war" got more intense with the McCarthyism of the early 1950s, military spending increased, creating the largest peacetime military establishment ever. Between 1950 and 1970 on average 60 percent of all government spending was on national security.

And while it was difficult to get Keynesian fiscal policies aimed at balancing unemployment and inflation through Congress, the "red menace" could always be invoked to justify a sort of military Keynesianism. A good example of this is the *Sputnik* scare in 1957, used to expand government spending and boost the economy just before an election year. The mobilization of fear to such a degree was made possible by the power of ideological manipulation afforded by television, and to a lesser extent other mass media and mass education. Symbolic of this fear was that by 1967 the United States had produced 32,500 hydrogen bombs, enough to destroy the world many times over in order to defend itself against communism.[83]

As previously mentioned, even Butz's new agricultural policies (1971–76) need to be placed in the context of the cold war. These policies meant that in many agricultural sectors farmers received half their income in the form of government subsidies (skewed heavily in the direction of the richer farmers). Seen from the point of view of the cold war however, massive food exports would make developing countries more dependent on the United States, and therefore more open to becoming part of the American "camp". In short, Butz's reforms turned food into a weapon in the cold war.[84] International US hegemony was also increased by policies that maintained the US dollar as the international currency by improving the balance of trade through agricultural exports. Finally, cheap food for workers could increase the profits of capital and thus strengthen the economy in general in the race to see whether the capitalist economy could outperform the communist economy.

It would seem then that the "welfare state" was actually to a much greater extent a warfare state. It is true that some welfare became available to those who most needed it, but in the main the welfare (taxpayers' money) went to the military industrial complex, to large corporations and to rich farmers in the form of subsidies. Large corporations received subsidies, tax breaks, the benefits of tied foreign aid, trade deals that opened foreign markets, import protections and cost-plus guaranteed profits from government contracts.

CONCLUSIONS

In this chapter, I have attempted to illustrate the ways in which the major conditions necessary for the existence of our current food system were established during the phase of consumerism, most characteristically developed in the United States between 1946 and 1970. When Marx referred to the indifference towards use-value characteristic of capital, he had in mind the priority placed on short-term profits in opposition to all other human values, and in particular the indifference of capital towards poverty and the plight of exploited workers. In a sense one can argue that for Marx capitalism would eventually come to an end because the social costs associated with social injustice would become blatant, leading to massive popular opposition to capitalism. From the point of view of our current situation, it seems that he may have underestimated the degree to which capitalism's atomizing forces, combined with strong technologies of ideological indoctrination, could weaken and undermine popular solidarity. Further, technologies of surveillance and force have made resistance to capitalism increasingly dangerous. Finally, the state has increasingly propped up capitalism in all sorts of ways.

Currently we are well into a period of history when our very survival depends on finding ways to move beyond capital's indifference to use-value, for we can no longer afford the rapidly escalating social costs, or more accurately, social destruction that capital's short-term profit orientation is generating. The most dramatic social cost is global warming, but there are many others having to do with increasing inequality and social injustice, with soil depletion and desertification, with the depletion of fresh water, with the depletion of oil, with pollution, with a rising global food crisis, and a chronic disease crisis often associated with obesity. In the coming chapters I shall explore in detail the mounting social costs that the current evolution of capitalism has generated in connection with agriculture and our food system.

This escalation of social costs really started to take off during the golden age of the phase of consumerism after World War II, an age characterized by a veritable orgy of profit making and capital expansion which was oblivious to many social and ecological costs. The introduction of profitable new products and technologies proceeded so rapidly that it seemed that no one could stop to think about testing the new commodities and new chemicals for their long-run consequences on human or environmental health. And the automobile was so popular that hardly anyone stopped to think about the long-term social costs of car-dependent development. It was full speed ahead, with blinkers that blocked out everything but profits and victory in the cold war.

It is this condoned single-mindedness, generated primarily by the spirit of capitalism, that enveloped agriculture and eventually food as well. The wake-up call to the massive increase in the use of chemicals in agriculture in ways that seemed indifferent to both the short-term and long-term dangers came in 1962, with Rachel Carson's book *Silent Spring*. At first, the book was denounced by all those sectors of the economy whose profits might be negatively affected by conservationist and anti-pollution policies. And while eventually certain of the more dangerous pesticides were banned, the agricultural policies favouring large industrial farms introduced in the early 1970s continued to favour the increased mechanization and chemicalization of agriculture. Large farms received large subsidies, making it possible for farmers to sell their crops for less than the costs of production and still do well. Essentially this meant that the American taxpayer subsidized the agricultural inputs of industry, particularly the food industry, so that industry could make larger profits. In Chapter 5 I shall discuss how American and European agricultural subsidies have undermined agriculture in many developing countries, where more often than not it is precisely the agrarian sector that is the key to development.

Part III

THE HISTORICAL ANALYSIS OF THE US-CENTRED GLOBAL FOOD REGIME

4 THE FOOD REGIME AND CONSUMERS' HEALTH

The World Health Organization (WHO) estimates that ... some 3 billion people, suffer from malnutrition of one form or another .... Hunger afflicts at least 1.1 billion people, while another 1.1 billion consume more than they need .... Hunger, overeating, and micronutrient deficiencies, for example, account for an estimated half or more of the world's burden of disease .... More than 5 million children die of hunger-related diseases each year, while survivors are often physically or mentally stunted .... Meanwhile millions of people in wealthy countries spend years or even decades late in life crippled with heart disease, diabetes, cancer, or other diseases attributable at least in part to overeating.[1]

It is an outrage that in the twenty-first century one child under the age of five will die every five seconds from hunger-related diseases .... Hunger will kill more people than all the wars fought this year. Yet where is the fight against hunger?[2]

The intimate connection between pangs of hunger suffered by the most industrious layers of the working class, and the extravagant consumption, coarse or refined, of the rich, for which capital accumulation is the basis, is only uncovered when the economic laws are known.[3]

"How capitalism creates hunger and obesity" is the subtitle of this book, and it is the main focus of this chapter, launching us from the theory of pure capitalism discussed in Chapter 2 and mid-range theory analysing the golden age of consumerism in Chapter 3. In the remainder of the book, I analyse the food regime over the past 30 years at the level of historical analysis. With this emphasis in mind, I start with two chapters (4 and 5) analysing the impact of the current food regime on human health – first the health of consumers and then the health of the workers who produce the food. The weave of history and health issues is probably most dramatic with the case of tobacco, which I examine not only because of its link to "land", but also to demonstrate the historical processes that allowed capitalism to compromise scientific research and democratic processes as well as human health. Although human health and environmental health are tied closely together, for analytic purposes I follow the two chapters on human health with a separate chapter (6) on the food system and environmental health.

Chapters 7–9 move away from the more biological aspects of human health and the environment to issues of individual choice, corporate power and needed transformations of the system. Because the idea of individual choice is so fundamental in both our popular culture and much social science literature, food, marketing and choice are addressed as the focus of Chapter 7. This focus leads to Chapter 8, which examines the enormous power corporations have, not only to shape choice, but also to manipulate the rule of law, democratic processes, the judicial system, the media and even science. The book concludes with Chapter 9, which proposes the sorts of changes needed to deal with the problems outlined in the book.

CAPITALIST AGRICULTURE

In order for agriculture to be managed in a capitalistically rational way, it would need to be operated in the same way as capital operates factory production. Because Marx was fully aware of how difficult and problematic this would be, he claimed that "the capitalist system runs counter to a rational agriculture". One of the aims of Chapter 2 is precisely to expand on this claim by Marx.

Parts of the food system, for example meat packing, became capitalist early on. Economic historians generally locate the origin of the assembly line in the disassembly lines developed in Chicago meat packing plants in the last half of the nineteenth century.

Despite such examples, it is important to remember that the modern food system as a whole rests upon agriculture, and that except for some sectors of the plantation system developed under colonialism, or the persistence of quasi-feudalism or quasi-slavery in some parts of the world, for the past 150 years agriculture in the United States and in much of the rest of the world has been carried out by non-capitalist family farms.[4] Capitalism had more success early on in subsuming agriculture in England than anywhere else because of the very large estates there, and the role that landlords played as a sort of buffer between the vagaries of competitive capitalism's pure profit orientation and farmers.[5]

At the level of historical analysis, capitalist and non-capitalist often shade into one another without a clear boundary. For example, if a family farm becomes large enough to hire wage labour, it increasingly becomes a capitalist farm. Or if a family farm becomes sufficiently subsumed to a larger flow of capitalist profit making, such that capitalist corporations largely determine inputs, production processes and outputs, in this case it also becomes increasingly a capitalist operation.

In the United States the family farm began to be seriously threatened during the "Dust Bowl" era of the 1930s. At this juncture it became increasingly clear that mechanized farms with irrigation would thrive, and that farm size needed to increase for mechanization to be affordable and efficient. Yet small and medium-sized family farms still predominated until the post World War II petrochemical revolution and the biotech revolution increasingly subsumed farming to capitalist industrialization. It was these new technologies, coupled with Secretary of Agriculture Earl Butz's policy changes in the early 1970s, that contributed to a significant collapse of the mixed family farm ("mixed" means a variety of crops and animals relating symbiotically) in the United States.[6]

By increasing the rate of profit in agriculture and by promising future increases through new technologies, the petrochemical revolution (coupled with seed engineering and irrigation) increasingly drew the immense investing power of capital into the agrarian sector. Fertilizers could magically increase soil productivity; pesticides could increasingly control every kind of pest, from diseases to weeds to insects to rodents, and new seeds made possible faster-maturing crops with higher yields. The hybridizing of seeds made it possible to produce corn that could be planted closer together, or wheat that would mature faster and was more cold-tolerant. The growing season could be extended, the maturation of a crop could be speeded up, and irrigation made agriculture less weather-dependent. For the first time in history, the natural qualitative/material constraints that had always figured so large in limiting the ability of capital in this sector seemed to be overcome. Now it seemed that human technology could at last subsume the vagaries of nature to the quantitative concerns of profit maximization, and nature could be forced to submit to the rapid increases in productivity needed by capital to keep up with industrial rates of expansion.

As is characteristic of capital in general, social costs could be ignored since either they were sufficiently long-term that damages would not show up immediately, they would be hard to trace, or they could by paid for by the taxpayer. The privatization of profits and socialization of costs made agriculture a veritable paradise for profit making, with the collateral damage deferred to future generations. Yes, there was some concern that insects were becoming increasingly resistant to insecticides, and that depleted soils needed more and more fertilizer, but two considerations calmed these concerns: petrochemicals were relatively cheap to farmers and they were highly profitable to corporations. Indeed, though problematic to farmers, particularly smaller farmers whose sales often did not cover the costs of production, the tread-mills of increasing rates of fertilizer and pesticide usage promised a bright future for the chemical corporate sector. From the point of view of capitalist expansion, the failure of tens of thousands of family farms could simply be viewed as the sort of "creative destruction" required by capitalist progress that always gets rid of the less profitable units of production.

Today the food industry, which is the largest industry in the United States, is not only largely capitalist, but also in capitalist fashion is triumphalist in celebrating its high level of productivity. Even when families still own farms, they often become subsumed to a capitalist flow-through system, where large corporations, by controlling inputs and outputs, reduce the farmer to being an appendage of corporate specifications that predetermine the farming process. In short, the family farm loses its autonomy and becomes totally embedded in the circuit of capital.

No time in human history can compare with the post World War II period when it comes to introducing so many new products and technologies with such abandon. The abandon that is characteristic of capitalism's rush to profit in general was now supplemented by the exigencies of a cold war fought in part as a competition in economic growth that pitted the United States against the USSR. While the ecological damage associated with the single-minded focus on growth in the USSR has received a great deal of publicity, a fair-minded tally might find the damage in the United States as bad or worse.[7]

THE CASE OF TOBACCO

Warren Buffett, who has made enormous wealth through investing, at one point in his career advised investors in the following words: "I'll tell you why I like the cigarette business. It costs a penny to make. Sell it for a dollar. It's addictive. And there's a fantastic brand loyalty."[8] There are four main reasons that I give so much attention to the cigarette industry in a book about agriculture and food:

- The cigarette is a good paradigm case of what I have been arguing about capital's indifference to quality of life issues except as they impact profit. In this regard it is also a good example of privatizing profits and socializing costs.
- Agriculture includes many non-food commodities, of which tobacco, cotton, crops for ethanol, flowers, trees for pulp or lumber and illegal drugs (opium, coca, marijuana) are the most important. Such commodities may take a good deal of arable land from food production in some circumstances. Also field workers, farmers and corporations can move back and forth between food and non-food crops as profitability alters.
- The cigarette industry has bought into the food industry to such an extent that the techniques that it first developed to protect the cigarette from marketing constraints are already appearing in efforts to protect junk foods from similar constraints.[9]

• The power that corporations have to run roughshod over the institutions of liberal democracy is particularly clear in the case of the cigarette industry's continued success in marketing its product and addicting a whole new generation in developing countries to a habit that poses grave health risks.

There was strong scientific evidence as far back as the 1930s that cigarettes are a cause of lung cancer, and now it is known that tobacco is a truly deadly commodity which contributes to many life-threatening diseases.[10] And yet cigarettes are so profitable and in some cases the state revenues from their sale are so large (especially in China), that they continue to be marketed throughout the world using the most advanced and effective marketing techniques.[11] In the past tobacco companies paid scientists to cast doubt on the health risks of cigarettes, and by doing so undermined the credibility of science.[12] And they have handed out millions of dollars to politicians to avoid legislation deleterious to the tobacco industry, thus undermining the credibility of democracy.[13] They have hired expensive lawyers who managed for years to persuade judges to rule out of court most epidemiological evidence demonstrating the connections between smoking and cancer, thus weakening the credibility of the courts.[14] They have manipulated the media to misinform, confuse and seduce.[15] And according to Devra Davis, the director of the Center for Environmental Oncology at the University of Pittsburgh and professor of epidemiology, they have set back public health by 50 years.[16]After a half-century of expensive and often abortive legal struggles, and hundreds of millions of deaths, a certain amount of cold water has been thrown on the marketing of cigarettes in North America, such that the rate of smoking has been more than cut in half. Yet, over 435,000 Americans still die every year from tobacco-related illnesses.[17]

According to US Federal Court Judge Kessler in her August 2006 decision which found the tobacco industry guilty of racketeering:

> over the course of 50 years, defendants [the cigarette companies] lied, misrepresented, and deceived the American public, including smokers and the young people they avidly sought as "replacement smokers," about the devastating health effects of smoking and environmental

tobacco smoke. [They] suppressed research, they destroyed documents, they manipulated the use of nicotine so as to increase and perpetuate addiction ... and they abused the legal system in order to achieve their goal – to make money with little if any regard for individual illness or suffering, soaring health care costs, or the integrity of the legal system.[18]

In developing countries, where there are fewer constraints, the cigarette corporations are using the most advanced marketing techniques to hook the youth on cigarettes. They are succeeding at the rate of 80,000–100,000 new smokers a day.[19] As a result, it has been estimated that in the twenty-first century over 1 billion people, mostly in developing countries (80 percent), will die of tobacco-related illnesses.[20] Running into opposition in advanced industrial countries and then shifting marketing to developing countries where regulations are weaker has also characterized the pesticide industry, as we shall explore later.[21]

While constraints have been placed on advertising and marketing cigarettes in the United States, it is significant that government subsidies to tobacco farmers in the United States were only ended in 2004. By then they were no longer needed because the price of tobacco was at such a high level that profits on an acre of tobacco were nearly five times higher than on an acre of corn, for at least some farmers.[22] At the same time, we should note that the US government does not subsidize fruit or vegetables.[23]

Land that is utilized to grow tobacco is land taken away from growing food.[24] Furthermore, as a crop, tobacco is hard on the fertility of the land and on the workers who are exposed to toxic chemical pesticides and must pick the large tobacco leaves by hand (nicotine poisoning is not uncommon amongst tobacco pickers).[25] As the demand for cigarettes expands, forests in developing countries are being cut down to provide land for tobacco farming and wood for the fires needed to cure tobacco.[26] Thus we see how even a non-food agricultural commodity can impact on food, human health and environmental health. And yet, it must be admitted, that the tobacco industry has acted in all this as any rational capitalist should. It has acted to maximize profits for its shareholders.

While the cigarette may seem to be an unusually blatant case, it does clearly bring out what I want to emphasize. For as we proceed, it will become apparent that how corporations have related to agriculture and food is in most respects not qualitatively different from how they have related to cigarettes. The effects of capitalist commodification and the primacy of profits that follow are similar across the board, and we are simply lucky if the rush to profit does not harm a lot of people before we have a chance to discover the toxic properties of any commodity. Further, once we have exposed some of the social costs of a commodity, there is no guarantee that government will act to constrain those costs,[27] for there is little likelihood that government will tax the commodity (at least where the corporations are powerful) sufficiently to cover the social costs, since this would likely sharply reduce profits.[28]

In part because in the United States the congressional route did not yield results, reformers often tried to utilize the courts to constrain the tobacco industry. But this is an extremely expensive and time-consuming route to take, given that powerful corporate sectors have the funds to hire the best lawyers, who can, at the very least, delay any award. Instead, in most cases, corporate lawyers have succeeded in getting the courts to accept that it is almost impossible to prove one-to-one relations between this cause and that effect (smoking this cigarette caused that cancer). Taking the juridical route also has the disadvantage of being able to only deal with particular harms in particular jurisdictions, and thus may not have much impact on the overall issue of long-term social costs.[29]

THE GLOBAL FOOD REGIME: A STORY OF IRRATIONALITY

Given that tobacco is only one agricultural crop, its cost to both the environment and human health is steep; and yet in these respects it is less costly than the global food system taken as a whole. It has often been noted that we can produce enough food to provide a healthful diet to everyone in the world without damage to the environment. Since good diet is the basis of human health, and since providing food in ways that are environmentally friendly is crucially important ecologically, a rational economic system would take these goals as the highest priority. Judged by such criteria our economic system is a miserable failure.

Defenders of our capitalist economic regime can of course point out that starvation appears to be a perennial problem historically. While there is some truth in this, it is also true that previous economic orders lacked the knowledge and technology that makes it possible for us to prevent malnutrition and starvation. This is something that we have the power to choose to do. Good intentions abound. Witness the 1996 World Food Summit, which passed a resolution to reduce hunger by half before the end of 2015. This resolution was then picked up and made one of the UN Millennium Development Goals, which among other things committed the world to reduce by half the number of people living on less than $1 per day by 2015.[30] This sort of commitment to change remains little more than a pose without an understanding of the deep causes of the problems and a commitment to policy changes that would at least begin to alter these causes.

Starvation as a process of malnutrition is currently the most immediate cause of human suffering and obstacle to human flourishing that the world faces.[31] Not only is it the most severe global challenge now, but without some significant changes in the short term, it will reach truly massive proportions in the near future as food prices continue to escalate. There are three basic causes of this escalation:

- Our food system is very petroleum-dependent, the price of petroleum is increasing, and by all accounts it will continue to do so.
- The "meatification" of the world's diet means that a higher percentage of grains are going to meat production.
- Most important are the American government's entirely preventable huge subsidies to ethanol producers in the United States, who in the near future might take 50 percent or more of the corn harvest. Because corn is a basic grain in the global food system, the prices of most other foods will rise as corn prices rise.

There is a fourth less basic but more immediate cause of some importance: financial speculation. When speculators see the above three causes at work, they believe that the prices of food commodities will go up. The resulting shift of financial investment into commodity futures can create a bubble that pushes prices yet higher. Because the prices of the major food grains are on the whole determined by speculators operating in the Chicago and New York commodities futures markets, they are subject to the vagaries of speculation in ways similar to stocks in stock markets. And while speculators may have caused some of the recent sharp upward spikes in food prices, a long-term upward trend in prices will likely occur not from speculation but from the petroleum dependency of the food regime, plus the conversion of what was, or could be, food crop land into the production of biofuels.

According to the FAO, 36 countries are already suffering severe food crises, and this is only the beginning.[32] And according to Donald Coxe, a researcher for the Bank of Montreal, "We are facing the real possibility of the worst global food crisis for which we have records."[33] This is not even taking into account the long-term negative impacts that global warming will have on food production.

According to Pinstrup-Anderson and Cheng, "every thirty minutes 360 pre-school children will die of hunger and malnutrition", adding up to over 6 million children a year.[34] Yet the news media in rich countries pay little attention to this massacre, which can only worsen with rising food prices. It is not unusual to find the business press in wealthy countries focusing on the money to be made from the booming prices of food commodities where people are hungry, or prices of water where people are thirsty. For example, a recent article in Toronto's *Globe and Mail* entitled "The hottest commodities are in your cereal bowl" points out that yellow peas, a basic staple in the East Indian diet, have increased from $400 a ton to $600 a ton in two months.[35] And according to Bank of Montreal's Donald Coxe, "Milk is the new oil. Milk demand worldwide is rising faster than oil demand."[36]

What rich country news media have been focusing on ad nauseam is the "obesity epidemic", as it has been labelled by the American Center for Disease Control.[37] The starvation "epidemic" can be held at arm's length because it is occurring mainly somewhere else, but the obesity epidemic hits home for North Americans. According to Lang and Heasman, "diseases associated with deficient diet account for 60 percent of years of life lost in the established market economies".[38] No doubt the health costs of obesity are and will become increasingly massive, but the starvation epidemic results in highly preventable immediate and severe suffering along with extreme long-term suffering for survivors. Because of penetration by the capitalist food system based in rich countries, many developing countries now have to deal with both widespread obesity and starvation (especially India and China).

Viewed positively, calling obesity an "epidemic" has the effect of drawing attention to an extensive, rapidly spreading and deeply threatening problem. At the same time, applying a medical metaphor tends to medicalize the problem, thus focusing attention more on treating the resultant diseases than on dealing with the causes. Using this kind of metaphor makes us think of obesity like the spread of a virus – something that simply happens to us. But obesity is something that we allow to happen, and while there may be many causes, I would argue that the primary cause is a capitalist food system that we have allowed to subject us. We do not have to accept this subjection.

Medicalizing problems tends to convert them into problems with extremely complex causes that only scientific experts can deal with. It is a way of depoliticizing problems and of obfuscating the search for primary causes. It is as if to find a cause is to demonize something or someone. But if the cause is a set of social relations as in the capitalist food system, then it is something we all participate in, and if we allow it to continue, then one would think that a least a significant number of us are accepting of it. I am not so interested in pointing my finger at the guilty ones as I am in explaining the social relations that cause our food system to operate as it does. In a sense I blame capitalism, but "capitalism is us" as we are shaped by social relations that we participate in shaping. Of course, there are always those classes and elites who have a great deal of power to do the shaping, while most of us must accommodate, for the most part, to being shaped. Mass mobilizations, however, can alter this.

It has not been sufficiently noticed that the obesity epidemic and malnutrition are interlaced. People who become obese from eating junk food may eat too many calories, but at the same time be starved of nutrients. And being starved of nutrients may be a cause of their eating too many calories. Further, we know that food laden with caloric sweeteners typically only satisfies hunger for a short time, as blood sugar levels soon fall, rapidly stimulating renewed hunger. In a food environment filled with highly sweetened foods at every turn, it is difficult to avoid eating excessive amounts of hunger-producing sweets. Finally, people often eat too much as a means of filling an emotional emptiness, but a capitalist social life that is both isolating and organized principally around an ever-increasing speeding up of producing, buying and selling commodities can itself be a major cause of feelings of inner emptiness.

The term "starvation epidemic" sounds somehow inappropriate, and this is because it does not make sense to medicalize something so systemically caused and so preventable as starvation. Opinion-forming elites in rich countries would rather not call a lot of attention to hunger and starvation precisely because it would raise such deep and compelling criticisms of the capitalist system which in many cases has played the main role in creating it. Further, many people profit both from the "toxic food environment" that helps generate obesity and from the many industries whose aim is to reduce it. Hungry and starving people can only be a source of profit to corporations that receive government subsidies to provide food aid. The profits in this sector are low because governments commit very little revenue to food aid. Further, starvation does not easily lend itself to a model of individual sickness and individual medical treatment, and even if it could, the poor could not afford treatment. From the point of view of distributive justice, there can be no justification whatsoever for the global massacre that is starvation.

I start with an examination of obesity, not because it is more important than the far more serious starvation in the world, but because I want to start with the United States as the hegemonic centre of global capitalism. Arguably it is obesity and not starvation, at least as seen from within the United States, that is a far more serious problem, even though over 10 percent of US households were food insecure in 1999, and by 2005 35.1 million Americans suffered from hunger.[39]

THE OBESITY "EPIDEMIC"

It will be helpful to begin by sorting out some common vernacular food expressions. As previously mentioned, "junk food" refers to food that is high in calories relative to nutrients, or in calories that are relatively empty of nutrients.[40] Perhaps the epitome of junk food is a soda consisting of sugar, water, artificial colour and artificial flavour.[41] The sugar in most soft drinks, high fructose corn syrup (typically around 15 teaspoons of high fructose corn syrup (HFCS) per 20 ounce bottle), gives it lots of calories but no nutrients. A triple-thick 32 ounce milk shake has 1,110 calories, and while it no doubt also has nutrients, these pale into insignificance relative to the calories.[42]

"Fast food" is food that is almost immediately available for consumption. Although the overwhelming majority of fast food in the United States is also junk food, it need not be. Fast food could consist of items high in nutrients per calorie, such as some ready-to-eat salads (assuming non-junk salad dressings). Fast food has become associated with the automobile, from which one can order at the first window, and pick up the food at the second, usually in less than two minutes.[43] The meal can be eaten while driving, which often fits with the fast pace of life characteristic of the late twentieth and early twenty-first centuries.

Finally there is "processed food", which tends to be less nutritious the more it is processed, although sometimes nutrients are added back in.[44] More processed white bread is less nutritious than less processed whole wheat bread. Whole and relatively unprocessed breakfast cereals are more nutritious than the highly processed ones, which often have a great deal of added sugar. Processing typically not only degrades the original nutrient complement of the food, it also often involves the addition of sugar, fat, salt or various chemicals. At the extreme, processed food may add so many calories and process out so many nutrients that it becomes junk food.[45] Thus it is very possible to have processed, fast, junk food all rolled up into one food item. The more processed the food, the more "value added" (not food value but money value); hence the food industry's embrace of processed foods. Yet the value added might in some cases be not even empty calories, but packaging. The grain costs only 25 cents in a 12 ounce box of cereal that sells for $3.50.[46] In other words, most of the $3.50 consists of the costs of processing, packaging, transporting, and retailing, plus a hefty profit.

It has often been pointed out that health correlates more closely with economic class or standard of living than with any other social variable.[47] There are no doubt many reasons for this, but I would suggest that a major one has generally been diet. Those with higher incomes can afford better diets, live in places where better diets are accessible, afford the education to know what a better diet is and afford the time it takes to invest in a better diet. It has been said that Americans are "overfed and undernourished" because they consume so many calories that are relatively devoid of nutrients.[48] While as a generalization this may be true, obesity rates themselves tend to be higher amongst the poor in the United States, and this is at least partly because junk foods are cheap, accessible, convenient and often quasi-addictive. With the spread of junk food and supermarkets selling "junky" processed foods to poorer countries, capitalism has played a big role in the "global obesity epidemic".

Margo Wootan, nutrition policy director of the Center for Science in the Public Interest (CSPI), commenting on fast food chain meals for children, claims that:

> McDonald's, Burger King, KFC, and other chains are conditioning kids to expect burgers, fried chicken, pizza, French fries, macaroni and cheese, and soda in various combination at almost every lunch and dinner …. Most of these kids' meals appear to be designed to put America's children on the fast-track to obesity, disability, heart attack, or diabetes.[49]

In the same news release, CSPI states that "Besides being almost always too high in calories, 45 percent of the kids' meals at the 13 chains studied by CSPI are too high in saturated and trans fat, and 86 percent are too high in sodium."[50]

Given that a diet high in sodium can contribute to high blood pressure, a major risk factor in heart disease, these findings suggest we are creating a disease-prone generation of children.

Of course, the consumption of junk foods is not the only cause of obesity, but it is doubtless a major cause. Obesity is a concern because it correlates closely with the incidence of numerous chronic diseases including diabetes, heart disease and cancer.[51] A study carried out by Jay Olshansky, professor of public health at the University of Illinois at Chicago, shows that when body fat is over

30 percent, on average, one's life will be ten years shorter.[52] As a result, there are strong reasons to fear that the rate of serious chronic illnesses will escalate dramatically with the tendency for capitalism to contribute to obesity, and that existing medical systems will simply not be able to bear the increased burdens of disease. (Arguably this is already occurring even in some wealthy countries.) For example, according to former US secretary of Health, Education, and Welfare, Joseph Califano, health care spending in the United States has increased by 1,000 percent since 1980,[53] and this increase is likely to continue in light of the fact that obesity rates for teens have tripled since 1980.[54] Popkin, a leading researcher on global food consumption, claims that "Medical costs of illnesses caused by obesity can bring down the economies of China, India, and many other developing countries."[55] According to the *Economist*, there are more new cases of diabetes in India and China than the rest of the world combined.[56] Furthermore, approximately one-third of China's population have high blood pressure, the major risk factor in heart disease.[57]

According to a paper published by the American Medical Association, one-third of the babies born in the United States in 2000 are likely to become diabetic.[58] It is even likely that for the first time in the history of capitalism in the United States, average life expectancy will decline, as the incredible growth of childhood illnesses such as autism, attention deficit disorder (ADD), allergies, diabetes, depression and asthma, coupled with the chronic illnesses of adulthood such as respiratory ailments, depression, cancer, stroke and heart disease, are spurred on by obesity, smoking and chemicals in the environment.[59]

The rate of depression has increased ten times in two generations, with 10 percent of American's suffering a major depression in any given year.[60] At the same time many anti-depressant drugs seem to increase appetite, thus contributing to obesity. The global incidence of adult-onset diabetes increased five times in the 13 years between 1985 and 1998.[61] These statistics are alarming, but a change in diet could alter them significantly.[62]

A person may be obese but malnourished from eating too many empty calories. Malnourishment may refer to a lack of calories as in hunger and starvation, but it can also be caused by an inadequate intake of micronutrients such as zinc, calcium, vitamin A, vitamin C, selenium and iron, which play a key role in human health.[63] The World Health Organization (WHO) estimates that more than 3 billion (or 50 percent) of the world's people suffer from malnutrition.[64] Although it has been estimated that over 1 billion people will die of tobacco-related diseases in the twenty-first century, an even larger number are likely to die from obesity-related diseases.[65] In the United States obesity rates have risen from 14 percent in 1978 to 31 percent by 2000 to 40 percent by 2004, or nearly tripled.[66] According to a report released by the WHO/FAO in 2001, chronic diseases resulting largely from poor diet contributed to 60 percent of the 56 million reported deaths worldwide and nearly half the global burden of disease.[67] Finally, of the ten leading causes of death in the United States, only two are not related to food or drink.[68]

SUGAR

In the future we may replace the phrase "sweetness and light" with "sweetness and darkness", because of the ever-darkening shadows that sugars are casting over the human prospect.[69] Sweetness seems to be the most universally desirable taste, to the point that sweet things may become quasi-addictive.[70] Further, there is some evidence that we become jaded by sweetness, such that the sweeter the foods we become accustomed to, the sweeter food must become to satisfy our sweet tooth. Newer breeds of fruits and vegetables tend to be sweeter than older breeds. For example, a recent breed of red grapes is 20 percent sugar compared with a standard 1940 variety that was 16 percent sugar.[71] Similar results could be found with many other fruits and vegetables, from raspberries to corn. Indeed, some fruit juices have more sugar than the typical 15 teaspoons in a 20 ounce bottle of cola.[72]

Eating sugar gives a burst of energy followed by a low, as insulin released by the pancreas lowers the blood sugar, leaving one hungry for more sugar. In experiments carried out by Carlo Colantuoni and associates at the Department of Psychology, Princeton University, and reported in the journal *Obesity Research*, rats were given large amounts of sugar and then the sugar was withdrawn.[73] With the sugar taken away, the rats manifested withdrawal symptoms similar to those found with morphine or nicotine. According to Aubrey Sheiham, emeritus professor of public health at University College, London, "as you expose yourself to sugar, your liking for it increases, and your taste threshold changes. You start needing more. Manufacturers have exploited that."[74]

Sugar, then, may have addictive qualities, particularly if we use the definition that an addiction is any "excessive appetite".[75] According to a recent article by Loefler, in terms of world health, sugar is more dangerous than tobacco, because while tobacco usually kills after the age of 60, sugar is a health burden throughout life, attacking the teeth of the young and contributing to all the diseases associated with obesity, many of which can have an early onset.[76] Sugar is also problematic because, with 40 percent of the world's people making $2 or less a day, sugar is generally the cheapest and therefore most accessible calorie. In Mexico, for example, more people drink cola than milk,[77] and in the United States the consumption of soft drinks by children doubled between 1993 and 2003.[78]

The main caloric sweetener in soft drinks is HFCS, a sweetener that has radically increased the consumption of fructose worldwide since the 1970s. There is some evidence that HFCS may contribute more to consumers developing diabetes than other sugars. Experiments have shown, for example, that HFCS does not trigger the body's "satiation reflex" the way other foods do.[79] According to Simin Liu, a scientist at the Harvard School of Public Health, the increased incidence of diabetes closely matches the increase of HFCS in our diet.[80]

The more sugar we have, the more we want. And it is this wanting, this wanting to the point of excess, that makes sugar-laced food so profitable to capital and so dangerous to humans. As a result, more and more processed foods are getting sweeter and sweeter, and consumers are getting fatter and fatter. Recently the US Surgeon General warned that soon obesity will kill as many as tobacco.[81]

According to Patti Randall, policy director of Baby Milk Action Group, because tastes are formed at an early age, it is no small matter that baby formula "can contain 60 percent more sugars than regular milk". According to Randall, "A bottle-fed baby consumes 30,000 more calories over its first eight months than a breast-fed one. That's the calorie equivalent of 120 average chocolate bars."[82] Given how early our tastes are formed, it is not surprising that "several research studies have shown correlations between bottle-feeding and subsequent obesity".[83]

Further, the high level of added sugars continues in baby foods, against efforts to limit them. It is well known that the United Nation's International Codex Alimentarius Commission, which sets global standards for foods, is heavily influenced by the food industry. And yet it is always a little jarring when this influence acts so blatantly against human health as it did at the November 2006 meeting of Codex. According to Lawrence, at this meeting "the Thai government introduced a proposal to reduce the levels of sugars in baby foods from the existing maximum of 30 percent to 10 percent, as part of the global fight against obesity. The proposal was blocked by the US and the EU,"[84] where the world's largest sugar corporations have their home offices.[85] This is simply one of many examples of the lobbying power of the sugar industry.

In another case, the American sugar lobby threatened to have the US Congress cut off funding to the WHO and FAO if they insisted on a sugar guideline in their 2003 report *Diet, Nutrition and the Prevention of Chronic Diseases*, which recommended limiting the daily average intake of added sugars to 10 percent of total calories.[86] This is a widely accepted standard, even though the average daily intake of added sugars by American teenagers is 20 percent of total calories.

In the United States one in three children eat fast food every day,[87] and 80 percent of all children have poor diets.[88] For example, in 1997 50 percent of the calories consumed by American children were from sugars and fats added to their food,[89] and it was children who ate or drank 25 percent of the salty snacks, 30 percent of the soft drinks, 40 percent of the frozen pizza and 50 percent of the cold cereals consumed in America.[90] Further, the number of overweight children has tripled in the United States since 1980.[91] These statistics are particularly telling because of the strong evidence that food preferences tend to be established early in life, and because children represent our hope for the future.[92] This hope cannot help be dimmed by the fact that one-half of the global population is under 25, and a significant proportion are living in poverty, a poverty that will severely limit their diets. Many more, who may or may not be poor, will also have to contend with a lifetime of health problems related to obesity.

Three-quarters of all Americans live within three miles of a McDonald's,[93] and two-thirds live within three miles of a KFC, Pizza Hut or Taco Bell fast food restaurant.[94] Because of proximity alone, it is not at all surprising that every day 25 percent of the US population eats fast food, and one-third of the total caloric intake is from fast food.[95] According to Nestle,[96] Americans consume an average 31 teaspoons of added sugars a day, and 40 percent of this is in soft drinks.[97] The rate of consumption of soft drinks per person averages 606 12 ounce cans per year. Teenage boys in the United States (aged 12–19) average 800 cans of soft drink per year,[98] and just to make this consumption more convenient there are over 3 million soft drink vending machines in the United States, many of which are in educational institutions.[99]

Furthermore, fat and sugar constitute more than 50 percent of the caloric intake of the average American, and now over two-thirds of all Americans are overweight.[100] In only 15 years, 1990–2005, obesity in the United States doubled to reach nearly 40 percent,[101] with the "very obese" (at least 100 pounds overweight) being the fastest growing group. Americans on average get 40 percent of their sugar from soft drinks. Indeed, of all the major fast foods, it is soda pop that has the highest profit margin, and hence is most profitable to increase portion size.[102] The standard soft drink in vending machines has gone from 8 ounces to 12 to 20, and studies show that portion size partially determines how much people eat or drink.

Coca-Cola and Pepsi are enormously profitable corporations which, by aggressively and successfully marketing their products throughout the world, have managed to capture 70 percent of the global soft drink market.[103] It is now in developing countries that soft drink consumption is increasing the fastest. Coca-Cola, the largest consumer of sugar in the world, and with the most recognizable brand name, sells over 300 brands of pop in 200 countries.[104]

While this appetite for sugar and the corresponding increases in obesity are relatively recent (globally per capita sugar consumption has increased 25 percent since 1961[105] and by 28 percent in the

United States since 1983[106]), diabetes is estimated to have cost the American health care system over $132 billion in 2002 alone.[107]

The incidence of obesity and diabetes is not blind to differences of gender, race or class. Obesity is considered a major cause of heart disease, the world's number one cause of death. Cancer, the number two cause of death, can be attributed to obesity as the primary cause in 14 percent of male cancer deaths and 20 percent of female.[108] And in the United States obesity rates vary directly with class and ethnicity. For instance, the obesity rate for black households with an annual income of less than $10,000 is 33 percent, for Hispanics 26 percent and for whites 19 percent.[109] In the United States a disturbing 32.4 percent of Mexican/American boys are obese by the 5th grade.[110] Finally, women who are overweight are five times more likely to get type-2 diabetes than women in the normal weight range and those with severe obesity are 50 times more likely to.[111]

Developing countries can even less afford to deal with the health consequences of obesity. In Mexico for example, 69.3 percent are overweight or obese and 14 percent of the population has type-2 diabetes.[112] Mexico is second only to the United States in obesity rates, and not surprisingly is also second in the consumption of soft drinks.[113] Indeed obesity in Mexico varies directly with how close Mexicans live to the US border. The Pan-American Health Organization conducted a study that showed that for the mostly Hispanic population that lives on either side of the US border, 74 percent of men and 70 percent of women are overweight or obese.[114]

Life expectancy in Russia was 70 years in the mid-1980s, but by 2002 it had fallen dramatically to 59.[115] While there are many causes of this remarkable decline in life expectancy, the aggressive marketing of cigarettes and junk food, along with the collapse of the state-supported medical system and radically increased economic inequality, no doubt played the main roles. Smoking rates, for instance, have doubled in Russia since 1991.[116]

Globally there has been a five-fold increase in the consumption of corn syrup since the early 1970s (in the United States a ten-fold increase) and a six-fold increase in cases of diabetes since 1985.[117] Globally, six people die every minute from diabetes, and such statistics are likely to increase unless there is a worldwide change in diet.[118] The International Diabetes Federation has predicted that at current rates of increase there will be 380 million people with diabetes globally by 2025.[119]

The international price of cane sugar fell from $2.60 per kilogram in 1974 to $0.06 in 1985, largely because of the export of highly subsidized EU beet sugar, and because of cheaper sucrose substitutes like HFCS.[120] A lower price for sugars encouraged the food industry to use more of it because of the high profits involved. Imagine the extra profits for the world's largest industrial consumer of sugar, Coca-Cola. At the same time, imagine the devastating impact of such low prices on cane sugar farms in the developing world and on sugar workers. Cuba, a country heavily dependent upon sugar, would surely have faced economic collapse had it not been for the support of the Soviet Union. When the Soviet Union withdrew its support of Cuba in the early 1990s, faced with economic disaster, Cuba developed what is perhaps the most resourceful and sustainable food system in the world.

In the United States, the inflated sugar prices due to government protection subsidize a small number of large sugar companies to the amount of approximately $2 billion a year. These subsidies go to a crop that in its refined state has lots of calories but no other nutrients, and in the current quantities being consumed threatens human health. In the case of sugar producers in Florida, its production threatens the future of the Everglades, from which it draws cheap water and to which it returns chemical pollution runoff.[121] During the Clinton administration, Vice-President Al Gore proposed a 1 cent tax on each pound of sugar to go to cleaning up the Everglades, but this proposal was defeated by the powerful sugar lobby.[122] Given the enormous subsidies received by the sugar industry as a result of protectionist legislation, it is not surprising that it made campaign contributions of $3.1 million to the 2004 federal election campaign.[123] It seems rationally inexplicable that taxpayers should give such enormous subsidies to corporations that make huge profits by producing a food that has zero nutritional value other than calories, is quasi-addictive and contributes to ill health.

It appears that the sugar corporations will not pay to clean up the Everglades, rather the tab will be picked up by taxpayers. In

July of 2008, Florida announced that it will pay US Sugar $1.75 billion for 187,000 acres of land in order to protect the Everglades. It will give US Sugar six years to wind down its business, before taking over the land. It is not yet clear whether or not Florida Crystals will also agree to some such arrangement.[124]

HFCS has increased rapidly in the American diet since it was developed in the 1960s, until today it constitutes 10 percent of the calories that Americans consume. As a consequence, Americans are consuming huge quantities of fructose, something new to humans in such quantities. There is growing evidence that it is having a negative impact on human health. Studies have shown that it can contribute to cardiovascular disease, kidney and liver disease, high blood pressure, systemic inflammation and increased formation of cell-damaging free radicals.[125] Other studies indicate that it is a risk factor in the burgeoning of obesity in the world, as it is the primary sweetener in the soft drink industry, which has expanded around the world.

MEATIFICATION AND FAT CONSUMPTION

Of course sugar is not the only culprit in the obesity epidemic. Fat is another, and the meatification of the US diet along with the increased consumption of dairy products, has played a part in this. Meat is a widely preferred food, and its consumption is a status symbol of being at least middle class in our world. In countries like China and India with rapidly growing middle classes, meat consumption is growing commensurately. The downside of meat production stems from its high social and environmental costs, which are generally not reflected in its market price. Never in world history have so many people eaten so much meat as in the United States over the past 20 years. Americans consume on average 220 pounds of meat per capita per year, or nearly two-thirds of a pound per day.[126] This meatification of the American diet is now spreading rapidly to the rest of the world, even though it is based on farming practices that damage human health, are unspeakably cruel to animals, contribute to obesity and cause enormous environmental damage. Despite these problems associated with such a high level of meat consumption, meat production is highly subsidized through government subsidies to farmers who produce feed grains (mainly corn and soy). Weis asserts that the global spread of the confined animal feeding operations (CAFOs) for the production of meat has become so central to the global food system that it deserves a special label: the "industrial-grain-livestock complex".[127]

Between 1965 and 2005 global soy production increased seven-fold primarily in order to provide more cheap feed to the meat industry, and not to feed the massive numbers of undernourished in the world.[128] Much of this new soy acreage came at the expense of deforestation in the Amazon basin, which has contributed significantly to global warming.[129] In addition the meat industry combined with fish farming takes up to one-third of the annual global fish harvest to use as animal or fish feed.[130]

Like sugar, fat plays a major role in making food taste better and hence has quasi-addictive qualities. The percentage of fat in the American diet has increased from 19 percent in 1977, to 38 percent in 1995, to 40 percent in 2005.[131] Between 1970 and 2002 the consumption of cheese alone increased from 11 lb per capita per year to 30 lb.[132] It is interesting to note that one-third of all vegetables consumed in the United States consist of French fries (25 percent), chips (crisps) and iceberg lettuce.[133] Also, it is worth noting in passing that although scientific experiments in the early 1970s found trans fats (hydrogenated vegetable oils) to be contributors to heart disease, governments have only recently begun to limit their use.

Meat in the United States has had an artificially low price because of government subsidies to farmers of corn and soy, the two principal feed grains. One estimate puts the savings accruing to industrial livestock firms over the nine-year period between 1996 and 2005 at $35 billion.[134] The result is that American taxpayers subsidize and thereby cheapen the cost of meat and dairy products, so that price becomes even further removed from real social costs.

CAFOs now account for more than 40 percent of global meat production.[135] This mode of meat production may maximize short-term profits by producing the most meat in the least time at the least cost, but there are many social costs not counted in the price of the meat. CAFOs crowd thousands of animals together at close quarters with little opportunity to move or do anything but eat and produce the stench of huge amounts of manure. Indeed 50 percent of cattle that are slaughtered in the United States pass through one of only 20 giant feedlots.[136] According to Nierenberg:

> Factory-farmed meat and fish contain an arsenal of unnatural ingredients, including persistent organic pollutants (POPs), polychlorinated biphenyls (PCBs), arsenic, hormones, and other chemicals. Meanwhile the overuse of antibiotics and other antimicrobials in livestock and poultry operations is undermining the toolbox of effective medicines for human use.[137]

Animal livestock receive 70 percent of all antibiotics utilized annually in the United States, or about 13 million pounds.[138] This is eight times more antibiotics than used for humans, and the trend has increased dramatically in recent years.[139] For example, according to Nierenberg, "On a per-bird basis, antimicrobial use by poultry producers has risen 307 percent since the 1980s."[140] This practice is dangerous because it can produce antibiotic-resistant organisms capable of sparking epidemics.

CAFOs are often dangerous for workers and for those living nearby or downstream because of the huge amount of waste that they produce. Often the smell of the waste is not only repellent, but according to Agriculture Canada the waste itself may contain infections that can be transmitted to humans, such as salmonella, anthrax, tularemia, brucellosis, erysipelas, tuberculosis, tetanus and colibacillosis.[141] One study found that 25 percent of hog house workers had breathing obstructions that could cause long-term lung damage.[142]

According to Dove:

> [Chicken and hog] factories do not produce meat more efficiently than traditional family farmers. The industry's willingness to treat the animals with unspeakable cruelty and to dump thousands of tons of toxic pollutants into our nation's waterways, and their ability to get away with it, however, has given it a dramatic market advantage over the traditional family farm. Indeed, the industry's business plan is based upon its ability to use its political clout to paralyze

the regulatory agencies, thereby escaping the true costs of producing its product.[143]

While there may be economies of scale and higher profits associated with CAFOs, we need to consider whether collateral costs make them worthwhile.

Although "couch potatoes" are not confined like animals in CAFOs, they might just as well be, given activity levels in some cases. Food industry representatives and health professionals often point out rightly that lack of exercise is also a cause of obesity. While it is difficult precisely to weigh causal factors, you would have to run half a marathon to burn off the calories of an average fast food meal.[144] It is no wonder, then, that Coca-Cola, a producer of products high in empty calories, focuses attention away from calorie intake and onto exercise by giving pedometers to schools.

Many studies show that when serving sizes are larger, people eat more. It is quite obvious that serving sizes have grown, whether it is soft drinks, hamburgers, French fries, popcorn at movies or muffins.[145] For example, the average size of muffins in the United States has increased 400 percent in the past 20 years.[146] In the summer of 2008, Pizza Hut began to forcefully market its new one pound P'zone pizza and dipping sauce, which contains 1,560 calories and twice the recommended daily intake of sodium.[147]

Obesity has increasingly spread to developing countries more or less in direct proportion as processed foods and junk foods have spread there. In Latin America food expenditure in supermarkets has increased from 15 percent in 1990 to 60 percent in 2000,[148] and at this rate must be much higher yet by now. Indeed, in Mexico 30 percent of the food peso is spent at Wal-Mex supermarkets.[149] It is perhaps not surprising, then, that low and mid-income countries are estimated now to have 80 percent of the world's cardiovascular disease, with India alone expected to have as much as 60 percent in the near future.[150] Both smoking and poor diet are major contributors to this trend.

The increasing meatification of the global diet is a causal factor in starvation, because more and more of the world's grain production is being used to feed animals, and in the process, not only are many of the grain calories lost, the resulting meat is not generally affordable for the poor. In other words, meat is not a very efficient source of calories. Meat is the preferred food of hundreds of millions of people, but we need to consider the social and environmental costs associated with high levels of meat consumption.

If everyone in the world ate as much meat as Americans, the total global grain harvest could only support 40 percent of the current population of the world. According to Roberts, 90 percent of the grain consumed in the United States is consumed in the form of meat or dairy products, and it takes 20 pounds of grain to produce one pound of beef.[151] Considering levels of hunger and starvation alone, this should suggest the need to reduce meat consumption. There are many other reasons as well. Meat production is very petroleum-dense, as is production of the main feed grains, corn and soy. Cattle, in particular, are implicated in greenhouse gas emissions: not only carbon dioxide from the use of petroleum, but also methane and nitrous oxide.[152] Packaging and refrigeration are also petroleum-dense. Meat production also utilizes enormous amounts of fresh water, and CAFOs pollute rivers and ground water. Further, CAFOs and slaughterhouses are very unsafe places to work. Also, being high on the food chain meat concentrates toxins such as pesticide residues, and the highly centralized meat production system can spread dangerous microorganisms far and wide. Finally, eating too much meat high in fat or salt can predispose people to a variety of diseases. The meatification of the global diet undermines both social justice (by making grain less available and more expensive) and the environment. Good meat in moderation is a wonderful food, but its consumption at a level above moderation is unsustainable.

HUNGER AND STARVATION

Starvation, in the sense of people being both underfed and undernourished, has existed a lot longer than the recent obesity "epidemic", and it has not received anywhere near as much press because it does not affect the privileged of the world. The number of people worldwide who suffer physical and mental illnesses or death because they cannot afford sufficient nutrients is growing every year, despite grandiose resolutions and efforts to alter the situation (like the UN Millennium Goals). Surely we might suspect that there is something about the system's deep structures that tends to frustrate and often nullify these good intentions.

It has been estimated that half of the earth's people make their living from the land, and that agriculture is the main source of income for 2.5 billion people, with 96 percent of the world's farmers living in developing countries.[153] Many of these men and women are desperately poor, in large part because of a long history of exploitation, which started with colonialism that goes back as far as the seventeenth century, colonialism that inserted them into a Euro-centred capitalist economy which cared much more for profits than human well-being.

As cited above, Jean Ziegler claims in a report presented to the UN Commission on Human Rights in 2004:

> It is an outrage that in the 21st century one child under the age of five will die every five seconds from hunger-related diseases .... Hunger will kill more people than all the wars fought this year. Yet where is the fight against hunger?[154]

The impact of lack of adequate food on human flourishing in the world is frightful to contemplate. Over 146 million pre-school age children suffer from chronic or acute hunger, and 18 percent of all hungry people are children under five years old.[155] The result is an early death for many, and for those who survive longer, physical and mental stunting affects 31 percent of all children in developing countries.[156] It has been estimated that given current trends there will soon be 1 billion people in the world with impaired mental development because of poor nutrition.[157] Malnutrition can also weaken the immune system to the onslaught of infectious diseases, such as malaria and tuberculosis, which are particularly severe in developing countries.[158] According to the FAO, malnutrition plays a role in more than 50 percent of the annual 12 million deaths of children under the age of five.[159] Further, as a result of vitamin A deficiencies, 500,000 children become partially or totally blind every year, while iodine deficiencies result in widespread brain damage.[160]

There are important gender differences with regard to lack of adequate food. Seventy percent of those living in absolute poverty globally are women,[161] and more than 60 percent of those suffering malnutrition are women.[162] In developing countries 25 percent of men and 45 percent of women have anaemia, but anaemia is far more dangerous to women, as an estimated 300 women die every day during childbirth because of iron deficiency.[163] In the face of these appalling statistics, the 1996 World Food Summit resolved to reduce the number of hungry people from 800 million to 400 million by 2015.[164] But today the number of hungry people in the world is increasing, and may have already topped 1 billion as a result of the burgeoning famine that is being created by rising food prices. The United Nations estimates that 1.2 billion people are living on less than $1 a day, while 2.8 billion, or 40 percent of the world's population, live on less than $2 per day.[165] When we consider that the young represent the future, it is disturbing to find that of the 1 billion young people between 15 and 24 worldwide, one half are living in poverty and will likely have poor diets.[166] In India alone 46 percent of children under three are malnourished, as arable land is increasingly used for export crops including non-food crops like flowers.[167]

As the highly subsidized global food regime, coupled with the "green revolution", increasingly undermines the smaller farms in both developed and developing countries, the rural poor are forced to move to city slums, where often their poverty is further exacerbated by the poor sanitation and crime associated with slums. During the first ten years of the North American Free Trade Agreement (NAFTA), 1,175,000 Mexicans were displaced from agriculture largely as a result of highly subsidized American agricultural commodities (especially corn) flooding into Mexico.[168] In this case, many poor Mexicans crossed the border to the United States in order to survive, while other Mexicans migrated from rural areas to the cities. Already one out of three urbanites worldwide (1 billion people) lives in a slum, and it is expected that by 2020 one half of the world's urban population will be living in slums or shanty towns.[169]

The recent policies to increase ethanol production from corn are likely causes of growing world hunger. Although ethanol is apparently no improvement over petroleum in contributing to greenhouse gas emissions, at the time of writing, the American government is giving huge subsidies to ethanol producers, who convert corn to ethanol. The United States produces 40 percent of the world's corn harvest, and in the past it accounted for 70 percent of global corn exports.[170] Other countries cannot compete with the immense subsidies received by American corn producers, which enable them to sell corn abroad at well below the cost of production and still make a handsome profit. As a result, the world food system has become rather dependent on the grain exports of the United States. Now suddenly this grain export is facing the prospect of being reduced as it is predicted that as much as half of the 2008 corn harvest will be used to produce ethanol.[171] This change is a major cause of skyrocketing food price increases worldwide, which threaten hundreds of millions of people with greater poverty and starvation.

Because of rising grain prices, the United States has cut its food aid by more than half from 2000 to 2007, and this is occurring at precisely the time that food aid is most needed – largely because of US ethanol policy.[172] It should also be noted that the United States requires that food aid be in-kind and be purchased from the United States.[173] This ensures profits for the US food industry, but it is often not the best way to proceed when food can be acquired regionally, particularly when regional producers need the extra income.

According to the World Bank, food prices have risen 83 percent in three years, and currently prices seem to rise almost daily, with the price of rice, the basic staple for two-thirds of the world's population, doubling between 1 March and 15 April 2008.[174] As a result 20 million children face starvation and over 1 billion people face the prospects of continual hunger.[175] In the mean time, investors are making a killing on commodity markets, causing prices to escalate even more. One investment company in Toronto recently recommended investing in water since there are critical shortages in more than 80 countries, which will surely increase prices not only of water but of food as well. Indeed, according to the *Toronto Star,* "The global water index is up 9.4 percent in the first four months of this year."[176]

SALT

Another area for concern is the quantity of salt and various flavoured salts in our diet. Most people think that salt makes food taste better, and there is nothing wrong with salt in moderation, but the use of salt in processed and junk foods has increased to the point of being a health threat. In the United States, 90 percent of salt consumed is already in processed or fast foods and only 10 percent is added at the table.[177] It is remarkable to consider that salt consumption in the United States increased by 20 percent between 1992 and 2002.[178] Salt does not appear to be a cause of obesity, but it has been known for a long time that salt makes people thirsty. The problem comes when the preferred drink to quench thirst is soda pop with its typical load of sugar, and increasingly this is the preferred means among today's youth. Salt, then, may indirectly contribute to obesity.

Excessive salt is perhaps far more dangerous as a cause of high blood pressure, the major risk factor in heart disease and strokes.[179] Unlike sugar, salt is unregulated and yet according to the WHO, high blood pressure is the leading risk factor for death in the world, and it is estimated that reducing salt consumption by half in the United States would prevent 150,000 deaths per year.[180]

SOY

Soy and soy byproducts are now integrated into 60 percent of all processed foods.[181] Between 1990 and 2005 global soy production doubled.[182] This intake of soy and soy products is unprecedented, since even in the Far East where soy has been consumed in the past, it has been consumed largely in fermented or modified forms and in nowhere like the quantity that we now consume it. Further, very little research has been done on the long-term health consequences of soy, even though it contains powerful vegetable oestrogens. Between 30 and 40 percent of all infants in the United States are raised on soy formula, in part because it is marketed and is given away in welfare programmes. And yet babies fed on this formula are receiving an amount of vegetable oestrogen that is the equivalent of an adult taking five birth control pills per day.[183]

When we consider the combination of oestrogen in soy, pharmaceuticals that get into the water supply, and all the endocrine disruptors in pesticides and plastics, we need much more research into their long-term impact on human health and the environment.

For example, it has been discovered that one-third of male fish in England are growing female reproductive tissues and organs. Should fish become desexed or unisexed they will become extinct. Among UK men, sperm counts fell by one-third between 1989 and 2002, and one in six couples now have difficulty conceiving.[184] While endocrine disruptors in pesticides and plastics or oestrogens in pharmaceuticals probably have far more impact on reproduction than soy oestrogen, there is still inadequate research on the possible long-term impacts of the amount of soy and soy by-products currently in our diet.[185]

PESTICIDES

The immense increase in pesticide use after World War II was part of the petrochemical revolution which at first seemed to promise a utopia of better living. In this case, the promise took the form of abundant cheap food. The immediate profits were such that capitalists rushed full speed ahead without considering the long-term costs of such a prodigal spread of possible and even probable toxic substances. Today, we are paying the price in cancer rates, weakened immune systems and a host of chronic diseases with earlier and earlier onset.

Pesticides can threaten human health in three ways: as residues in foods, as toxic exposure to workers, and as a build-up of toxicity in the environment or in the human body. In this chapter I shall focus mainly on the first. While there are many types of pesticides, the three most common are insecticides, herbicides and fungicides, with each category containing numerous carcinogens, endocrine disrupters and poisons with long staying power.

It is difficult to prove a relation between a particular pesticide and a particular disease when often very small amounts may constitute the main contributing factor in the appearance of a disease many years after exposure, and when all humans on earth have absorbed at least 250 synthetic chemicals.[186] According to WHO, unacceptable levels of pesticides have been found in babies worldwide, and it has been found that Americans on average carry 13 pesticides in their bodies.[187]

As mentioned above, it was only in 1962, with the publication of

Rachel Carson's *Silent Spring*, that public notice was taken about the possible damage from pesticide use. In this case, the focus was mainly on DDT; and despite the strong evidence of its damaging effects, it took over ten years to get it banned in the United States (it was banned in 1973). As is generally the case with pesticides, it is often possible to market a pesticide banned in the United States in developing countries, just as the shrinkage of the cigarette market in the United States has led to a shift towards marketing in developing countries where controls are weak or nonexistent. For example, in 1990 the United States exported 52 million pounds of pesticide banned in their own country.[188] While this is good for the profits of the producing corporations and is therefore capitalistically rational, it implies a kind of racism. We know better than to poison ourselves, but it is OK if poor people in other parts of the world poison themselves. Given the increasing globalization of the food system, however, we may import food with residues of pesticides that we have banned. Of course, this in no way damages corporate profits, since it is consumers and taxpayers who generally pay health costs.

As organisms build resistance to pesticides, more and more have to be used. In the past two decades in the United States, petrochemical pesticide use has increased 33-fold to 1.2 billion pounds of poison a year, or 20 percent of the global total.[189] California with its enormous food sector utilizes 25 percent of the annual pesticide consumption in the United States.[190] Since some pesticides accumulate in the food chain over time, the higher on the food chain people eat, the more pesticide they ingest. In the average North American diet, 55 percent of pesticide residues come from meat (for example, beef concentrates pesticide residues from feedstock consisting mainly of corn and soy), 23 percent come from dairy, and the remainder from grains, vegetables and fruits.[191]

According to the US Department of Agriculture (USDA) the most heavily sprayed crop is corn (not per acre but in total amounts), followed by cotton (the largest amount per acre).[192] Five of the nine pesticides sprayed on cotton have been classified as carcinogenic by the US Environmental Protection Agency (EPA), including one that is so dangerous that it is no longer used.[193] According to the EPA, 60 percent of herbicides currently in use, 90 percent of fungicides and 30 percent of insecticides are carcinogenic.[194]

There are three main problem areas with pesticide residues in food:

- Who decides the allowable limits of pesticide residues?
- How do we test enough to protect the consumer, since we cannot test all food for such residues? What might be a safe limit for a healthy adult may not be safe at all for a child or for someone with a compromised immune system.
- How do pesticide residues interact with other chemicals that have been ingested?

Existing practices suggest that the food system in the United States does poorly in dealing with these problems:

- Those (corporations) that stand to profit from higher limits have far too much influence on limit setting.[195]
- Nowhere near enough money is spent on developing an effective food inspection system.
- Most allowable pesticide exposure is far too high for children and people with compromised immune systems.

The absence of adequate research and safety standards is especially critical since in the past two decades alone, pesticide use in the United States has increased enormously, in large part because of growing resistance of pests to pesticides.[196]

A study of 2,400 Americans six years old and older, carried out by the US Center for Disease Control in 2002, found 81 different toxic chemicals in the bodies of those tested. According to the report, for many compounds by themselves or in combination, the long-term impact of low dose exposure is unknown. There is some concern that pyrethroids, one of the main classes of pesticides to replace DDT, were found in most bodies. While they do not persist in the environment for years as DDT does, in high enough doses they are toxic to the nervous system and at low doses they may alter hormones.[197] A study by Toronto's Environmental Defence carried out in 2006 measured the toxic chemicals in the bodies of members of a number of typical families.[198] On average, adults carried 26 carcinogens in their bodies and children 19, adults 18 hormone disruptors and children 14, adults 8 respiratory toxins and children 6, adults 26 reproductive/development toxins and children 20, adults 14 neurotoxins and children 11.[199] In this case, many of the toxins were not necessarily pesticide residues in food or water, since there are many sources of toxic chemicals in the environment, including those associated with food packaging or cooking, such as non-stick surfaces of cooking utensils. Bisphenol A is a hormone disrupter found in plastic food and drink containers including plastic baby bottles. Perfluorinated chemicals can cause cancer and can affect child development. They are found in non-stick coatings on cookware, fast food packaging and microwave popcorn bags. Phthalates are hormone disrupters that may cause birth defects and affect child development. They are found in some food packaging. Polybrominated diphenyl ethers can cause cancer and are hormone disrupters and neurotoxins. Stored in animal fat, they can be found in dairy products, fish and meat.[200] According to Rick Smith, Executive Director of Environmental Defence, "We are the guinea pigs in the largest uncontrolled science experiment in history."[201]

As more research is done on the health effects of chemical pesticides and fertilizers, what we are learning is becoming more and more disturbing. Despite the increase in alarming findings, this area of research is greatly underfunded, suggesting that we have only examined the tip of the iceberg. For instance, a recent study carried out at the Indiana University School of Medicine discovered a link between rising premature birth rates in the United States and nitrates from fertilizers that had drained into the drinking water. One out of every four wells tested was found to have unacceptably high levels of nitrates.[202]

FOOD ADDITIVES

Unlike pesticides, food additives are intended to be ingested, and therefore one might think that they would be thoroughly tested for both short and long-term toxicity to determine safe levels of exposure, either by themselves or in combination with other chemicals. Alas, for many food additives this has not been done, which means that we are carrying out potentially damaging experiments on ourselves. Of the 540 food additives that have been approved, there is uncertainty about the safety of approximately 150.[203] It was only when "In some school districts, more than 10 percent of all children are on it [Ritalin] at some point in their lives"[204] and Attention Deficit Disorder (ADD) had become so prevalent, that it was discovered that something so common and widespread as artificial food colouring is likely a causal factor, although the toxic properties of petroleum-derived artificial colours had been suspect for some time.[205] The artificial sweetener aspartame is another additive that has been approved in the United States despite evidence of its having carcinogenic properties. According to American epidemiologist Devra Davis, "All of the studies that found aspartame safe happened to be sponsored by industry. Every single one that questioned its safety was produced by scientists without industry ties."[206] Commenting on artificial sweeteners, we find an article in the *Economist* asserting:

> But a spate of scientific studies has raised doubts about artificial sweeteners. Some studies have linked the chemically derived sweeteners to cancer in lab rats, and others claim, that such sweeteners, by "tricking" the brain without satisfying the body's cravings for sweet treats, may actually promote overeating.[207]

MICROORGANISMS

Because toxic microorganisms in food cause almost immediate and sometimes extreme illness in consumers, they usually get the most press. It is difficult to get accurate statistics on food-borne illnesses, because if they are not severe, they often go unreported. Thus, the estimate of an average of 76 million food-borne illnesses a year in the United States is likely an underestimate, while the averages of 325,000 hospitalizations per year and 5,000 deaths are based on hospital records.[208] Given the concentration within the food industry, the potential for contamination is great. For example, in the beef industry, one infected beef carcass can contaminate eight tons of beef.[209] It is similar with packaged ice cream, which caused a salmonella outbreak in 1994 that infected 220,000 people in 41 states.[210] Between 1976 and 1996 salmonella illnesses in the United States increased six-fold.[211] In 2006, 146 people in 23 states became ill from the potentially lethal pathogen E.coli, which contaminated the California spinach crop.[212] In 2008 a major outbreak of salmonella, seemingly from tomatoes, threatened to bankrupt the big Florida tomato growers that supply tomatoes to fast food chains.[213]

The situation with the control of microorganisms in the US food system is well summarized by Nestle, who writes:

> At the beginning of the twenty-first century efforts to prevent microbial contamination of the food supply continue to be held hostage to industry obstructing intervention, agencies competing for scarce resources, inspectors defending obsolete job descriptions, courts defending obsolete laws, and a Congress more anxious to protect the sources of campaign contributions than the health of the public.[214]

Nestle presents evidence to support her claim that in general the food industry opposes pathogen control measures that might reduce profits or interfere with the rights of private property to take care of business as it sees fit.[215]

LOSS OF NUTRIENTS

In recent years new seeds and animals have been bred to create fruits, vegetables and meats more suitable to advanced industrial processes and profit making. For example, today chicken boilers reach 2 kilograms in one-third the time it took in 1946,[216] and calves, who would in nature feed on grass, can be grown to 544 kilograms in only 14 months through a diet of corn, soy, antibiotics and hormones.[217] Tomatoes have been bred to be tough enough to be machine harvested when green and then later gassed to turn red.[218] Also they have been bred to have a longer shelf life and to have a standard size and shape. At the same time, many have lost nutritional value. For example, the decline of micronutrients in our fruits and vegetables is alarming, with double digit declines in the percentage of such important micronutrients as iron, zinc, calcium and selenium.[219]

I am sure "green revolution" was not coined to refer to picking tomatoes when they are green. But because of the needs of machine harvesting, standardization, transportation and longer shelf lives, many fruits and vegetables are picked before they are ripe, and in the case of tomatoes that means green. While to some extent the loss of taste that results is covered up by breeding varieties that are sweet even when green, important sun-related nutrients like anthocyanins and polyphenols are lost.

Halweil argues convincingly that the single-minded focus on increased yields (which bring increased profits) has greatly increased the quantity of food available at the cost of its quality in terms of nutrient density (nutrients per calorie). For example, new varieties of corn, wheat and soy, bred to increase yields, have lower protein and oil content, and high-yield tomatoes are lower in vitamin C, lycopene and beta-carotene.[220] And according to Pawlick, today's tomatoes compared with those in 1963, have 30.7 percent less vitamin A, 16.9 percent less vitamin C, 61.5 percent less calcium and 22.7 percent less protein, while salt content is up 200 percent.[221] In terms of daily nutrient intake, studies have shown that 30 percent of Americans do not have a sufficient daily intake of vitamin C, 42 percent are insufficient in vitamin A, 50 percent in calcium, 55 percent in magnesium and 94 percent in vitamin E.[222] It has been estimated that nutritional deficiencies in the United States alone cost $120 billion per year in health care costs and lost productivity.[223]

Similarly, high-producing dairy cows produce less protein and other health-enhancing elements, while at the same time the stress they are under to produce so much milk makes them vulnerable to diseases.[224] Part of the stress arises from the widespread use of bovine growth hormone, the use of which requires no labelling, despite the fact it has been outlawed in almost every other country, and has been linked to premature puberty and cancer in humans.[225] Finally, by nature cattle eat grass, but in feed lots they are forced to eat corn and soy, which can cause them to become sick; hence, massive amounts of antibiotics not only speed up growth, but also reduce the percentage of "downers".[226]

For human health, taking vitamin supplements may help, but they are not the same as getting the nutrients from whole foods. According to Halweil:

> Supplements may not be as bioavailable, typically contain no fibre, and do not also provide a myriad of phytochemicals

and related nutrients found only in whole food.... A recent article in the *American Journal of Clinical Nutrition*[227] looking at the benefits of whole-grains in reducing heart disease suggested that it isn't the fibre or additional nutrients or phytochemicals in whole-grain that confer protection against heart disease, but the combination of the three which act "in synergy with each other" when eaten as part of whole food.[228]

The rush to expand quantity and the indifference to quality, so typical of capitalism, are what lie behind the focus on yields as opposed to nutrient density. Pushing this tendency to the extreme, we get junk food high in calories with zero or low nutrient density. In general, food processing decreases nutrient density, but so does the artificial intensification of many natural processes. Dairy cows that on average yielded 5,000 pounds of milk per cow per year in 1900 are now forced to produce 22,000 pounds of milk per year.[229] In 1930, laying hens averaged 93 eggs per year and this has now been increased to 252 eggs per year.[230] Similarly beef cattle are brought to slaughter much faster through the feed lot system, which takes a grass-eating animal and pours huge amounts of corn, soy, hormones and antibiotics down its gullet to bring it to weight in a quarter of the time.[231] The resulting meat not only has a higher content of saturated fats, but also has fewer micronutrients and fewer omega 3 fatty acids.[232] A British study showed that the average iron content of beef went down 54 percent between 1940 and the present.[233] While nearly every industrial researcher wants discoveries that will increase immediate profits, according to Halweil, "there are few systematic breeding efforts currently in the United States to raise nutrient content of major foods".[234]

Industrial farming that relies on nitrogen-potassium-phosphorus (NKP) natural gas fertilizers and petroleum-based pesticides, when coupled with irrigatin, may not add organic matter back into the soil, thus causing it to be drained of micronutrients:

> The large amounts of organic matter returned to the soil in organic farming systems encourage healthier, more robust roots, higher levels of available micronutrients, water

infiltration and retention, and below ground microbial activity that can help increase crop nutrient density.[235]

Soil improvement, by adding the right sorts of organic matter, is an essential step in increasing the nutrient density of our foods. Also essential to growing nutrient rich foods are healthy root systems (often weakened by chemical fertilizers, pesticides and irrigation) that can take full advantage of improved soils.

As previously argued, the green revolution in retrospect was not so green after all. Yes, food yields were increased enormously, but primarily in staple grain crops where new hybrid seeds replaced seed diversity with monocultures that required increased chemical inputs. As a result, not only were the increased yields less nutrient dense, the diets of entire populations were altered. For example, in South East Asia per capita grain consumption has gone up 15 percent in the past 40 years, while per capita consumption of legumes went down over 50 percent.[236]

GENETICALLY MODIFIED ORGANISMS

The use of genetically modified organisms (GMOs) in agriculture raises many issues about environmental impact and the concentration of corporate power, but in this chapter, I am only concerned with their health impact on consumers of food. There are only two types of GMOs in widespread use: one type makes crops immune to the herbicide Roundup which gets rid of weeds, and the other type is Bt which makes crops poisonous to a range of insects.

There is evidence that many people not previously allergic to soy are allergic to GM soy.[237] Soy allergies increased 50 percent in the United Kingdom just after GM soy was introduced. Ironically or perhaps not so ironically, the US government does not require biotech companies to test their GMOs for allergens.[238] Given that soy and soy derivatives are in 60 percent of all processed foods, soy allergies can be very problematic.[239]

The spread of Roundup-ready GM seeds has led to exponentially mounting sales of Monsanto's herbicide Roundup. The only problem is that the principal ingredient of Roundup, glyposate, has been found to have adverse effects in all five of the basic categories of toxicity: subchronic, chronic, carcinogencity, mutagenicity and reproduction.[240] While the persistence of Roundup in the environment seems to vary enormously, the EPA rates it as extremely persistent, with a 100-day half life.[241] Because Roundup-ready GM crops increase profits for some farmers, usage is increasing. The EPA estimated its use in 1998 at 38–48 million lbs and growing by 20 percent annually.[242] In 1997 Roundup was the highest cause of pesticide-induced illness in California.[243] Farmers have suffered miscarriages, premature births and lymphoma due to contact with Roundup,[244] and this is not surprising since an independent scientific study found that Roundup is an endocrine disruptor.[245] It is highly toxic to fish, kills beneficial insects and there is now evidence that weeds can develop resistance to it.[246] Despite all of the above, most likely because of Monsanto's influence in Washington, both Roundup-ready GMOs and Bt GMOs were approved without any independent government testing, and Roundup is not included in government monitoring of pesticide residues in foods.[247] Because Monsanto convinced government officials that genetically modified seeds are "substantially equivalent" to non-GMO seeds, no approval from the Food and Drug Administration was required:

> In the US, the wording of the Food and Drug Administration's approval statement for new GM crops says that they believe that the corporations have performed all necessary tests to be in compliance with existing safety law.[248]

SUPERMARKETS

It is easy to be impressed by the tens of thousands of items in an average American supermarket, but much of the food is a rearrangement through processing of a small number of basic ingredients.[249] Think, for example, of the enormous array of chips (crisps), breakfast cereals, snack foods and candies which in actuality differ very little. They all have a preponderance of some combination of highly processed grains, fats, sugars, salt, artificial flavouring and various chemical additives which function to colour, preserve, texturize and so forth. What they tend to have in common is a high ratio of calories to nutrients and quasi-addictive qualities. Twenty-five percent of all supermarket items contain corn and 60 percent of processed foods contain soy (most likely GM soy, since over 93 percent of soy acreage in the United States is GM).[250]

Supermarkets play a major role in the American food regime since that is where 40 percent of all food is purchased.[251] Supermarkets typically sell a high proportion of highly processed, highly packaged and highly transported foods. In other words, supermarkets are largely purveyors of unsustainable petrofoods and unhealthy processed foods.[252] The average supermarket item has travelled at least 1,500 miles, and that takes a lot of fossil fuel.[253]

Only four companies control 83 percent of the breakfast cereal industry which is so important to the diet of children.[254] The tendency of this industry has been towards more and more highly processed cereals, with many cereals achieving junk food status because of added sugars, even with their various health claims. By the late 1980s, 92 percent of the products for sale in supermarkets were processed, and processing often means loss of nutrients.[255] Further, it is estimated that 80 percent of processed foods contain GMOs, though there is no way of knowing which ones, since there is no labelling requirement for the presence of GMOs in food even though there are people allergic to GM soy.[256]

The supermarket industry is highly concentrated and is becoming more so, with the recent addition of Wal-Mart as the single largest chain. In the United States five corporations control 42 percent of grocery sales, and such large corporations typically contract for fruit and vegetables with large industrial farms located in California, Florida, Mexico or Chile.[257] This is no doubt one reason that on average 20,000 small farmers go out of business in the United States every year. And the death-rate of small farms in developing countries has even greater impact, because there are few other options for making a living.

FAST FOOD CHAINS

The food served by many fast food chains is almost synonymous with large servings and with the junkiness of foods high in sugar, fat and salt.[258] The car/suburbanization/television complex that developed during the 1950s also fuelled the development of fast food chains. The leading chains are all burger chains (the three largest in order are McDonald's, Burger King and Wendy's), specializing in burgers, French fries and soda pop. Yum! Brands is a consortium of fast food chains that includes KFC, Pizza Hut, A&W, Long John Silver and Taco Bell, which taken together make it the largest restaurant company in the world with over 34,000 restaurants in 100 countries.[259] McDonald's has over 31,000 restaurants in 100 countries, Burger King has 11,200 in 66 countries and Wendy's 6,700 globally.[260]

It is not just the high ratio of calories to nutrients in most food that is served, but also the portions themselves have increased in size as much as five times since the 1950s and 1960s, when the fast food system was just getting off the ground.[261] The basic reason for this is that larger portions are more profitable since the costs of the food make up only about one-third of the costs of running a fast food restaurant. The profits particularly expand with French fries and soda pop, because the food inputs are so cheap with these products. For example, frozen French fries can be bought at 30 cents a pound and then sold at $6 per pound.[262] And Burger King has shown that even supersizing hamburgers can increase profits with its recent announcement that its already large "Whopper" will be accompanied by the he-man's "Triple Whopper". It cannot be too surprising, then, that Americans today are eating on average 12 percent more calories per day than they were in the mid-1980s, when the trend towards larger portions got kick-started in Texas "where everything is bigger".[263]

It is interesting to consider the extent to which fast food restaurants are typically subsidized by the government. Restaurant lobbies have played a major role in successfully opposing increases in the minimum wage, and this has kept their costs down. But more importantly their food inputs are significantly cheapened by government subsidies. Starmer argues that the chicken broiler industry benefits from subsidized feed grain to the tune of $1.25 billion a year.[264] The fast food industry also receives $1 billion a year in small business loans to its franchisees from the US Federal Government.[265]

One consequence of changed eating habits is a gradual loss of cooking skills. As people eat out more and more and rely on convenience foods like frozen pizza at home, less time and effort goes into home cooking. For example, in Britain in 1980 the average time per day spent cooking was 60 minutes, but by 2002 this had fallen sharply to a mere 13 minutes a day.[266]

Feeding over 1.3 billion mouths in China has recently been the big attraction for fast food chains. Yum! Brands has already opened 2,600 restaurants there, with most of its three new restaurant openings per day outside the United States occurring in China.

CONCLUSIONS

The key message of this chapter is that the current global food regime has generated an enormous global health crisis consisting of two interrelated problems, one of obesity and the other of starvation. In contrast, we would like to see a world in which every woman, man and child could access sufficient nutritious food in an environment that encourages healthy eating and that produces the food in ecologically sustainable ways. According to the United Nations, food should be a basic human right, but so far this right remains purely theoretical.[267]

Capitalists continually point to the incredible technological progress and wealth generation of the capitalist system, but they never point to its enormous failures when it comes to distributive justice and democracy. It is with food, the basis of human life and health, that these failures have the most damaging consequences. And because the food system is so closely integrated with the natural environment, its petrochemical basis has dangerously polluted the environment and contributed to global warming. The debt to future generations is even more severe as petroleum is a non-renewable resource that we are fast depleting.

Because of its short-term profit orientation, I believe that capitalism is not consistent with a human right to food or with sustainable agriculture. We should not deceive ourselves that the human right to food of good quality and sufficient quantity provided in sustainable ways can remain anything but a purely formal right within the current economic system. I don't mean to suggest that we could or should change the economic system from top to bottom all at once, but we do need to chip away at it with radical reforms that begin to redistribute wealth and food world-wide. Such reforms will not be possible without very significant mobilizations that will advance democracy. In saying this, I do not mean to devalue even the smallest steps towards reform provided they are in the direction of social justice, human health and sustain-ability. Over time many small steps can add up, and can gradually mobilize more and more people, even if in the short term, headway may be halting.

Let us consider an example. Parents across the United States have mobilized to try to get junk foods out of schools, but because of the power of food corporations, their efforts have often been partially or wholly thwarted. In order to deflect the rising public outcry against the advertising and marketing of junk food to chil-dren, some corporations have declared that they will no longer target children under 12 in their television advertising of junk foods. The problem is that although they may not "target" the under 12 age group, this group will still be exposed to many television ads for junk foods even if the ads are not specifically aimed at them. There are many ways of marketing junk food to children besides television commercials during child programming. As with ciga-rettes, the popular uprising may eventually succeed in constraining the marketing of junk foods, but I suspect that success will only occur after many battles.

In the next chapter, I want to indicate some of the ways in which our food system has failed not only consumers, but also those who toil on the earth to produce the food. It has failed family farmers in the United States and around the world, and also field workers hired by capitalist farmers. The two principal failures are: lack of adequate income for small and medium-sized family farm-ers; and field workers with low wages and poor working conditions, including the dangers of exposure to petrochemical pesticides.

5 THE HEALTH OF AGRICULTURE AND FOOD WORKERS

Moreover, labour economists point out that California agribusiness in particular does not want so much a stable supply of labour, but rather a dependable system of constantly disposable and replenishable labour. Foreign labour is best for their needs precisely because it represents a never-ending pool and because the constant replacement of such labour ensures that the entire workforce will, in the classic phraseology of those who are familiar with the bottom line of illegal or legally admitted but not totally free labour, "work hard and scared."[1]

The trillions of dollars spent supporting farmers in rich countries have led to higher taxes, worse food, intensively farmed monocultures, overproduction and world prices that wreck the lives of poor farmers in the emerging markets.[2]

In those countries where capitalism is most fully developed, it has been a long uphill battle for workers to achieve wages and working conditions that are more than minimally acceptable, and even where achieved, it is only in certain sectors. In countries where capitalism penetrated not as an industrial revolution but as colonialism, the legacies of forced labour, racism and foreign domination have in many cases made it nearly impossible to establish even minimally acceptable wages and working conditions for many workers. And where neo-colonialism has been overlaid with the "green" revolution, which the United States exported to much of the world, yields have increased for richer farmers, but at a great price: ecological unsustainability of agriculture, export-oriented crops taking priority over domestic food crops and the deepening impoverishment of the majority of farmers, many of whom have ended up in city slums.

Although the United States is considerably less hegemonic than it was during the golden age after World War II (1946–70), as we approach the end of the first decade of the twenty-first century, it is still considerably more powerful and influential than any other economy in the world. I therefore start my analysis with a focus on food workers in the United States.

Because food is so basic and important to consumers, and because we live in the age of consumerism, in which capitalism celebrates its vast provision of consumer goodies, most books on food devote little attention to food workers. In my research I have found it difficult to find thorough studies of food workers, and as a result this chapter is shorter than I would like it to be. At the same time, I hope to have given the topic enough attention to underline its general importance. For instance, one-third of all workers in the world work in fields,[3] and over 2.5 billion people worldwide, depend on agriculture for their main source of income, making it by far the largest sector of economic activity.[4] If we include people who make a living from fishing, from food transport, food processing, food retailing and food serving, the numbers swell. We need to understand and improve the situation of workers in the areas of agriculture and food provision if we are to make the transformations required to achieving a world where distributive justice and human well-being are significantly advanced.

WORKERS IN THE US AGRICULTURAL AND FOOD SYSTEMS

The real incomes of US workers increased over a 25-year period after World War II, but since then there has been little increase, while the real incomes of the upper 5 percent of Americans have increased enormously.[5] The job security of the 1950s and 1960s now appears to be historically exceptional. Many better-paying jobs in manufacturing have been lost either because manufacturers have moved production offshore to low wage areas or because manufacturing is increasingly automated.[6] According to Schlosser,[7] real wages for the average worker in the United States have not increased since 1973. Since 2000 most of the new jobs have been created in health care, the food/hospitality sector, policing/military/prison/security sector or retailing, and typically these are among the lowest-paying and least secure jobs.[8] Agricultural field workers constitute the lowest-paid major category of workers, while workers in fast food chains receive the second-lowest average pay.[9] In fact, there is a tendency for workers up and down the food chain from field to table to receive low wages, and for undocumented workers in the United States this can be less than the US minimum wage of $5.15 per hour, which was only recently slightly raised for the first time since 1 September 1997.[10] According to an article in *Business Week* published in 2004, 24 percent of all American workers earn annual wages that place them below the poverty line,[11] and the median paycheque for working wives in 2001 was only $18,000 per year.[12]

I have presented reasons that capitalism pays food workers particularly low pay, yet if we think about it rationally, it is perhaps more than a bit ironic given that food and drink are not only basic necessities of human life but also their quality impacts hugely on that life. In a rational economy workers in the food sector would be paid handsomely for the extremely valuable work that they do. Currently in both the United States and globally the treatment of many food workers often seems to be a throwback to the early days of capitalism before workers had won any rights at all. This is particularly the case with undocumented workers.

Field Workers

It is estimated that there are over 12 million undocumented immigrants and migrants in the United States, who because of their lack of legal status are vulnerable to employers who would enhance profits by ignoring rights won by citizens who have legal standing.[13] Such workers can be deported if they complain about low pay, unsafe working conditions, too long hours or the intensification (speed-up) of work.

California produces more than half of all fruits, vegetables and nuts grown in the United States. Many of these crops are labour-intensive, and as of 2005 over 90 percent of all field workers in California were undocumented.[14] Back-breaking work for long hours in the hot sun is rewarded by an average income of $7,500 per year,[15] an income that is well below the poverty line of $10,488 for a single person.[16] More dangerous than sunstroke or heat exhaustion are the continuing exposures to chemical pesticides that result in over 300,000 poisonings a year in the United States.[17] Agricultural field work is one of the most dangerous categories of work, and field work in California has a death rate five times higher than the average for all other industries taken as a whole.[18] And it is not only the field workers that are exposed to pesticides, but also those who live near enough to the fields to be affected by the runoff and wind-blown drift from spraying. For example, of 60 children of Latino farm workers in North Carolina, 90 percent had pesticide metabolites in their urine – a serious risk factor for long-term health.[19]

Employers are motivated to hire undocumented workers because vulnerable workers can be paid less and employers can be saved the costs of ensuring safe working conditions, giving them a competitive advantage over employers who hire documented workers. Since undocumented workers mean higher profits, their use has spread from fields to slaughterhouses to fast food restaurants. In order to stem the flow of "illegal aliens" across the Mexican border, President G.. W. Bush has expanded the H-2A program that brings "contract" or "guest" workers across the border to work for specific employers for specific time spans.[20] But such workers cannot change employers, cannot bargain collectively, are subject to deportation or blacklisting if they complain, and have limited remedies in the face of abuse.[21] In short, the degree of power that this programme grants employers places workers under a kind of compulsory servitude, since they are dependent on the employer who sponsored their entry.[22] This mode of attaining field workers is rapidly gaining in popularity, and in 1998 there were already 10,500 such guest workers in North Carolina alone.[23]

Some field workers employed by sugar companies in the Dominican Republic are for all intents and purposes little better off than the slaves brought from Africa to work in this industry from the seventeenth to the nineteenth centuries. The sugar industry is centred in Florida, where four main companies dominate. Because the industry is protected from foreign competition, it charges up to three times the going international price for sugar, which amounts to a subsidy of from $1–3 billion a year to grow a crop that has lots of calories but no other nutrients.[24]

In the 1980s the working conditions in the Florida sugar plantations were so slave-like that a public outcry began to increase in volume.[25] The response of the sugar industry was to mechanize the harvest. But the American sugar industry in the Dominican Republic has not moved in the direction of expensive mechanization because their workers received in 2004 on average $2 for a twelve-hour day cutting cane in the hot sun.[26] There are approximately 650,000 sugar workers on the plantations in Dominican Republic, mostly from Haiti. Desperately poor Haitians cross the border to find work. Once hired by a sugar plantation, their passports are taken away and they are not allowed to leave the plantation on which they are housed in small shanty towns.[27] They lack good water and medical care, and must buy food from the company store which typically overcharges.[28] These slave-like conditions are only possible because of the extreme poverty in Haiti which forces people to accept almost any conditions just to survive.

Family Farmers

US agricultural subsidies go to the largest and richest farmers, leaving smaller family farms to go bankrupt. American agriculture loses on average approximately 20,000 farms per year, and this is largely because the smaller family farm cannot compete with large industrial farms.[29] Larger farms can more easily afford and utilize the latest high-tech combines (which may cost over $800,000) and other expensive mechanical equipment, costly chemical inputs, costly seeds and the latest irrigation equipment. Also, a subsidy system that rewards high yields has encouraged large farms. For example, in 2005 the federal government spent over $20 billion in agricultural subsidies.[30] Forty-six percent of subsidies went to corn, 23 percent to cotton, 10 percent to wheat and 6 percent to soybeans. The largest 10 percent of farms got 72 percent of the subsidies and 60 percent of farms got no subsidies at all.[31] It is difficult for smaller farms to survive since, as a result of subsidies to the large industrial farms, the selling price of their crops can be lower than the costs of production.

The American cotton industry is also shamelessly subsidized by the federal government, and this encourages overproduction and prices lower than the cost of production. In 2005 the US Congress decreased the maximum subsidy to cotton farmers from $360,000 per farmer per year to $250,000.[32] From 1996 to 2006 world cotton prices dropped by 50 percent, and by 2002 US cotton was dumped on the world market at 61 percent below the cost of production,[33] ruining many small producers in developing countries. It has been estimated that US cotton subsidies cost African countries $250 million a year by lowering the international price of cotton.[34]

The average worth of cotton farmers in the United States is $800,000, and yet between 1995 and 2003 they received $14 billion in subsidies, with 75 percent of the subsidies going to 12 percent of the richest farmers.[35] There are 25,000 cotton growers in the United States, with the largest 12 percent receiving high subsidies;[36] whereas there are 11 million cotton growers in West Africa, receiving no subsidies and having to sell their crops at international prices deflated by American growers being able to sell below cost of production and still make large profits because of subsidies.[37] It is estimated that the desperately poor cotton farmers of Mali lose $30 million a year as a result of American subsidies.[38] Because of low cotton prices and their resulting indebtedness, over 1,200 cotton farmers in India committed suicide over an 18-month period.[39] Another study of the 100,000 Indian farmers who committed suicide between 1993 and 2003 came to the conclusion that the main cause was debt.[40] Sadly, it is not only cotton that is exported at below cost of production. The same occurs with all of the major grain crops produced in the United States. For example, in 2002 wheat was exported at 40 percent below the cost of production.[41] Indeed, farmer debt is a global problem since even in the United States it is typically the large farms that get the subsidies.[42]

Subsidizing cotton also subsidizes agrochemicals, as cotton is the heaviest user of chemical pesticides per acre of crop. Cotton is grown on only 2.5 percent of the world's agricultural land and yet it uses 8 to 10 percent of all chemical fertilizers and 22.5 percent of total world consumption of pesticides.[43] It takes about one-third of a pound of chemicals to produce one T-shirt, and five of the nine pesticides used to grow cotton are carcinogenic.[44] Further, the production of a single T-shirt generates ten times its weight in CO_2.[45]

By 1990 20 percent of farm households in the United States had incomes that put them below the poverty line.[46] Fifty years ago North American farmers got 40–60 percent of the money spent by consumers on food, but today they average only 3.5 percent, which is about the same as Third World farmers.[47] And there are extreme cases as with French fries, where the potato farmer gets 2 cents out of a $1.50 order of fries.[48] No doubt falling incomes and large debts are a major contributing factor to the fact that suicide is the leading cause of death among US farmers, and their suicide rate is three times the average for the general population.[49] Also it is a reason that the average age of a farmer in Iowa is 52 and steadily increasing.[50]

Capitalist Farms

Increasingly farming is becoming a "flow-through" system in which corporations sell expensive input packages to farmers who will meet the output requirements of large corporations that either process or market the farmer's product. This largely removes control over farming from the farmer. An industrial tomato farm, for example, must produce tomatoes that meet the price and quality requirements of a fast food chain, but in order to do this, it must be large enough to have the resources to buy an expensive input package which includes hybridized seeds, pesticides, chemical fertilizers, an irrigation system and a variety of tractors and mechanical inputs. The farmer's job is simply to implement the input package in order to produce the tomato that the fast food company has contracted the farmer to produce. All of the risks of the chemical inputs and the enormously hard field work fall on the workers, who make a pittance, while the corporation executives sit in their air-conditioned offices and rake in the profits. With many pre-purchase agreements, the only cost that the farmer can cut is labour costs, thus ensuring the lowest possible pay for field workers. The farmers simply implement the input package and most importantly manage the field workers in order to get the contracted-for output.

The fast food giant Yum! Brands, for example, buys all of its American produce from one company (Unified Foodservice Purchasing Co-op) which in turn buys all of its tomatoes from six growers.[51] Since only very large farms can contract in this way, small farms are displaced. In Florida where most of the large growers are located, the number of tomato farms decreased by 38 percent over the five-year period between 1992 and 1997.[52]

Slaughterhouse Workers

Tyson Foods, the largest meat processor in the world, does not need direct subsidies, although it profits indirectly from the subsidies given to animal feeds. Some of its workers have been undocumented and yet even with such vulnerable workers, the job turnover is 75 percent annually because the pay is low, the work is demanding, and the working conditions of slaughterhouses are dangerous.[53] Between 1980 and 2000 the profits of the chicken industry tripled, while the real wages of 250,000 poultry workers in the United States remained unchanged, and the pace of work intensified dramatically.[54] Intensification implies speeding up of the already dangerous disassembly line:

> line workers can hang chickens at a pace of 40 birds a minute .... They stand in the same place and make the same series of motions for an entire shift. If you stay in these jobs long enough, you will inevitably develop serious injuries associated with this repetitive motion.[55]

According to a 2005 Human Rights Watch report on the US meat and poultry industries:

> Nearly every worker interviewed for this report bore physical signs of a serious injury suffered from working in a meat or poultry plant. Automated lines carrying dead animals and their parts for disassembly move too fast for worker safety. Repeating thousands of cutting motions during each work shift puts enormous stress on worker's hands, wrists, arms, shoulders and backs. They often work in close quarters creat-

ing additional dangers for themselves and coworkers. They often receive little training and are not always given the safety equipment they need. They are often forced to work long overtime hours under pain of dismissal if they refuse. Meat and poultry industry employers set up the workplaces and practices that create these dangers, but they treat the resulting mayhem as a normal, natural part of the production process, not as what it is – repeated violations of international human rights standards.[56]

The need to increase profits leads to increasing the speed of the line, which is one of the main reasons why the work has become so dangerous. Some beef disassembly lines disassemble up to 400 cattle an hour, and at that rate it is not rare for workers to take amphetamines just to give themselves the energy to keep up.[57] According to Nierenberg:

> Every year, one in three meatpacking workers suffers an injury on the job. But because many of these workers are undocumented immigrants or struggle at the very bottom of the economic ladder, many don't report their injuries, making the actual numbers far higher.[58]

Supermarket Workers

While the health and safety issues are less extreme in the supermarket sector, real wages are low and will probably get lower because of the influence of Wal-Mart in this sector. Wal-Mart now controls over 20 percent of all grocery sales in the United States, and this share is increasing. The anti-union, low-wage policies of this largest of all corporations are likely to impact the supermarket sector in general. Other supermarket chains will need to find ways of cutting their labour costs in order to compete with Wal-Mart. Given that it already has 4,000 stores in the United States, Wal-Mart's anti-union policy cuts deeply into the right to unionize.[59] In this situation it will be difficult for unionized workers in this sector to keep their unions, or to keep the improved wages and working conditions that their unions have won for them. It needs to be pointed out, that even with unions, the wages and working conditions in this sector are already far below the average for industry.[60]

Fast Food Workers

The 3.5 million fast food workers in the United States earn on average less than any large group of workers except migrant field workers.[61] McDonald's hires about 1 million workers annually (second only to Wal-Mart), but this needs to be considered in a context where the annual turnover of workers is 300 to 400 percent. The high turnover, the part-time nature of much of the work, and the fact that about two-thirds of fast food workers are under 20 have been enough to keep unions out of the fast food sector.[62] As a result, it is this sector that pays the minimum wage to the largest percentage of workers, and this is significant to profits given that between 1968 and 1990, the real value of the minimum wage fell by almost 40 percent.[63] No wonder the National Restaurant Association has lobbied so determinedly against any increase in the minimum wage, and this may also partially explain why between 1997 and 2007 there was no increase in the federal minimum wage of $5.15/hour despite ongoing inflation.[64]

The fast food chains have in the past received up to $2,400 per worker from federal programmes for "training" them.[65] When "The Work Opportunity Tax Credit Program" was renewed by Congress in 1996, it provided as much as $385 million in subsidies for 1997.[66] According to Schlosser, "Fast food restaurants had to employ a worker for only four hundred hours to receive the federal money – and then could get more money as soon as the worker quit or was replaced."[67] It is perhaps not surprising, then, that typically a fast food worker lasts only three or four months before quitting or being fired.[68] Often fast food restaurants further pad their profits by keeping shifts under four hours so that breaks are not required and few if any benefits need be provided to workers.[69]

WORKERS IN THE AGRICULTURAL AND FOOD SYSTEMS OF DEVELOPING COUNTRIES

Ninety-six percent of all farmers live in developing countries and 70 percent of these are women.[70] Despite the fact that half the world's people make their living from the land and work incredibly hard, the global food system is structured in ways that leaves most of these people in grinding poverty. Ironically the very people who produce the food in the developing world often cannot afford enough food for a good diet. Indeed, 80 percent of the world's population live in countries where economic disparity between rich and poor increased between 1990 and 2003.[71] Given these basic facts, it is shocking how little international support agriculture has received in recent years. Indeed, the small US aid package to agriculture in developing countries has been cut in half since 1986, and global foreign aid for agriculture in developing countries was cut by 57 percent between 1988 and 1996.[72] According to Patel, nearly all farmers in the world carry a debt load, and in many cases a truly crushing debt.[73]

The Global Food Regime and Developing Countries

Before focusing on food workers in developing countries, some of the general dynamics of the capitalist global food system need to be clarified. A good starting point is the impact of structural adjustment policies (SAPs) on developing countries. In the late 1970s the World Bank and the International Monetary Fund (IMF) developed increasingly interventionist SAPs to set the conditions for developing countries to get further loans or get better repayment schedules for existing loans in response to the "debt crisis" of the time. In the previous period, developing countries had been encouraged to deepen their debt load by financial institutions that needed to loan out the enormous volume of petrodollars arising from the quadrupling of oil prices in the early 1970s. But as it became increasingly clear that many developing countries could not even pay the interest on their loans, the World Bank and IMF required (among other things) that they develop export-oriented agriculture in order to earn foreign exchange to pay off their debts. With many developing countries expanding their export capacities for tropical commodities like coffee, prices fell from the resulting glut, making it increasingly difficult for these countries to develop or to pay off debts. Given that agriculture is the weightiest sector in the economies of over 80 developing countries, the results were in many cases close to catastrophic.[74] Indeed, according to Robbins, "The collapse of tropical commodity prices represents the most formidable obstacle to efforts to lift huge numbers of people out of poverty and yet, mysteriously, the problem has received almost no attention from the world's mainstream media."[75]

Because this has meant a huge drop in export revenue for deeply in debt developing countries, they have been forced to adopt extreme austerity measures, cutting back on health, education, welfare and infrastructure in order to pay their creditors.[76] For example, by 2002, coffee prices were at 14 percent of their 1980 price, while cocoa was at 19 percent and cotton at 21 percent.

Developing countries could not by and large compete with the major grain crops grown in the United States such as corn and wheat because they are so highly subsidized (farmers receive on average 50 percent of their income in the form of government subsidies).[77] The subsidies result in large surpluses that are then sold abroad at below the cost of production, thus lowering the global price for these commodities. For instance in 2002 US corn cost $2.66 a bushel to produce, but could be bought on the international market for $1.74 a bushel.[78]

By the late 1990s, 30 percent of agricultural income in the United States came from exports.[79] As a result, many developing countries became increasingly dependent on US food imports. The same countries currently face serious famines as a significant portion of US corn is now being diverted into ethanol production with the predictable result that food prices are rising globally. When the price of a basic grain like corn goes up, the prices of other basic grains will also go up. For example, rising corn prices will mean that farmers will grow less wheat and more corn, causing the price of wheat to go up as well.

Even to compete amongst themselves in producing tropical commodities, because of the "green" revolution, developing countries often had to invest heavily in agro-industrial seed, and mechanical and chemical inputs that would only be possible for the larger wealthier farms. Further, the green revolution became a substitute for much-needed land reform in many developing countries. As a result, huge numbers of people were driven off the land as only the richer farmers benefited. According to Davis:

the Third World now contains many examples of capital-intensive countryside and labor-intensive deindustrialized cities.[80] As large numbers of small farmers have been forced off the land, city slums have grown to the point that now one-third of all the world's urban dwellers live in slums, and this percentage is expected to increase in the near future.[81]

The North American Free Trade Agreement (NAFTA) has impacted upon Mexico much as SAPs have affected other developing countries. As previously mentioned, when NAFTA was ratified by Canada, Mexico and the United States, subsidized US corn began to pour into Mexico where corn is not subsidized, and corn imports from the United States tripled in a short time. As a result, over only a ten-year period 1.7 million Mexican farmers were forced off the land as the United States came to supply Mexico with 25 percent of its corn.[82] Many of these farmers crossed the border to the United States, as indicated by the statistics that estimate that only 7 percent of the 900,000 migrant farm workers in the United States prior to NAFTA were undocumented compared with 50 percent of the 2 million migrant farm workers in the United States ten years later.[83] Since NAFTA 80 percent of rural Mexicans live in poverty, and Mexico, which prior to NAFTA was nearly self-sufficient in food, now imports 40 percent, mostly from the United States.[84]

In Mexico a small number of farmers have become very rich, while the vast majority either barely survive or have had to leave the land altogether. While the export-oriented petroagriculture that has been introduced is highly profitable to a handful of farmers in the short run, in the long run it is radically unsustainable. From another perspective, the system helps the United States improve its balance of trade deficit at the expense of Mexico, which must export petro-foods in order to help pay for the increasing import of foods from the United States.

Banana Workers

A number of Central American countries grow a lot of bananas; and because the banana corporations have so often intervened politically in these countries to get their way, they have sometimes been labelled "banana republics". Dole, Del Monte and Chiquita brands control the large North American banana market, where bananas are the most consumed fruit. Bananas are the world's fourth largest agricultural commodity after wheat, rice and corn, and Dole and Chiquita control 50 percent of the banana trade.[85] Much banana production is plantation-scale with labourers hired as needed, usually from small villages near the plantations. They are typically paid very low wages for work that is physically demanding and dangerous. Banana workers in Ecuador, for example, earn only one-half of what is required to support a family of four.[86]

Banana trees, like many other plants, can be set back, stunted or even killed by nematodes – very small worms that attack the roots. As a result, Dow Chemical and Shell Oil thought they had struck it rich when they developed a pesticide to get rid of the nematodes. Although tests on rats in the mid-1950s caused retarded growth, smaller testicles and cancer, the pesticide was approved for use by the Department of Agriculture in 1961.[87] According to Barry Levy, former president of the American Public Health Association, Nemagon should never have been approved.[88]

Nevertheless, from the 1960s through the 1980s Nemagon was utilized extensively on plantations in Nicaragua, Costa Rica, Panama, Ecuador, Guatemala, Dominican Republic, St Lucia, St Vincent, Burkino Faso, Ivory Coast and the Philippines.[89] In 1975 the US Environmental Protection Agency (EPA) determined that Nemagon was a carcinogen.[90] In 1977 it was found that 35 workers out of 114 working in the US factory producing Nemagon had become sterile, but it was not until 1979 that it was banned in the United States.[91] The workers sued Occidental Petroleum, their employer, which was forced to pay millions in compensation.[92]

As has been the case with many toxic pesticides that have been banned in the United States, this one continued to be used outside the United States. An estimated 65,000 people worldwide have been affected by this toxic pesticide with, for example, 67 percent of the banana workers in Nicaragua suffering sterility as well as a host of debilitating and deadly diseases.[93] Thirty-three percent of the women working in banana plantations that used Nemagon have uterus or breast cancer, and many badly deformed babies have been born to those women who are still alive.[94] According to Berube, in 2002 after the longest civil action in Nicaraguan history, a court ordered Shell, Dow and Dole to pay $489 million in damages to banana workers afflicted with diseases and disabilities caused by exposure to Nemagon.[95] The corporations rejected the settlement, arguing that the Nicaraguan court system was not competent to reach a fair settlement.[96] In the meantime, over 2,000 banana workers have died in Nicaragua from exposure to this pesticide and that number is increasing by the day.[97]

Twenty-five percent of the bananas consumed in the United States and European Union come from Ecuador, the largest banana exporter in the world. A Human Rights Watch[98] team visited Ecuador in 2001. They discovered children (as young as eight, with most starting at ten or eleven) working in the banana plantations. Children often worked twelve-hour days and were continually exposed to the pesticides used on bananas.

The cases of Nicaragua and Ecuador are not alone. In Costa Rica 20,000 men have become sterile as the result of exposure to pesticides banned in the United States.[99] The World Health Organization (WHO) estimates that there are on average 3 million pesticide poisonings worldwide each year, and 250,000 deaths.[100] One study found that 91 percent of cotton field workers in India suffered health disorders due to pesticide exposure.[101]

Cocoa Workers

Eleven million people in West Africa are dependent on cocoa for their livelihoods, but they receive only 3.9 percent of the final price to the consumer for their cocoa beans from the giant firms that control the global chocolate market: Nestlé, Cadbury, Mars and Hershey. In fact the profits are so slim or non-existent that some cocoa farmers in Ivory Coast (which produces 45 percent of the global supply of cocoa) have come to rely on child slavery to work the fields, including dispersing some of the 30 pesticides used to grow chocolate.[102] Of course, nothing would do more to end the practice than simply to pay cocoa farmers a fair price for their crop so that they could afford to hire adult wage labour.[103]

There are approximately 600,000 cocoa farms in Ivory Coast,

most of them small family operations, where often the children participate in the labour.[104] This could be OK, but too often the children do dangerous work such as spreading toxic pesticides without adequate protection. According to a recent study, 21 percent of the pesticides are applied by children under ten and another 50 percent by children aged ten to 14.[105] If cocoa farmers were paid enough for their cocoa beans, they could afford to pay good wages to adult workers to do these jobs. Because farmers are poor and need the labour of every family member, children often cannot attend school. But worst of all is the trafficking of as many as 15,000 children (estimates range from 10,000 to 15,000) as young as twelve from desperately poor countries like Mali to work as slaves on cocoa farms.[106] This desperate effort to find cheap labour is spurred by prices for cocoa that often give the farmer an income that is less than the costs of production.[107]

The major chocolate producers have been pressured into accepting a protocol that would certify chocolate as being free from the worst forms of child labour and that would be in place by 2005. As of 2007 no such certification system was operating, as is indicated by a BBC news report entitled: "Slavery behind Easter chocolate".[108] While the situation in the cocoa industry is particularly disturbing, there are many other instances of child labour being exploited in developing countries. According to Human Rights Watch, there are up to 30,000 children as young as eight doing brutal sugar plantation work in El Salvador, and the situation is no better in Brazil.[109]

Tobacco Workers

In the 1950s and 1960s tobacco was one of the major subsidized crops in the United States, with US tobacco farmers growing 77 percent of total world production.[110] Subsidies to tobacco farmers continued until 2004, and ironically since 2005, tobacco acreage has expanded 20 percent even without subsidies. This is because the profits from growing tobacco, were, until recently, as much as five times those for growing corn.[111]

Its continual efforts to increase profits have caused Big Tobacco to not only shift its immense marketing power to the youth of developing countries with great success, but to shift much of the growing of this most labour-intensive crop to low-wage developing countries. It was in the mid-1980s that President Reagan launched the marketing offensive, which threatened economic sanctions for any country that did not open its market to American cigarettes.[112] In opposition, the Surgeon General at the time declared, "I don't think we as citizens can continue exporting disease, disability, and death."[113] His words, however, had no effect in the face of one of the most profitable and addictive commodities ever invented and one of the most powerful corporate lobbies in existence.

The shift to growing the crop in developing countries has occurred over the past 20 years, and this has meant, for example, that African production has doubled, with most of the growth occurring in Malawi, Zimbabwe and Tanzania. Malawi depends on tobacco for 50–70 percent of its export earnings.[114] But, as already mentioned, growing tobacco has led to deforestation to both grow the crop and provide wood for the curing of tobacco.[115] A tobacco crop takes nine months of labour intensive work to grow. Because the leaves ripen at different times, it needs to be hand-picked. Further, because tobacco is a pesticide-intense crop, tobacco workers are exposed to both toxic pesticides and nicotine poisoning from contact with the leaves. That is why in the United States today most tobacco workers are migrant workers under the strict discipline of their employers, and that is why so much growing of tobacco has shifted to low-wage areas where workers have little legal protection.

The marketing of cigarettes continues unabated in most developing countries, where now over 50 percent of men smoke, and in places like Russia, Indonesia, Philippines, Bolivia and Chile, where 30 percent of the children between 13 and 15 smoke.[116] Cigarettes will eventually kill 50 percent of those who fail to quit.[117]

Coffee Workers

The international trade in coffee is the most valuable of any agricultural commodity.[118] Like cocoa it is mostly grown on small family farms, with over 25 million families dependent on coffee for their main source of income.[119] While Brazil and Viet Nam produce the largest coffee crops, coffee farming is dispersed around the world in many semi-tropical or tropical climates. When SAPs became more widespread and invasive in the early 1980s, many developing countries (such as Viet Nam) were encouraged (forced?) to expand export-oriented agriculture to pay their debts. Since they could not compete with the heavily subsidized major grain and sugar crops of the industrialized countries, they were limited to tropical agricultural commodities. One of these was coffee, and the expansion of coffee farming has generally resulted in a downturn of prices, thereby inviting debt and exposing the destructiveness of the SAPs programmes. The world price of coffee peaked in 1954, but a system of international quotas was developed in 1973 in an effort to limit price fluctuations.[120] When this system was ended in 1989 the global price of green coffee beans fell by 50 percent,[121] finally reaching a 30-year low in 2002, resulting in many coffee-producing families selling their crops at less than the cost of production.[122] Millions of families fell into the most dire poverty, some were forced off the land into expanding urban slums, and yet others turned to more lucrative illegal drugs in order to survive. The hugely profitable mega-corporations, Kraft, Nestlé, Sara Lee, Procter & Gamble and Tchibo, which control over 50 percent of the coffee market, have done little to ease the plight of coffee-producing families.[123] Kraft and Nestlé, which control 49 percent of the roasting, are among the small number of importers and roasters that control 78 percent of the total revenues received from selling coffee.

Ethiopia, thought to be the birthplace of coffee, is one of the most coffee-dependent countries, with coffee accounting for 67 percent of its export earnings.[124] It seems more than a little absurd that a country that has faced such severe famine would devote so much of its best farmland to growing coffee for export, but such are the imperatives of the current international debt regime. Indeed, Ethiopia would not be so poor if its coffee farmers got more than 1 percent from the cost of a latte, or if bean sorters got more than 96 cents a day, or if workers loading sacks on trucks got more than $2 per day.[125]

Ethiopia is one of 80 countries in the world whose economy depends heavily on agriculture, and yet the centrality of agriculture to development has often been slighted by economists. The fate of Ethiopia's economy depends largely on the speculative fluctuations of the coffee futures market.[126] In many cases, were the direct producers to receive a fair share (say 30 percent instead of 3 percent) of the retail price, the world would be a very different place. The fact of the matter is that for most of the tropical commodities grown in developing countries, there are huge profits for the transnational corporations that control the consumption ends of the food chain, while the producer ends receive a pittance. For example, when the price of green coffee beans fell by 50 percent from 1989 to 1991, there was only a decline of 1 percent in the price to the final consumer, with the corporations pocketing the difference.[127]

Tea Workers

Nearly all tea came from China until the British developed large tea plantations in India in the mid-nineteenth century. Globally more people drink tea than any other beverage, and now over 50 percent of the world's tea comes from India, Bangladesh and Sri Lanka, where typically tea workers survive on less than $2 per day for extremely demanding labour.[128] Tea pluckers are mostly women, who carry heavy baskets on their backs supported by straps across their foreheads. They are exposed to pesticides and repetitive stress injuries, and respiratory diseases. Tea sorters are particularly prone to respiratory illnesses caused by continual exposure to tea dust. On most tea plantations the living conditions for workers are very poor, which further exposes workers to malnutrition, poor sanitation and respiratory illnesses.

Palm Oil Workers

Recently there has been a rapid expansion of palm oil plantations, with Indonesia and Malaysia supplying 85 percent of the world market.[129] It is now the world's leading vegetable oil, replacing soy oil which was previously number one. But this sudden expansion is resulting in either deforestation or the use of crop land that might otherwise produce rice or other food crops. Much of the palm oil is slated to be converted into biodiesel fuel even though "biodiesel results in as much as 2 to 8 times more carbon emissions" than standard diesel fuel.[130] No doubt profits can be made from palm oil, but in the light of growing global famine and growing global warming, it is shameful to destroy tropical forests in order to produce palm oil.

Wages are low for the field workers in the palm oil plantations, where exposure to toxic pesticides is a continual cause of sickness and death. For instance, in Malaysia as many as 30,000 women work every day spraying the fields with an array of chemicals, including the potentially fatal paraquat.[131]

Pesticide Use in Tropical Settings

Industrial coffee production is third after cotton and tobacco in the intensity of its use of pesticides per acre, while banana production is close behind. It is worth noting that these are all produced in developing countries and are highly labour-intensive with the exception of cotton, which is largely mechanized in the United States and some other parts of the world, but often not in many tropical developing countries. Labour intensity in these cases generally means that workers are exposed to numerous toxic pesticides, turning the fields bearing these crops into fields of sickness and death. There are several reasons that this state of affairs has developed:

- Long after toxic pesticides have been banned for use in the United States or some other country of origin, they are often still marketed in countries where either they have not been banned or where controls are weak.
- Workers in developing countries are often not well informed about the hazardous toxicity of the chemicals they are using.
- Even where workers can afford to buy or are provided with protective clothing and masks, the heat in tropical fields makes the use of protective clothing impractical.
- Pesticides in the air and ground water pollute the surrounding countryside where workers and their families live.
- Given the low price of their crop, farmers cannot afford to lose any produce to pests, and are thus tempted to use pesticides that they would rather not use.
- Sometimes children, who are particularly vulnerable to pesticides,

are exposed because poor families need the labour of all family members to survive, because families live near the fields where pesticides are used, or because children are to varying extents enslaved.

CONCLUSIONS

Food not only connects human health to environmental health, it is also among the most labour-intensive of all commodities. The final consumer in most instances is unaware of the exploitation of labour that occurs at almost every step in the food chain from field to table. Food is so basic to human flourishing, that one would expect that in an enlightened society all those participating in the food chain would be well paid as a reward for their important and often very demanding work. Instead in our technologically sophisticated capitalist economy, we find the opposite – food chain workers are among the most exploited, the most impoverished and the most exposed to hazardous chemicals. In my opinion this is a highly perverse outcome that speaks volumes about the social injustice that our economic system generates.

In the final chapter of this book, I shall discuss some possible new directions for the provisioning of food. There is one basic point, however, that I should like to at least introduce here. We would be foolish to think that we could rely upon markets alone to solve our food provisioning problems, since so many problems have been caused by markets. Later I shall argue at length that more than anything we need a massive shift of wealth from the private to the public sector, and from the rich to the poor. We need large increases in government spending on research to improve food provisioning. We need to facilitate effective agricultural extension services on a global scale to help develop cooperative relations among farmers, between farmers and consumers, and to synthesize the latest scientific knowledge with traditional knowledge in order to develop the most organic and/or sustainable farming techniques possible. We need a strong and independent public sector that has the money and will to test the long-run impact of chemicals utilized by the food and agricultural industries. Where necessary we need to subsidize family farms to ensure an annual income well above locally defined basic needs for food, shelter, education, transportation, health and recreation. In other words, we need to ensure that all food-chain workers receive an income that will enable them and their families to lead decent lives. This cannot be done if their standard of living is dependent on commodity prices in the New York or Chicago commodity exchanges or on the enormous bargaining power of giant corporations.

6 AGRICULTURE, FOOD PROVISIONING AND THE ENVIRONMENT

Unless greenhouse gas emissions begin to decline within the next decade, we risk triggering a runaway disruption of the world's climate, one that could last centuries and that our descendants would be powerless to stop ... changes in the concentration of carbon dioxide, methane, and other less common gases could trigger an ecological catastrophe of staggering proportions.[1]

instead of a conscious and rational treatment of the land as permanent communal property, as the inalienable condition for the existence and reproduction of the chain of human generations, we have the exploitation and squandering of the powers of the earth.[2]

The great question of the seventies is, shall we surrender to our surroundings, or shall we make our peace with nature and begin to make reparations, for we still think of air as free. But clean air is not free, and neither is clean water. The price tag on pollution control is high. Through our years of past carelessness we incurred a debt to nature, and now that debt is being called.[3]

The above quotation from President Nixon's State of the Union Speech in 1970 suggests that the central environmental concern was pollution. Words are cheap, and in practice little was done to address pollution by Nixon or any president since him, for it would have been

[146]

very costly to have made any significant headway in addressing our debt to nature even in 1970. Thirty-eight years later pollution is only one dimension of the multidimensional ecological disaster that we face, which includes the prospects of global warming, depletion of non-renewable resources, land degradation, species loss, shrinkage of fresh water supplies, toxic chemicals in the environment and inadequately tested new technologies such as GMOs. It is not as if many voices have not raised these problems over the years and many good intentions been formulated, but as I have argued, capital's central imperative is intense competition to maximize short-term profits, and unless this imperative is countered by very strong forces, it will tend to override all opposition.

While the problem of putting short-term profits ahead of environmental concerns is a problem which is characteristic of capitalism in general, in this phase of history it is exacerbated by the petrochemical revolution, which made profits depend increasingly on speeding up the rate at which commodities were produced and new commodities introduced. This general rush meant that the toxic properties of more than 1,000 of 80,000 chemicals in widespread use were not well tested as individual chemicals much less in combination with other chemicals.[4] In most cases this has meant that toxicity is discovered only after widespread damage to human health has caused alarm. Even so radical an innovation as transgenic organisms was rushed into use without adequate testing for their possible dramatically damaging and irreversible consequences, largely because corporations had invested so much in developing them that they could not afford a long delay in profiting from their use, and because these same corporations have enormous influence in government circles.[5]

A central problem with our current food system is its dependence on petroleum at a time when the price of petroleum will continue to climb because of dwindling supplies relative to demand, and at a time when burning fossil fuels contributes to global warming. Breaking the food system's addiction to petroleum is both necessary and difficult.

PEAK OIL AND BIOFUELS

Over the past 40 years the US consumption of fossil fuel has increased 20-fold.[6] Given the extent to which the US economy, including agriculture and food, is tied to petrochemicals, and the likelihood that passing the "peak oil" point globally will lead to large and permanent price increases of petrochemicals, without radical changes, the prospects for the US economy are bleak. In the 1940s for every barrel of oil spent searching for oil, 100 barrels of oil were produced, and now for every barrel of oil spent, we get only 10 barrels.[7] As we reach the point of "peak oil", it takes almost as much oil to expand the supply as is gained by the new supply. For example, the ecological damage involved in retrieving oil from the Alberta oil sands, and the amount of energy it takes to produce a single barrel of oil from the tar sands, raise serious doubts about the desirability and viability of the entire project.[8]

The Canadian oil sands are enriching many people at immense long-term environmental costs. It now takes one barrel of oil to produce three barrels of oil from oil sands, and as a result, three times the quantity of greenhouse gases are produced per barrel of oil from oil sands than for conventional oil.[9] Further, because it takes up to 4.5 barrels of water to produce one barrel of oil from oil sands, aquifers are being drained and huge toxic tailing ponds are created.[10]

While there has been awareness of the problem of peak oil along with the problem of global warming for years, the lobbying and propaganda power of the oil, chemical and auto industries have delayed for at least two decades most efforts to wean the US economy and especially agriculture off petroleum. The efforts that are being made now either switch from one problem to an equally damaging one (substituting ethanol for oil), or tend to be too little and too late when we consider the enormity of the problem.

If we add up all the fossil fuel energy that is utilized to produce and transport food in the current American agriculture/food regime, we find that it accounts for approximately 20 percent of all fossil fuel consumption in the United States.[11] That is a lot of fossil fuel considering that the United States, with only 5 percent of the world's population, consumes 20 percent of all fossil fuels consumed worldwide annually.[12] The current US agricultural/food regime utilizes petroleum products in four main ways:

- the production of chemical fertilizers and pesticides
- the running of tractors and other farm equipment

- transporting crops to storage, processing (including meat production), or wholesale markets
- transporting food commodities to final points of sale.

I want to reiterate the claim made by Cornell professor David Pimentel: that if the entire world adopted the US agricultural/food system, all known sources of fossil fuel would be exhausted in seven years.[13] While the US agriculture/food regime is heavily addicted to petroleum (and natural gas), it is worth noting in passing that as of 2004 the US military was the single largest consumer of oil in the world at 85 million barrels per year, and this no doubt has something to do with the Bush regime spending $1 billion subsidizing oil drilling in the Gulf of Mexico in 2004.[14]

The green revolution increased the energy flow to agriculture four-fold between 1945 and 1994, such that so much petroleum is utilized in the US food system that the resulting food that we eat can accurately be called "petrofood".[15] Cook estimated in 2004 that US agriculture uses 15 million tons of petroleum-based fertilizer each year, but since the amount used tends to increase each year, it no doubt will be appreciably higher in 2008.[16] In 1990, 1,000 litres of oil were used on average to grow each hectare of crop,[17] and it took on average 400 gallons of oil per year to feed each American.[18] It takes a surprising 2,200 calories of hydrocarbon energy to make a can of Pepsi.[19] The fact that food travels on average 1,500–2,000 miles from field to table in the United States, mostly by truck,[20] not only means that a lot of oil is used, but diesel fumes are produced, which have been discovered to be one of the causes of asthma.[21] Usually the processing of food takes a lot of energy. For example, a pound of breakfast cereal made from wheat takes 32 times more energy to produce than a pound of flour.[22] Finally, meat and dairy products typically require a large amount of additional fossil fuel energy for refrigeration.

Meat production is particularly costly in terms of fossil fuels. It takes on average 35 calories of fossil fuel to produce one calorie of beef, 68 calories to produce one calorie of pork.[23] The production of one kilogram of beef produces 36.4 kilograms of CO_2, and it takes 100 calories of grain to produce 4 calories of beef.[24] According to Nestle, it takes 200 gallons of petroleum to raise one 1,200 pound steer in a feedlot.[25] Indeed confined animal feeding operations (CAFOs) which produce most of the US meat, utilize huge amounts of energy, on top of which they produce 600 million tons of waste a year which has to be disposed of in some way that does not contaminate the environment too much.[26] The impact of the meatification of America's diet is well summarized by Weis's claim that:

> In the USA, for instance, livestock consume roughly 70 percent of all domestic grains, including an even higher percentage of maize – a crop that alone consumes about one-third of US crop space, 40 percent of nitrogen fertilizer and more total herbicides and insecticides than any other crop.[27] Resource demands are further magnified by the intensity of water consumption and pollution from factory farms and slaughterhouses and the energy needed to control the temperature of factory farms and run the slaughter process. As a result of the additional grain and the resource budgets of these industrial systems it has been estimated that an edible unit of protein from factory-farmed meat requires 100 times more fresh water [it takes 3,000 litres of water to produce one kilogram of beef][28] and more than eight times the fossil-fuel energy than does an edible unit of protein from grain.[29]

It is not surprising that many people advocate a change in the American diet toward more local food and less meat.

But the reality of peak oil and dependence on petroleum imports has sparked another even more damaging strategy – the production of biofuels (for example, ethanol). As pointed out earlier, so far the central US strategy for weaning its economy off of petroleum is the substitution of ethanol, the production of which is encouraged by large government subsidies, despite the fact that ethanol is very hard on the environment, that switching to non-food crops increases the price of food, and that ethanol contributes more to global warming than petroleum.[30] The United States accounts for 50 percent of the global production of ethanol, and the world production of biofuels rose by 20 percent in 2007 for the sixth consecutive year of double-digit growth.[31] In other words, the world has already moved down a path that holds great dangers.

The damage from ethanol production is multifaceted:

- Oil palm and soy used for diesel ethanol have resulted in tropical deforestation, currently a major contributor to global warming.[32]
- Corn, the main crop used for ethanol production in the United States, uses huge amounts of fossil fuels and water.[33] In total, corn consumes more chemical fertilizers and pesticides than any other crop in the United States. It takes on average 230 lbs of nitrogen fertilizer to grow an acre of corn in the United States, and typically 50 lbs end up in the environment, where it can convert into nitrates that experiments have implicated in miscarriages and cancer, or into nitrous oxide (N_2O), a greenhouse gas, 70 percent of which comes from agriculture.[34] Corn grown in drier areas such as Oklahoma uses on average 2,900 gallons of water per bushel.[35]
- Ethanol production itself is problematic. According to a report by the Global Forest Coalition, "Many ethanol refineries are powered by coal, which results in emissions of mercury and other toxins, as well as greenhouse gases.[36] In April 2007, the US Environmental Protection Agency (EPA) relaxed air release regulations on ethanol fuel refineries, which release particulate matter, ethanol vapours, carbon monoxide, volatile organic compounds and several carcinogens .... Refineries also place immense demands on water supplies."[37]
- The release of N_2O from fertilizer use "is 296 times more potent as a greenhouse gas than carbon dioxide (CO_2), and persists for an average of 100 years .... A recent study of N_2O emissions from agrofuels revealed that some contribute up to 70 percent more to global warming via N_2O emissions than they do to cooling via avoided CO_2 emissions through the use of agrofuels."[38]
- Biofuel production in Brazil, which utilizes primarily sugar cane and soy, has not only contributed to deforestation, but also has expanded monocultures and driven the poor from the land, thus exacerbating a land distribution problem where

3 percent of the population control two-thirds of the crop land.[39]

- Most important in terms of immediate human suffering, the switch of crop lands from food crops to agrofuel crops is perhaps the single greatest cause for the increased cost of food that is currently triggering global famine. It is for this reason that "Jean Ziegler, The UN's Special Rapporteur on the Right to Food, called the diversion of food crops into agrofuel production a 'crime against humanity.'"[40]

Biofuel production in the United States receives an incredible $7.14 in subsidies for the energy equivalent of one gallon of gas. Imagine if this were not subsidized and consumers had to pay this much for a gallon of fuel for their cars. From the point of view of the US government, which wishes to increase biofuel production five-fold by 2017,[41] ethanol production may make some political sense as a means of making the United States less dependent on Middle-Eastern oil, but it makes almost no sense from the point of view of concern for social justice or the environment. As previously mentioned, the US policy of handing immense subsidies to the richest corn farmers with the greatest yields has in the past generated the production of large surpluses of cheap corn. Typically, 25 percent of the US corn crop has been surplus traded abroad, and this surplus constitutes 70 percent of the global trade in corn.[42] As a result some countries have become partially dependent on food imports from the United States. Now all of a sudden 33 percent of the corn harvest is going to ethanol production (projections for 2008 increase the percentage to 50) and this could mean a significant reduction in exports, a reduction in corn reserves (so far accounting for half the fall in global grain reserves) and significant price increases for food.[43]

President Bush has tried to downplay the impact of biofuels on global food prices by claiming that they only account for 3 percent of the increases. It is not surprising then, that the American government should pressure the World Bank to suppress its report claiming that biofuels account for as much as 75 percent of the global rise in food prices. The report was ready for release in April 2008, but it was kept secret and would perhaps never have been released had it not been leaked to the press in July 2008.[44]

Seeing these trends, speculators have quite realistically bid up the price of food grains at the Chicago Board of Trade and other commodity futures markets. According to the *Economist*'s[45] food-price index, prices have increased in real terms (accounting for inflation) by 75 percent since 2005. But when 2.8 billion people out of a total global population of 6.5 billion are living on less than $2 per day, significant increases in food prices can only lead to hunger, starvation and global famine. According to the FAO, the food price index rose by 40 percent in 2007 alone (of course not solely caused by the shift to ethanol), and now 37 countries face a serious short-fall in food supplies.[46] And this situation is further exacerbated by an 80 percent increase in shipping costs because of the price rises of petroleum.[47]

The pressure to increase ethanol production will also increase the price of food in the United States, where 16 percent of families are already food insecure.[48] For not only is corn the main feed grain for nearly all CAFOs, but also 25 percent of items in the supermarket contain corn or corn derivatives in some form or other. The price increases of petroleum, coupled with US government subsidies for ethanol, increase the costs of petrofoods, but also make it more prof-itable to grow non-food crops. Since capitalism is driven to follow profit rates, if left to its own devices it will necessarily produce massive global hunger and starvation.[49] In a book published in 2006, before the increases in global food prices, Pfeiffer predicted that "the coming decade could see massive starvation on a global level such as never experienced before by the human race".[50]

While the price rise of oil and the diversion of corn to ethanol production are the main causes of food price increases, there are other causes as well. For example, AIDS in Africa, worsened in the past by the pharmaceutical industry's failure to make affordable drugs available to Africans, has decimated the agricultural work force. Further, regional conflicts fuelled by the arms trade, oil, diamonds, poverty and border disputes often rooted in colonialism and neo-colonialism, have also seriously disrupted farming. Other causes of food price increases include urbanization and the accom-panying meatification of global diets which diverts grains to feed animals, speculation in commodities markets and extreme weather associated with climate change.[51]

For the reasons given above, ethanol is counterproductive with regard to global warming.[52] Were it not for the annual subsidies approaching $10 billion to corn farmers that enables the price to go below the cost of production, the price of food would go up yet more.[53]

GLOBAL WARMING

Global warming is the greatest threat to the quality of life for humanity as a whole in all of human history, and it will not take much warming for it to be catastrophic. Nine of the ten warmest years on record have occurred since 1990.[54] Since 1990, carbon dioxide emissions have doubled and the rate of increase is still accelerating despite the Kyoto Accord.[55] When we should be cutting emissions by 5–10 percent a year, worldwide emissions are accelerating.[56]

Because there are so many causal variables and possible tipping points (feedback loops that increase each other at a greater and greater rate), it is difficult to predict the timing and the precise consequences of global warming. For example, some of the earth's great sponges for absorbing carbon dioxide are the oceans, but as they warm, they will absorb less, and the added carbon dioxide in the environment will increase global warming yet more, thereby heating the oceans so that they absorb still less. There are many such vicious circles interconnected with each other in ways that multiply the effects of global warming.

The melting arctic ice cap will contribute to warmer oceans, which in turn will contribute to faster and more extensive melting. Greenland's ice sheet is melting faster than anyone expected, and should it all melt, the oceans will rise more than 7 metres or 23 feet.[57] The predictions for the rise in ocean levels this century varies from a few metres to a truly catastrophic 25 metres.[58] Many experts believe that global warming in excess of 2 degrees centigrade could trigger extremely dangerous changes in weather and ocean levels, and that we have less than ten years to substantially reduce greenhouse gas emissions.[59] It is important to know that even if we stopped all greenhouse gas emissions now, the full impact of the greenhouse gases already in the atmosphere will not be felt until 2050.[60]

It is particularly important that the United States take the lead in the global effort to reduce greenhouse gas emissions, because it emits 20 percent of the world's greenhouse gases, and it is still the dominant capitalist power in the world. So far, it is fair to say, the United States has been a major obstacle in the global effort to reverse trends towards global warming.[61] China and the United States are followed by Indonesia and Brazil[62] as the emitters of the largest quantity of greenhouse gases. Given China's fossil fuel-based rapid growth, it is not surprising that it has risen to number one in total emissions, but it is still far behind the United States in per capita emissions. Indonesia and Brazil, however, follow not so much because of the size or rapid growth of their economies, but rather because of deforestation, which is undermining the very habitability of the earth. According to a recent UN report, deforestation is occurring at such a rapid rate in places like Borneo and Sumatra that their previously large tropical forests will be gone in 15 years.[63]

Meat production is another source of greenhouse gas emissions, and the United States is the dynamic centre for the spread of a meat-based diet in the world. Livestock globally produce 18 percent of greenhouse gas emissions caused by deforestation, the production of petroleum dense feed grain crops, the high energy needs of CAFOs and methane gas emissions (livestock produce 16 percent of global methane gas, or 100 million tons/year).[64] Methane gas has 23 times greater impact on global warming than carbon dioxide, and a single cow averages 500 litres of methane a day.[65] The good news is that cattle raised organically on grass produce 40 percent less greenhouse gas and require 85 percent less energy from birth to slaughter.[66] Finally, as previously mentioned, significant amounts of an another greenhouse gas, nitrous oxide (N_2O), are emitted from the use of nitrogen fertilizers in the production of feed grains.[67]

Global warming will seriously affect the world's principal grain crops – wheat, rice and corn – as they will not grow at high temperatures. When average daytime high temperatures exceed 36 degrees centigrade the yields of these crops begin to fall, and at 40 degrees photosynthesis shuts down all together.[68] Other important crops will also be adversely affected by increased average temperatures. For example, for every 1 degree average temperature rise, the yields of tea and coffee drop 10 percent, and tropical countries in general which already have high average daytime temperatures will be particularly adversely affected by global warming.[69] It has been estimated that as early as 2020, global warming will reduce Africa's crop yields by 50 percent.[70]

Global warming is already causing an increased number of extreme weather events along with drought in some parts of the world and flooding in others. For instance, since 1974, category four and five hurricanes have nearly doubled.[71] Two hundred leading researchers on global warming have signed a statement declaring that we have a "decade to avert climate catastrophe".[72] The statement claims that:

> millions of people will be at risk from extreme events, such as heat waves, drought, floods and storms; our coasts and cities will be threatened by rising sea levels; and many ecosystems, plants and animal species will be in serious danger of extinction.[73]

LAND AND DEFORESTATION

We can lose fertile agricultural land in many ways. One way is to cover it with cement or blacktop. For example, between 1947 and 1978 in the United States a total land area the size of Ohio and Pennsylvania combined was covered with blacktop.[74] Fertile land can also be lost because of toxic waste, as an estimated 100 trillion lbs exist at sites scattered across the United States.[75] Land can have its topsoil eroded, or it can be lost for agricultural use because of:

- changing weather
- the drying up of water sources
- compaction
- salination as a result of irrigation.

With the loss of topsoil, the earth loses its sponge-like character, requiring more irrigation and more chemical fertilizer as more of it runs off. This run off eventually reaches rivers, which reach seas, resulting in algae blooms that suck up the oxygen, creating "dead zones". In this way the chemicalization of the land creates dead land which ultimately contributes to deadened oceans.

An estimated 67 percent of the world's agricultural land is

degraded, 40 percent is seriously degraded, and in Africa an alarming 80 percent is degraded.[76] All in all 25 percent of global irrigated land is degraded, and the 20 percent of all agricultural land that is irrigated produces 40 percent of the world's food.[77] The US prairies, the grain basket of the world, have lost 50 percent of their top soil, largely from farming practices that fail to replace sufficient organic matter in the soil, but instead dump more and more chemical fertilizer onto soil which, lacking in organic matter, drains away faster and faster.[78] Organic matter in the soil acts as a sponge, soaking up and retaining water and resisting wind erosion. Without it, the water quickly drains away eroding the soil, such that the less organic matter, the faster the erosion. The seriousness of soil erosion in undermining food production and water availability is seldom fully appreciated. It has been estimated that desertification globally removes more than 100,000 square kilometres a year from further agricultural use.[79]

In some cases deforestation is the first step towards desertification, and the main cause of deforestation is our current capitalist food system. Because the rainforests play such a crucial role in regulating global weather, they have sometimes been called the earth's "thermostat".[80] And yet, according to the Stern Report,[81] the short-term profit orientation of our system has led to the deforestation of 50 million acres a year, an area the size of England, Wales and Scotland put together. As much as 70 percent of this area of deforestation is utilized to raise cattle or feed (mostly soybeans) for cattle, such that for each quarter pound of beef, 55 square feet of rainforest are lost and 500 pounds of CO_2 is released.[82] It has been estimated that as much as 25 percent of annual greenhouse gas emissions come from deforestation.[83]

Arable land can be lost to non-food crops as well. One instance of this is tobacco, but there are many others. The massive conversion of potential food crop land to the production of ethanol was discussed earlier. Another such conversion is the use of arable land for tree plantations to feed the pulp and paper industry. The pulp and paper industry, the fifth largest industrial consumer of energy globally (using 20 percent of the world's harvested wood) and one of the most polluting, has plans for massive industrial tree plantations and pulp mills primarily in the global South where pollution controls are less strict (Brazil, Uruguay, Chile, Australia, South Africa, Viet Nam, Indonesia, India and Laos).[84] Industrial tree plantations require large amounts of chemical fertilizers, insecticides and herbicides. Tree plantations developed extensively in the south of the United States since 1990 have increased the use of chemical fertilizers there by 800 percent.[85]

FRESH WATER

Farming takes a 70 percent share of total global freshwater consumption and 85 percent of the annual water consumption in the United States. And the consumption of water for food production is increasing dramatically with the meatification of the world's diet.

It takes vastly more water per food calorie to produce meat than grain. For example, beef production takes 3,000 litres of water per kilogram,[86] and the production of a single hamburger takes over 10,000 litres of water.[87] The global spread of the factory-farm meat-based diet is currently a powerful global trend; and yet this is occurring in a world where 2.3 billion people have inadequate access to fresh water and over 1 billion people are hungry. One-third of all cropland globally is used to grow animal feed, and in the United States 70 percent of the annual grain harvest is so used.[88] One calorie of factory-farmed meat protein takes 100 times more water and eight times more fossil fuel than one calorie of protein from grain.[89] The 1,000 tons of water that it takes to produce one ton of grain is not used very efficiently given the amount of grain that it takes to produce one kilogram of meat.[90]

The supply of fresh water is an increasing global concern, and global warming is a factor as it can cause drought. For example, it is the Indian Ocean that is warming the most rapidly, and one result of this is that the Sahel in Africa has lost much of its rainfall, causing famines in East Africa and in countries bordering on the Sahara.[91] This drying up of parts of Africa has resulted in an increase of dust in the atmosphere globally by one-third, which is one source of increasing respiratory problems worldwide.[92]

Drought in many parts of the world has led to the depletion of underground aquifers, and the use of river water for agriculture has resulted in the radical shrinkage of large lakes such as Lake Chad and the Aral Sea. It has been estimated that at current rates of usage there are only 30 years of water supply left in the giant Ogallala aquifer, the largest underground lake in the world, which provides much of the American midwest with water.[93] Given that it has been estimated that one in five irrigated acres in the United States receives its water from the Ogallala aquifer, the drying up of this aquifer will have a huge impact on American agriculture.[94]

Las Vegas is dependent for 90 percent of its water on Lake Mead which has now lost half its water, and depends on the flow of the Colorado river, which may have a permanently diminished flow because of global warming.[95] This is also occurring in California, where cities and farmers are vying for a limited water supply. In some areas the water use by agriculture is subsidized to the extent that farmers pay as little as 1 percent of what households pay per gallon of water.[96] Indeed, without the steady flow of highly subsidized water, the profits of Californian agriculture would be undermined.

According to the EPA, the number of chemically polluted streams in the United States increased ten-fold between 1993 and 2003.[97] The largest polluters are the CAFOs, which produce 1.4 billion tons of manure per year.[98] Rivers and streams are also polluted by the chemical runoff from agriculture. The run off of nitrogen fertilizers is particularly problematic because of the deadly algae blooms that result.[99]

THE OCEANS

According to an article in *Nature*,[100] climate change is reducing the productivity of plankton, organisms which form the base of oceanic food chains and which absorb carbon dioxide. Another important index of the health of the oceans is coral, 40 percent of which is dead or dying.[101] Coral cannot thrive in water that is too warm or is polluted, so that even a small amount of additional global warming will kill off most of it. It is predicted that a 1 degree rise in ocean temperature will kill 82 percent of the Great Barrier Reef.[102] Coral is also being destroyed by algae blooms caused by both nitrogen fertilizer runoff and the dumping of sewage in the ocean. Algae blooms cause dead zones by sucking most of the oxygen out of the ocean. An algae bloom the size of New Jersey lies just off the gulf coast in the Caribbean.[103] It is fed largely by chemical fertilizer runoff carried by the Mississippi river. In only two years between 2004 and 2006 significant low-oxygen dead zones in the world's oceans increased from 149 to 200.[104]

According to Worldwatch, 29 percent of the ocean species fished in 2003 had collapsed by 2006 (collapse = 10 percent or less of peak abundance). Further, only 10 percent of the large fish that existed in 1950, exist today,[105] while two-thirds of ocean fisheries are fully exploited.[106] Some traditional fisheries are now closed as a result of overfishing, and an article in *Science*[107] predicts a complete collapse of fish and seafood species by 2048. Despite this sobering information, the United Nations failed to support a ban on the highly wasteful and destructive practice of bottom trawling. Bottom trawling for only one kilogram of prawns on average causes 10 to 20 kilograms of other species (including 150,000 sea turtles a year) to be discarded.[108]

Unfortunately it is meat and seafood that are the most rapidly growing food items in the world's diet,[109] and only seven nations take two-thirds of the annual global fish harvest.[110] Existing fishing practices are not energy-efficient, with fishing fleets utilizing 12.5 times the calories of energy that can be derived from the fish caught.[111] Given the nature of current industrial fishing, the oceans will soon be emptied of larger wild fish.

The growing practice of fish farming is also impacting on wild species by polluting the oceans. It is predicted that wild salmon will soon be extinct off the coast of British Columbia because of sea lice produced by salmon fish farming. Industrial fish farming can produce a lot of fish cheaply, and it can also pollute surrounding waters with biocides, manure, sea lice and disease. Fish farmers who raise carnivores consume more fish than they produce, with the result that now 37 percent of the global fish catch is used to feed fish and animals. For instance, it takes five tons of wild fish to feed one ton of farmed salmon.[112] Ecologically friendly fish farming may be possible, but so far it is rare.

SPECIES LOSS

To the extent that agriculture is tied in to deforestation and global warming, it is complicit in the serious species loss that results from these conditions. For instance, one-third of the 6,000 known species of amphibian are threatened with extinction,[113] as are 20 percent of bird species.[114] It has been estimated that 67 million birds die each year from habitat loss, pesticides, global warming and other toxins in the environment.[115] In some parts of the world birds eat large numbers of insects that eat crops. In this way their loss can impact on agriculture.

I have already mentioned capitalism's tendency to homogenize for the sake of the standardization required for mass, speeded-up production, but applied to agriculture the result has often been species loss and monoculture. Besides the loss of wild species, then, there is a tendency to reduce the genetic diversity of domesticated seeds and animals as well, leaving us open to diseases that cannot be effectively combated by shifting to a gene type that is resistant. Currently, for example, there is only one species of banana widely grown in the world, and in the near future it is predicted to be wiped out by a black fungus.[116] And because of the role of wheat in the world's diet, much more serious is a wheat fungus that appears to be spreading from Uganda to the rest of the world, and that can wipe out as much as three-quarters of a wheat crop.[117]

GENETICALLY MODIFIED ORGANISMS

GMOs are sometimes more accurately labelled "transgenic organisms" to emphasize the insertion of genetic material from one species or genus into another. Chapter 4 raised the concerns about allergenic properties of GMOs, but there are much greater concerns about their possible long-term ecological consequences. For instance, it is possible that new more resistant superbugs or super weeds could develop that would not only nullify the benefits of GMOs, but could also set back farming which is based on non-GM crops. Bt cotton plants are such that the entire plant is poisonous to various insects for the entire growing season. Bt crops were introduced into China in 1997, but by 2004 farmers were again spraying large amounts of insecticide because a secondary insect moved into the slot left by the bollworm killed by the Bt.[118] In India, large numbers of cotton farmers were persuaded that the increased yields that they would harvest from planting Bt cotton would help them to begin to pay off their crushing debt load. When they discovered that the Bt cotton plants were more prone to disease and that the yields were lower, many faced debts that they could not pay. The result was a very high suicide rate amongst cotton farmers, and it was later discovered that "90 percent of farmers who had committed suicide in Andhra Pradesh and Vidharba had been growing genetically modified cotton".[119]

Since the development of GMO seeds has been driven by profit, the focus has been on the big four temperate climate crops – corn, canola, cotton and soybeans; and only two traits – insect resistance and resistance to herbicides. Focusing on other crops and other traits might make sense from the point of view of developing countries, but since they typically lack the funds, developing GMOs in these directions would not be profitable.[120] It is unlikely, for example, that we will see drought-resistant and higher-yielding sorghum in the near future. In this case, perhaps their poverty is a protection for developing countries against possible long-term destructive consequences of utilizing GMOs.

The ownership of 90 percent of transgenic traits globally by Monsanto gives this corporation enormous power and enormous profits. As a capitalist corporation, it is rational for it to maximize profits by focusing on the largest crops produced mainly by industrial farming, where the big money is. Further, it has managed to tie in GMO seeds with a herbicide it also produces, enhancing its profits yet more. GM seeds engineered to tolerate the herbicide Roundup require farmers to buy an expensive seed/herbicide package. So far GM crops are simply a way of internalizing into living organisms ways of resisting (RoundUp) or displaying (Bt) petrochemical toxins, while recent research has shown that properly grown organic crops can not only give life back to the soil and begin to detoxify the environment, but also can produce three times as much food as conventional farming.[121]

Surveys show that between 90 and 95 percent of Americans want foods containing GMOs to be labelled, but so far the power of the corporations appears to be defeating the democratic will of the people.[122] A further consequence is that if someone is allergic to GM soy, they have to avoid all soy, since there is no way of knowing which products have GM soy and which have non-GM soy (by now nearly all soy in North America has become GM).

Though not an expert, I have doubts about the advisability of the entire GMO project, because of all the unknowns associated with plunging radically new genetic organisms into environments whose genetic make-up has for the most part evolved slowly over the centuries. I have even graver doubts, because the project is directed by corporations whose main aim is profit maximization and not necessarily the flourishing of humanity as a whole.

WASTE

As suggested by much that I have written, our existing food system is wasteful of the earth's resources, but it is also wasteful of food. Over 5 billion pounds of food are lost per year at the retail level,[123] 91 billion pounds are lost by consumers and food services, and of 1 million restaurants in the United States, each averages 50,000 pounds of waste per year.[124]

Another source of waste is packaging, particularly in the case of plastics that do not easily biodegrade. Some headway has been made in the area of recycling because in some cases this can be profitable enough to be capitalistically organized. Also consumers can be easily made to feel guilty about the concept of waste, and can feel virtuous when not wasteful. They can be pressured to recycle either by making it easier for them, or by requiring it by law, as we see in some jurisdictions where consumers must take their own reusable bags when they go shopping. However, if we look at the entire life-cycle of most commodities from the point of view of their environmental impact, in most cases the potentials for recycling have hardly got off the ground.

By 2004 CAFOs produced 40 percent of the world's meat, and the percentage is no doubt significantly higher by now.[125] Not only do CAFOs use enormous amounts of grain, antibiotics, water and energy, but also as CAFOs become larger and larger, it becomes more and more difficult to dispose of the waste they create. By the early twenty-first century, half of the beef cattle in the United States were being raised on only 20 feedlots, creating serious pollution problems, as discussed earlier.[126]

Waste can be viewed as a very general problem since in many ways our existing systems of agriculture waste petroleum, water, land and human energy.

CONCLUSIONS

In this chapter I have presented a brief and condensed summary of the ways in which our current food system is unsustainable. Capitalist agriculture is not only a major contributor to global warming, it will also become a casualty of the higher temperatures and the ever more frequent droughts and floods that will become the inevitable result of global warming. It follows that farmers will need special supports in the future, and our petroleum-based system of food provisioning will need to be transformed. While global warming carries with it the most catastrophic long-term consequences, there are also many other urgent ecological problems that are emerging from our food system.

It is disturbing to see the degree to which political leaders hesitate to redirect resources towards solving the health, social justice and environmental problems that we face. For example, committing to cutting greenhouse gas emissions in half by 2050 can be just a way of putting off dealing with the problem until it is too late. In the mean time, politicians can make all sorts of minor "green gestures" and let governments in the 2040s worry about reaching the target. While it is impossible to predict exactly how long it will take for the seas to rise 5 metres, for the average global temperature to rise by over 2 degrees Celsius, or for weather to turn truly vicious, so far there have been enough urgent warnings from experts on global warming, that it would be rational to take radical action now.

Our most intimate connection with the environment and our greatest impact on it arises from our system of food provisioning. It follows that this must be at the centre of our economic concerns, if we want future generations to continue to flourish on this earth. We cannot continue to base our agriculture on the depletion or degrading of non-renewable resources, whether they are fossil fuels, tropical forests, fresh water, land, sea or air. We also should not count on GMOs to solve all problems with food provision. Arguably, so far they have done more harm than good. Indeed, they pose grave risks and unknown dangers unless we solve more of the problems associated with plunging wholly new genetic organisms into environments whose evolutionary balances can be severely disrupted by their presence.

7 FOOD, MARKETING AND CHOICE IN THE UNITED STATES

In the standard approach to consumer policy, laissez-faire, or leave alone, is the near-universal prescription. This ideology of non-interference holds that one should be able to buy what one likes, where and when one likes, and as much as one likes, without so much as a glance from others. Consumption is arguably the activity our society deems most purely personal, outside the legitimate interest of society or government. Ironically it is considered even more private than sex.[1]

With a single-minded competitiveness reminiscent of the California gold rush, corporations are racing to stake their claim on the consumer group formerly known as children. What was once the purview of a few entertainment and toy companies has escalated into a gargantuan, multi-tentacled enterprise with a combined marketing budget estimated at over $15 billion annually – about 2.5 times more that what was spent in 1992. Children are the darlings of corporate America. They're targets for marketers of everything from hamburgers to minivans. And it's not good for them.[2]

A few giant corporations control much of what children eat, drink, wear, read, and play with.[3]

One of the most hallowed yet hollow conceptions of mainstream economic theory is "consumer choice" or "consumer sovereignty".

[165]

It is not that choice is a bad thing or does not exist, rather it is the huge exaggeration that each individual's choice somehow wells up purely internally as a preference schedule that the individual, at least in principle, rationally follows with full knowledge of each commodity. In this manner the purely private and inner desires of each individual are sanctified and are translated by "consumer sovereignty" into the driving force of capitalism that ultimately insures the maximization of every individual's private desires. What is wrong with this picture? Nothing except that it totally distorts what actually goes on and results in the extreme valorization of a childish possessive individualism. In other words, individuals are given a sense of empowerment that is largely false, and individualism is sanctified at the expense of the general welfare. Further, it is a fiction that makes capitalism seem to be much more democratic than it actually is.

Consumers' needs, wants and desires are almost totally socially constructed in their historical specificity. They are constructed by the actual array of commodities available, by their price, by the socioeconomic status of the consumer and by marketing or sociocultural practices that shape desires. American consumers in 1870 would not place an automobile high on their preference schedule, nor in the computer age would they likely pine for a mechanical typewriter. People might want to take public transportation to work if offered the option, but lacking adequate public transportation, they may be forced to struggle with gridlock every day in their personal car. The desire for a leopardskin coat is not likely to be high on the want list of poor women. Marketing may convince a young boy that it is "cool" to smoke cigarettes, and images of beauty may be a conditioning factor for a young girl to adopt a very restrictive diet.

Individuals are also socially conditioned from infancy to need or want certain things. Children can be and are manipulated by the marketing industry to establish early – and the marketers hope lifetime – consumption patterns or brand loyalties. Social status connected with the ownership of certain commodities is socially constructed as well – in clothing fashions and with any other commodity connected to status. Some commodities such as sugar and tobacco have addictive qualities, which shape desire. Consumers may be seduced into believing that certain commodities will bring pleasures that they turn out not to bring.

It is extremely rare that consumers are fully informed about the commodities they are consuming. Even if a consumer would like to consume in ways that would promote social justice and environmental health, in order to do so, they would need to know the entire life cycle of the commodity, its environmental impacts and its impacts on human flourishing. In the petrochemical age, knowing the life cycle and impact of commodities is particularly difficult. Given that so few chemicals have been fully tested for their long-term health impacts, we often are unaware of the chemical components of many commodities, and the many petrochemicals that are at least to some degree toxic. Further, we may be forced to consume a commodity even if we are very critical of its life cycle, simply because a commodity of that type with a more acceptable life cycle is not available.

Consumers may be offered an array of brand-named commodities that give the impression of choice, but differ very little from each other. Advertising will attempt to valorize very fine distinctions in order to establish brand loyalties, so that some consumers will come to love Pepsi-Cola and hate Coca-Cola. It is even possible that the ability to make such choices will help consumers to think of themselves as autonomous and empowered.

Consumers might prefer to eat organic foods, but find them too expensive. "Preference schedules" tend not to include things that a consumer is not likely to ever afford. Ethiopian peasants are not likely to save for a personal jet. More likely, they will have almost no choice, for their choice will be translated into trying to find enough to eat day in and day out. For 2.8 billion people who earn $2 or less a day, their "preference schedules" are limited to the desperate needs of survival in the face of inadequate food, clothing or shelter. Choice hardly comes into it, and their choices in no way make them a sovereign force that ensures that the economy meets their needs.

CHOICE AND THE CASE OF TOBACCO

No doubt having choice is important to us. For example, a consumer may value being able to choose between a plasma screen or LCD screen television. But we need to remember that even to be in a position to make such a choice has already been heavily conditioned by one's socioeconomic status, which in turn depends on accidents of birth in historical time and place. According to Brandt, "the cigarette came to epitomize this crucial aspect of the consumer culture, in which advertisers manipulated meaning and experience, creating needs and consumer loyalties", and "cigarette brands and their aggressive promotion were a primary example of the 'invention' of choice".[4] Edward Bernays, a pathbreaking expert on marketing for American Tobacco in the early 1940s, coined the concept "engineering consent" to describe the *modus operandi* of marketing in fabricating the notion of consumer sovereignty. As Brandt puts it so well:

> With the term "engineering" Bernays specified the instrumental precision with which he aspired to operate; in "consent" he implied that, ultimately, individual autonomy persisted despite the power of corporate manipulation … the illusion of agency was a critical component of the consumer culture.[5]

There are two reasons for this discussion of choice. One is that I want to emphasize the extent to which advertising and marketing influence and even manipulate choice. The other is to emphasize the extent to which powerful corporations turn individual choice into a religious fundamental when it comes to defending themselves against government regulation. For example, a propaganda ploy frequently used by tobacco (and many other) corporations, has been that "individual freedom" includes the freedom to choose to smoke and that therefore any constraints placed on smoking interfere with individual freedom. Big government is pictured as nearly totalitarian when it interferes in any way with the consumers' right to consume almost anything no matter what the individual or social costs. Thus cigarettes continue to be marketed in the United States even though, according to Davis, "one out of every two men and one out of every three women will develop cancer in their lifetime", and cigarette smoking is still the leading cause of cancer.[6]

I mention tobacco again not only because it is an agricultural crop, but also because it presents the paradigm case of an industry that has done the most to develop modes of advertising and marketing to circumvent popular efforts and government efforts to limit the damage of such an addictive and deadly commodity.[7] The tobacco industry is a good example of how far profitable corporations will go to defend their profits even when the social costs of the commodity they produce are enormous. Indeed, one could say that from the point of view of capitalism, the tobacco industry is acting perfectly rationally.

Before discussing these ploys, it should be pointed out that the tobacco industry pioneered many modern advertising and marketing techniques. For example, because there was not much difference between one cigarette and another, tobacco corporations began early on to develop advertising aimed to create brand loyalty by having famous people endorse a brand, by creating slogans or jingles ("Lucky Strike means fine tobacco"), or by creating associations with certain lifestyles (Marlboro country). Never mind that the original Marlboro man died of lung cancer.

When tobacco companies were criticized for producing a commodity that caused lung cancer,[8] they worked on many fronts to undermine the critics or to make superficial changes (filter cigarettes) that might give the impression that whatever dangers might have existed had now been removed. In order to combat scientific findings that linked cigarettes to cancer, they paid lots of money to scientists who would in return declare that much more research needed to be carried out before any definitive causal connection could be found between an individual's smoking and their cancer.[9] Since cancer can be the result of a large complex of factors operating over a long time, it was argued that it was not possible to single out cigarettes as the main cause. The cause might be carcinogenic chemicals in the environment and not cigarettes at all. We were to ignore that fact that a person who smokes 25 cigarettes a day has 50 times as much likelihood of contracting lung cancer as someone who does not smoke.[10] While the first ploy was to cast doubt on a proven probability by asserting the impossibly high criterion of causality, the second ploy was to focus attention away from cigarettes onto other possible causes. All of these ploys were facilitated by the ability of large corporations to manipulate the media.[11]

A third ploy was the use of high-paid lawyers to defend tobacco companies against litigation that aimed at sueing the companies for producing a commodity that damaged health. The lawyers managed to persuade the court system to accept such a high standard of causality that it was almost impossible to prove a causal connection between smoking and a particular case of cancer. Further, the lawyers argued that smokers needed to accept full individual responsibility for their choice to smoke in the first place, then to continue smoking. Philip Morris went so far as to mobilize the patriotism and sacredness associated with the American constitution to draw up a smoker's Bill of Rights.

A fourth ploy was to pay off politicians to speak well of the tobacco industry, to support consumer rights to smoke and to oppose legislation that might damage sales of cigarettes, such as higher cigarette taxes. Brandt reports that in the 1996 presidential race the republican candidate, Robert Dole, received $477,000 in contributions from the tobacco industry and flew on its corporate jets 38 times. When asked about the health risks of smoking he said, "We know it's not good for kids. But a lot of things aren't good ... some would say milk's not good."[12] According to former Secretary of Health, Education and Welfare under President Carter, Joseph Califano:

In late June, 1995, John Boehner, then an Ohio Republican representative and later House Majority Leader, walked the floor of the House of Representatives handing out checks from Philip Morris to individual members as they were debating legislation that the tobacco company opposed.[13]

A fifth ploy was to gain a good public image through philanthropy, particularly by supporting mass entertainment, such as sporting and cultural events. In this way smoking could be associated with having fun and tobacco corporations could be seen as good corporate citizens. Further, if they sponsored family events they could reach children without being criticized for aiming their advertising at children.

These ploys were amazingly successful in prolonging the booming cigarette sales in the United States. Sales of cigarettes peaked in 1975, over ten years after the Surgeon General's report of 1964, which declared that smoking causes cancer.[14] Tobacco farming continued to be heavily subsidized by the federal government until 2004.[15] Also, when debate first occurred about placing health warnings on packages of cigarettes, the US Department of Agriculture, which administered the tobacco price support system for farmers, strongly opposed the health warnings.[16] The health warning that finally was approved, "Caution: Cigarette Smoking May Be Hazardous to Your Health", was seriously weakened by the "may be" favoured by the cigarette industry. And finally the Reagan presidency utilized the enormous economic clout of the United States to force other countries to open their markets to American cigarettes at a time when this would help reduce the large and growing US trade deficit.[17]

The cartoon figure Joe Camel was introduced by R. J. Reynolds in 1986 in order to appeal to the youth who would constitute tomorrow's smokers. Vying in effectiveness with the Marlboro Man as an advertising symbol, Joe Camel helped increase Camel's share of the underage market from 3 percent in 1986 to 13 percent by 1993.[18] As public outrage grew, R. J. Reynolds was eventually forced to remove its giant figure of Joe Camel from Times Square, and the momentum of the protest led to banning all cigarette billboards by 1999.[19]

While it is the cigarette industry that perfected the means to protect their interests against citizens and the government, powerful corporations in other sectors including agriculture and the food industry now utilize similar methods when their profits are threatened. Some of the more blatant examples already mentioned include the sugar industry's successful efforts to block setting international standards to limit sugars to 10 percent in baby food and to establish a norm that would aim to limit daily intake of added sugars to 10 percent of total calories. Also it is worth noting the success that the same industry had in blocking the proposal to have the US industry pay 1 cent for every pound of sugar sold in order to provide funds to clean up damage that the sugar industry has done to the rapidly deteriorating Everglades in Florida.

MARKETING

Since the costs of marketing and advertising are tax deductible, and since both have been proven effective in increasing profits, large corporations spend a lot on them.

Food is the most advertised commodity in the United States, and food corporations spend on average over $36 billion a year on marketing and advertising.[20] Seventy percent of this goes to advertise convenience foods, candy and snacks, soft drinks, desserts and alcohol.[21] Coke and McDonald's are among the top ten in corporate spending on advertising in the world. Further, soda pop, which is one of the most profitable "junk foods", is also the largest source of sugar in the American diet, and therefore one of the most significant contributors to obesity. Purveyors of sugar such as Coke try to deflect attention away from junk foods and on to lack of exercise as the principal cause of obesity. As previously mentioned, Coke has gone so far as to contribute step-counting pedometers to schools.[22]

According to Putnam,[23] television is addictive (like junk food), with the average American devoting 40 percent of their free time to watching television; this comes out to an average of four hours a day. The average American is exposed to more than 40,000 television commercials a year, and 42 percent of families with children have the television on most of the time; 60 percent have it on during meals.[24]

MARKETING TO CHILDREN

The doors were opened and commercialism was invited to invade the lives of children by two fundamental policy changes made by President Reagan: the deregulation of advertising on children's television and the cutback in spending on schools.[25] The potential impact of the first is obvious, and the second led schools to scrounge for money by allowing brands to advertise and market on school property.

In the brave new world of hyper marketing, children are seen primarily as conduits between commercial advertising and the family purse,[26] or to put it more strongly, they became "profit centres for the food industry".[27] According to a recent estimate, children under 14 influence as much as 47 percent of US household spending.[28] According to Linn:

> kids today are growing up in a marketing maelstrom. That children influence more than $600 billion in spending a year has not been lost on corporate America, which seeks

to establish 'cradle to grave' brand loyalty .... Every aspect of children's lives – their physical and mental health, their education, their creativity, and their values – is negatively affected by their involuntary status as consumers in the marketplace.[29]

The food environment has been described as "toxic", but the same could be said for the impact on children of the culture of commercialism; it is no exaggeration to speak of a toxic "commercialization of childhood".[30] While there are many indicators of this toxicity, from skyrocketing obesity rates (which have tripled since 1980) to high rates of attention deficit disorder (10 percent in some school districts), perhaps the most telling is Schor's finding that "Today's average (i.e. normal) young person between the ages of nine and seventeen scores as high on anxiety scales as children who were admitted to clinics for psychiatric disorders in 1957."[31]

"Brand loyalty from cradle to grave" captures the intent of marketing research which shows that toddlers are requesting brands as soon as they can speak. Surveys show that 60 percent of American children aged under two watch television, and 26 percent have their own televisions.[32] Once children can speak, they on average request over 3,000 products per year.[33] Also they are doing more shopping at younger ages, as evidenced by data showing that children between the ages of four and twelve increased their purchases between 1989 and 2002 by 400 percent.[34] According to one estimate, marketers and advertisers will spend $15 billion directed at children in 2004 as compared with only $100 million spent on television advertising in 1983.[35] A new and important marketing category is the "tween" market which extends roughly from ages five to twelve. According to leading marketing expert, Martin Lindstrom, "by 2003 80 percent of all global brands required a tween strategy in order to keep up with the competition".[36]

Food marketing is particularly aimed at children as food tastes and eating habits formed early in life are hard to break and tend to be enduring. Clearly the food brands that can tap into the human craving for fats, sugars and salts the earliest will be the big winners – kids' number one spending category (at one-third of the total) is sweets, snacks and beverages.[37] A 1999 study found that 63 percent of the advertisements on children's television on Saturday mornings were for food.[38] A recent study of the total media exposure of American children aged 8–18 found that it has increased by one hour in the past five years to 8.5 hours per day.[39]

This barrage of advertising, not only in the media but also in every conceivable public space, is apparently successful, as the consumption of soda pop in the United States doubled between 1993 and 2003,[40] and over the past two decades the percentage of calories children consumed from snacks has increased by 30 percent.[41] Part of the "success" of advertising to American children is their increasing consumption of junk foods, such that, of children aged between six and twelve, only 12 percent have a healthy diet.[42] According to the Center for Science in the Public Interest, "a quarter of children between the ages of five and ten show early signs of heart disease, such as high LDL (the 'bad' cholesterol) or elevated blood pressure".[43]

Further, although tobacco companies have not been able to legally aim advertisements directly at children (as was done in the past with figures like Joe Camel), until recently it was legal to pay for product placement in movies. For instance, Sylvester Stallone was paid half a million dollars to smoke in five films.[44] In 1990 the tobacco industry agreed to a "voluntary" ban on cigarette product placements in movies. Despite the ban, between 1988 and 1997 actual placements nearly doubled, with 85 percent of the top 250 movies containing smoking.[45]

Now, by the eighth grade (13–14 years old) in the United States 7 percent of the students are regular smokers.[46] Product placement in films and on television has become an important means of marketing. For example, in the extremely popular television series *American Idol*, the judges sit sipping cups of Coca-Cola during the show. The National Football League seeks to require that journalists wear corporate names and logos during football games. As of 2003, there were already over 100 product placement agencies operating across the media.[47]

Tobacco companies have also utilized the lesser constraints on marketing cigars and chewing tobacco to get at children. Flavoured chewing tobacco and cigarillos are now widely accessed by children who, once addicted to nicotine, might on coming of age shift to cigarettes.[48] In this way a whole new generation of potential smokers is being nurtured despite all the constraints on marketing cigarettes to children.

Ironically fast food companies have found toys made by children in China to be powerful marketing instruments with American children. For example, McDonald's sells or gives away 1.5 billion toys a year, typically produced in China by children who are paid as little as 20 cents an hour.[49] The super exploitation of children in one part of the world feeds the supercommercialization of children in another part.

With the general shift of wealth from the public to the private sector, schools have suffered enormously from underfunding. Since increasingly it is the private sector that has the wealth, it has been necessary for schools to turn to this sector for financing, and marketers are responding with almost unlimited ways of commercializing the times and spaces occupied by schools. Schools are selling ad space on buses, in stadiums, inside school buildings, in washrooms and in classrooms. "Box tops for education" programmes encourage kids to return branded box tops to schools where they can be converted to cash.[50] And in some cases teachers have found they can supplement their incomes by allowing food ads to be placed on their cars.[51]

Schools have also made money by selling pouring rights to Coke or to Pepsi, which in return for a monopoly on selling drinks in the school, offer the school a certain amount of money. Thus it happened that schools became a place for soft drink vending machines, which at their height found their way into 94 percent of American high schools.[52] Snack foods and fast foods also found their way into vending machines and school cafeterias, and schools reportedly received $750 million a year from purveyors of these foods.[53] Until the recent concern about obesity gave rise to movements for change, 95 percent of California high schools carried fast food and soft drink vending machines.[54] The growing concern is evidenced by movements of parents in the United States to remove junk foods from schools, and by consumer groups in 20 countries urging Coke and Pepsi to limit soft drink marketing to children.[55] Given the power of the junk food corporations and the policies that have underfunded education, it may take some time for these struggles to be successful.

Corporate brands have also taken advantage of the need for good educational materials, to provide them free of charge, but not free of the promotion of brand names or corporate interests. For example, Schor reports that Exxon offers a curriculum that "implies that fossil fuels pose few environmental problems and that alternative energy is costly and unattainable",[56] "a Kellogg's breakfast curriculum presents fat content as the only thing to worry about when choosing breakfast food",[57] and "a first-grade reading curriculum has the kids start out by recognizing logos from K-Mart, Pizza Hut, M&M's, Jell-O, and Target".[58] Corporations gain from producing educational materials because it is a way of imprinting brand names on the minds of the young, and because the cost of providing educational materials is tax deductible.

Channel One in the United States gives television reception products to schools in exchange for having students watch ten minutes of news and two minutes of commercials on 90 percent of all school days. According to Channel One, 40 percent of all teens view its programmes. A good deal of the advertising is for junk foods, and it has even aimed military recruiting messages at its captive audience.[59]

> As one marketing expert says, corporations are "trying to establish a situation where kids are exposed to their brand in as many different places as possible throughout the course of the day or the week, or almost anywhere they turn in the course of their daily rituals."[60]

Young girls are particularly stressed by the contradiction between the slender bodies required by beauty images, and the continual bombardment of messages to eat more junk food. One result of this is that 40 percent of nine and ten-year-old girls in the United States are on a diet,[61] and another result is at least some contribution to the out-of-control feelings that tend to underlie anorexia and bulimia. On the Fiji islands, anorexia and bulimia were practically nonexistent in 1990 when US television was introduced. Three years later 11.9 percent of Fijian girls were bulimic.[62]

One would think that the high correlation discovered between consumerism and emotional problems might in part explain the disturbing figure that 21 percent of American children aged between 9 and 17 suffer a mental or addictive disorder with at least minimum impairment.[63]

CHOOSING JUNK FOODS

In this chapter I have emphasized the marketing of food and tobacco to children for two primary reasons. First, half the world's population is under 25 and it is these young people who are the hope for the future.[64] Second, the younger the target group, the more easily they can be manipulated towards cradle to grave brand loyalty.

But in terms of food in particular, we need to ask, if junk food is so unhealthy, why do so many Americans eat so much junk food? Is it simply the rational choice of well-informed consumers exercising their sovereignty? Or is it because they just don't care about their health or have some sort of unconscious death wish? Clearly neither of these explanations will do. I shall offer eight reasons.

- Junk food is cheap, and the majority of Americans have to watch their budget carefully.
- The high sugar content of baby formula and baby food can predispose one to crave foods high in sugars throughout life.
- Often it is sugars, fats and salts that make foods taste good to us to the point that we crave them or become quasi-addicted to them.
- Marketing and advertising assault us from infancy to old age. Next to Santa Claus, Ronald McDonald is the most recognized figure in the world, and the golden arches are more widely recognized than the Christian cross.[65] Parents often give in to nagging children when it comes to completing a toy collection offered by a fast food chain.[66]
- Americans lack the time to shop for food and prepare home-cooked meals. Life on the run means that there is not enough time even for life's basic functions like sleeping and eating. Many do not get enough sleep and also cut back on time spent eating. Fast foods often enable one to eat in the car while travelling from one task to the next.
- Junk food is everywhere, and depending on where you are, it may be all that is available. In sports venues, airports, train stations,

highway service centres, department stores and even schools, junk foods may be the main foods or only foods available.

- Some widely prescribed drugs like antidepressants increase appetites and food cravings.
- Feelings of inner emptiness and meaninglessness (created partly by capitalist commercialism, I would argue) can lead one to seek the consolation of food and a feeling of fullness or of fulfilment from eating.

CONSUMER SOVEREIGNTY

To symbolize their solicitousness towards consumers, retailers often say "the consumer is king". If this leads to retailers treating consumers better, then it is perhaps a good slogan, even if it is misleading. Consumerist capitalism has been sanctified by a fundamentalist belief in the private ownership of capital combined with markets as the economic route to affluence for all. As mentioned in the introduction to this chapter, one of the most basic beliefs and most mythical aspects of this new economic religion is that of "consumer sovereignty". According to the notion of "consumer sovereignty", capitalists can only profit by meeting consumer preferences, and hence it is such preferences which ultimately drive the system. While criticisms of "consumer sovereignty" have been scattered throughout this chapter, here I want to focus on the concept a little more systematically.

Consumers can only cast "dollar ballots" for commodities that are offered for sale and that they can afford; they may not be fully informed about the human or environmental costs involved in producing the commodity; and they may not be fully informed about the human or environmental costs involved in using the commodity. No doubt many Africans who are HIV positive would like to buy drugs that would slow down or prevent the development of full-blown AIDS, but of course in most cases they cannot afford them. The rush to produce tens of thousands of new chemicals after World War II resulted in about 1 percent being given complete toxicity tests.[67] Since many carcinogens only show their effects after several or even many years, or in combination with other chemicals, untested chemicals essentially get tested on humans. After enough people exposed to a particular chemical get sick or die, the chemical becomes suspect and tests are carried out. Potentially profitable chemicals are rushed into production since every day of production lost amounts to losing the potential profits from that production forever. The problem is that among the petrochemicals are some of the most toxic substances ever produced. Surely a sovereign consumer would not voluntarily condone the spread of toxic chemicals that could bring illness and death to many people?

It is rare that consumers are both fully informed and have the resources to care about all the social and environmental costs of a commodity. Purchasers of a cotton T-shirt may not know that the cotton came from Nicaragua where workers in the cotton fields have suffered from pesticide poisoning. Purchasers of a chocolate bar may not know that the chocolate came from a farm in Ivory Coast employing child slaves. People who are obese from the frequent consumption of junk foods may not be able to afford or have the time to prepare more nutritious food. It would be very difficult to find out if the hamburger you are eating in a fast food chain comes from a steer that was raised on marginal grassland that was once rain forest. The owners of gas-guzzling 400 horse-power sports cars may so delight in its speed and power that their small addition to long-run global warming may seem to them to be a harm of far less significance than their immediate pleasure. Consumers may be vaguely aware that wages and working conditions are very bad in the toy industry in China, but China after all is not only far away but also has a very different culture. Most consumers are by now aware that something called "global warming" is taking place, but the likelihood that oceans may rise 15 or 20 metres by the end of the century may be of little concern because they will be dead by then. In contrast, car owners may be very concerned about global warming, but still must use their car to get to work unless a convenient public transportation alternative exists. Finally, some cigarette smokers may be fully aware that smoking may result in a painful and early death, and yet still be too addicted to smoking to stop.

It is in the interest of capital to shift as much responsibility as possible to the individual consumer. Indeed, an ideology of extreme individualism is one of capital's favourite ways to shift burdens of responsibility away from itself to the individual consumer. The myth of consumer sovereignty assumes that the consumer is responsible. But given the existing "toxic culture of consumerism",[68] and the horrific global inequality that continually pushes people toward consumption choices that undermine human and environmental health, it is unwise to think that global warming can be significantly reduced simply by enlightened individuals changing their consumption patterns.

A much more effective strategy of change would be to look at ways of making corporations and markets more democratically accountable.

CONCLUSIONS

While some consumers are likely to make huge efforts to become more green, capital knows that with its marketing power and with existing widespread poverty, most people will not make radical changes in their life styles. Non-junk foods cost more in the short term, as do fuel-efficient appliances. If the individual is the main focus for change, then change is not likely to be effective, not only because of the unrealistic burden on individuals, but also because we are asking individuals to struggle against the root causes of the problem which remain intact.

The costs of obesity are translating primarily into medical costs, which in many countries are either partly or mainly subsidized by the government, or in other words "socialized". And from the point of view of capital, the more costs that can be socialized, the higher their profits. Capital benefits enormously from workers being educated and trained at public expense, or from cheap inputs such as land, water or electricity that are subsidized by government, or from publicly funded roads, publicly funded waste disposal or outright government subsidies. Thus it is always in the interest of capital to socialize as many costs as possible, and at the same time to privatize as much profit as possible. Corporations that produce and market junk foods do not have to pay even part of the medical costs of obesity.

Obesity is profitable not only for the purveyors of junk foods that are the principal feeders of obesity, but also for corporations and professions that offer all sorts of commodities and services that make up the enormous weight-reduction industry. In short, capital profits from being a cause of obesity and from individuals spending their hard-earned money trying to avoid the worst effects. Clearly we need to find ways of making corporations and markets more democratically accountable and of finding stronger modes of democratic decision making, and these changes especially need to occur at an international level since many problems that we face are global problems that require global solutions.

8 CORPORATE POWER, FOOD AND LIBERAL DEMOCRACY

When General Pershing was asked what the nation could do to assist in the war, he issued his famous plea to the home front: "You ask me what we need to win this war. I answer tobacco, as much as bullets."[1] Bull Durham tobacco came out with the slogan, "When our boys light up, the Huns will light out."[2]

[T]he US taste for Coca-Cola was first chorused in the theatre of the Second World War. The drink itself wasn't given away during the conflict, but General Marshall went to great lengths to make sure that it was freely available to buy wherever US troops were stationed. The Coca-Cola Company was exempted from sugar rationing so that it might produce a drink that came, for US soldiers, to signify the very lifeblood of the country.[3]

Cigarettes became commodities of mass consumption in the trench warfare of World War I, and Coca-Cola became a commodity of mass consumption in World War II. Both are stimulants, which is important in warfare, and both can be injurious to health, though in the short term are "pick-me ups". Further, they are both examples of consumption by mass contagion when the mass reaches out to a commodity that offers some comfort in the face of enormous stress. In this case, they gave birth to some of the most profitable and largest corporations in the modern world, and they are good examples of how politics and in this case the ideology of patriotism can and do create markets.

[182]

In the history of capitalism the balance of power between government and capital has continually shifted, but after 30 years or so of neo-liberalism and the continual global expansion of corporate power, corporations have perhaps never before been so powerful relative to government. The institutions of American liberal democracy have increasingly lost whatever autonomy they once had. The rule of law has increasingly become the rule of law in the interest of corporations; scientific research to advance objective knowledge has become science to advance the objects of corporate profit making; and law-making assemblies have become far more accountable to corporations than to the public interest.

From the point of view of capitalism, the totalitarian state is often feared and loathed, but what if the giant corporation should become totalitarian in more refined, subtle and manipulative ways which make its boardroom power even more difficult to see or counter? This is precisely what has happened and is increasingly happening. There was a time after World War II when the American government had the power to at least constrain and regulate some activities of the corporate sector. One might say that the state was to a degree relatively autonomous from capital. But this has changed, and in recent years the state has lost much of its power to act as a check on capital. This has happened at the same time as the social and environmental costs connected to many forms of short-term profit making have skyrocketed, and this is why forceful and radical political interventions against such catastrophic costs are urgent. While it is important as a first step to find ways to hold corporations accountable to democratic controls, in the long run corporate structures will need to be reorganized. This will become necessary in order for humans to flourish in the future. Paradoxically, corporations have so much control over our economies and our very thinking that very few existing politicians would even dream of policy alternatives that would touch corporate power, much less propose policies that would actually hold corporations democratically accountable.

It is not only the relative autonomy of the state that has been undermined, but also the relative autonomy of science, the legal system and the media. Liberal democracy has always had its own internal tensions between liberalism and democracy because many

conceptions of liberalism contain radical notions of individual freedom as non-interference, while conceptions of democracy often
emphasize the importance of equality which may imply interference precisely because of the extreme inequalities generated by
capitalism. For example, from an idealization of the capitalist
market, it is easy to extract a conception of possessive individualism that might support certain conceptions of individual rights and
freedoms deemed important to liberalism. However, if capitalist
markets generate great inequalities of economic and political
power, then individual rights and freedoms are likely to become
increasingly meaningless to those who lack power.

Yet most would agree that there are certain ideals of liberal
democracy that need to be strengthened, such as:

- the rule of law
- individual and social rights
- separation of church and state
- commitment to advancing the objectivity of science
- a questioning and probing media
- concentrations of power accountable to the people.

Although there has always been a tension between these ideals
(some more than others) and capitalism, I believe that capitalism is
now strongly undermining the headway towards them that has been
made in the past, particularly in the United States. It is beyond the
scope of this book to argue systematically and at length for this
position, but in this chapter I want to present an initial sketch of
how corporate power is undermining some of the most promising
ideals of liberal democracy.

There are four institutional clusters that are central to the way
in which capitalism is compromising liberal democracy:

- The cost of electoral campaigns in the United States has
  become so enormous that elected politicians are directly
  beholden to the corporations that provide most of their
  campaign funds.
- Because large corporations have the wherewithal to sue for
  large amounts of money and to successfully fight off suits filed

against them, they have partially compromised the systems of civil and criminal law.

- The large shift in wealth from the public sector to the private sector means that scientists are increasingly dependent on corporate funding for their research, which can thereby be strongly bent away from truth seeking in a direction that will support corporate interests.

- The American media as a critical force has been severely blunted by the fact that it is financially dependent for funding from corporate advertising, and it often practises a kind of self-censorship to please its corporate sponsors and to avoid the ever-present threat of expensive lawsuits from corporate interests which may feel in some way disparaged by the media.

The ideals of liberal democracy have often been criticized from the left, but for the most part that is because liberal democracies have so seldom come close to living up to these ideals. The shattered ideals relate to the shocking degrees of inequality that capitalism creates when left to its own devices, and the enormous power that corporations have to corrupt liberal democracy from top to bottom.

CORPORATIONS AND GOVERNMENT

To start with I want to clarify some terminology. Throughout this book I include non-food agricultural industries such as tobacco and cotton alongside food agricultural industries because in most respects all agricultural industries share a good deal in common. This is why it was not difficult for Philip Morris to utilize its immense profits to buy up food corporations, making it the largest food corporation in the United States, while at the same time maintaining its cigarette division. Furthermore, there are borderline cases such as sugar, which has calories and is eaten like food, but like cigarettes is addictive, unhealthy and provides calories but no other nutritional value. While I occasionally refer to coca and opium because they are agricultural crops and because poor farmers sometimes turn to them when they cannot make a living growing food crops, their illegality gives them a special role globally and in the US prison-industrial complex. This places them in a separate category which needs extensive analysis of its own.[4]

There are several reasons that the American state has become increasingly subject to the will of corporations:

- It is widely recognized that for the most part state regulatory agencies have become constituted so as to be particularly sympathetic to the interests of the corporations they are supposed to regulate. More often than not it is the regulators who are regulated by those they are supposed to regulate.[5]
- The cost of election campaigns has become so exorbitant that politicians have become deeply dependent on corporate donations in order to run their campaigns. This financial dependency places them in a position where they need to be in agreement with their corporate supporters even when the corporate position is obviously opposed to the long-term common good.
- Powerful corporate lobbies not only direct members of Congress to vote in particular ways, they also participate in proposing and writing legislation.
- Large corporations have the power to threaten their critics with enormously expensive lawsuits, and they have the money to buy expensive lawyers to shape the law to their advantage in many cases. Corporations have managed to stretch libel law in the courts such that it becomes more and more dangerous even to criticize them, thus undermining the freedom of speech.[6]
- The threat to sue has been utilized enough against the media, that they now tread with extreme caution and censor themselves when voicing criticisms of powerful corporate sectors.[7]
- Corporations can easily access the media to get their messages across and to shape public opinion.[8]
- Corporations have organized groups of scientists and think tanks to influence public opinion and to provide Congress with supposedly "authoritative" information which advances their short-term corporate profits even when the long-term social costs may be immense.[9]

Corporations in the agriculture/food sector have become huge. For example, Monsanto, Archer Daniels Midland, ConAgra and Cargill are giant corporations involved in many dimensions of the food system from seeds to retail sales. In 1996, ConAgra controlled 25 percent of the US feed and fertilizer markets, 53 percent of refrigerated foods, and 22 percent of all grocery products.[10] In global agricultural commodity trade five corporations control 60 to 90 percent of all wheat, maize and rice trade; three corporations control 80 percent of the banana trade; three corporations control 83 percent of the cocoa trade; and three corporations control 85 percent of the tea trade.[11] Such corporate concentration often gives corporations the power to set low prices for primary producers, squeezing them for all their worth. Also it gives them considerable power to set prices paid by consumers, as we have seen in the case of coffee, when the price of green coffee beans plunged dramatically but not the final price paid by consumers. Finally, we have seen how with the production of many agricultural products, the larger the factory-farming operation, the larger the subsidies received. Subsidies are particularly important for corn, soy, wheat, cotton and sugar; whereas fruit and vegetables receive next to no subsidies.[12] Even Wal-Mart receives indirect subsidies from the social services received by its underpaid employees. It has been estimated that Wal-Mart employees receive $86 million a year from California's public assistance programs, including the many employees who use food stamps.[13]

In order to try to stem the catastrophic global epidemic of diseases brought on by the enormous increase in cigarette smoking, the WHO developed a Framework Convention on Tobacco Control (FCTC) which articulates core principles and policies that signatories should attempt to implement in accord with the realities of each country. The tobacco industry strongly opposed this convention, and when opposition failed, it sought to water it down. George Dalley, a management consultant for the tobacco industry, argued in 1984 that "nationalism and aspiration for development and a higher standard of living will lead third world governments to resist the efforts of the do-gooders from WHO to impose a smokeless society upon them".[14] Expressed using somewhat different rhetoric, the British American Tobacco Company referred to the FCTC as "a form of moral and cultural imperialism .... Imposing western priorities", and lacking "respect for cultural diversity".[15] Despite these rhetorical blasts, 150 countries have signed the FCTC, but because of the influence of the tobacco industry in the corridors of power, the United States only signed it after it was starting to look bad as one of the few holdouts.[16]

As outlined in Chapter 4, there have been similar political manipulations by the sugar industry. When the WHO and FAO prepared a report[17] recommending international guidelines that would recommend that on average daily intake of added sugars be limited to 10 percent of total calories, the American Sugar Association threatened to lobby the US Congress to pull its funding from the WHO and FAO if they did not alter their report and raise the guideline to 25 percent.[18] Similarly when Thailand proposed to *Codex Alimentarius* that the maximum sugar in baby food should be reduced to 10 percent from its existing 30 percent, the proposal was blocked by the European and American sugar industries.[19] In this case the industry had so much influence with *Codex Alimentarius* to begin with, there was no need to threaten withdrawal of funding in order to block the proposal. And this occurred despite the fact that babies who develop a sweet tooth are likely to have it for life, making them particularly susceptible to obesity.

A *New York Times* article in 2004 referred to the food pyramid that is supposed to guide healthy eating as "the food pyramid scheme".[20] It pointed out that seven of the 13-member panel responsible for constructing the pyramid were connected to the food, drug or dietary supplement industries. Among the nine tips for healthy eating that accompanied the pyramid was, "Choose carbohydrates wisely for good health." The *Times* article suggested that this wishy-washy statement should have been replaced with something more direct like "reduce added sugars".

According to Schor:

> The restaurant and beverage companies have also founded a political front group, the Center for Consumer Freedom, which espouses extreme right-wing views. The Center ran print and radio advertising ridiculing the public health agenda and the scientists and medical professionals who are trying to help Americans achieve healthier eating habits.[21]

Corporations typically argue that they are not responsible for the health of the individual, and that each individual must take full responsibility for their food consumption, and yet historically they have fought against better food labelling laws.[22] They have also fought against more effective inspections of slaughterhouses or tighter controls on food safety in general.[23] According to Schor, "Biotech giant Monsanto has been suing small dairies that inform consumers that their milk is produced without bovine growth hormone" [BGH]. The company has been vigilant in its attempts to oppose labelling, and for good reason. Since 1994, when Monsanto's recombinant BGH was approved, it has been outlawed in every other industrialized country", and it has been linked to toxic effects on cows, contamination of milk by pus and antibiotics and increased levels of cancer-causing agent IGF-1.[24]

The giant agricultural corporation Archer Daniels Midland, which produces 25 percent of US ethanol, played a leading role in persuading Congress to provide large subsidies for the construction of ethanol plants and for the production of ethanol from corn as a substitute for petroleum-based fuels.[25] The auto corporations also strongly supported this move, because for them it meant less pressure to convert to radical increases in miles per gallon, and gave them more time to sell gas-guzzling SUVs and high-performance sports cars – vehicles where they have in the recent past made the most profit.

CORPORATIONS AND THE LEGAL SYSTEM

In 1996 Texas cattle ranchers sued Oprah Winfrey over remarks she made about mad cow disease. They sued under Texas's "food disparagement law", arguing that Oprah did not present the issue in a way favourable to US beef, thus disparaging their cattle. After 35 months of litigation, 75 volumes of court records, and millions of dollars in non-recoverable lawyer's fees, Oprah won the case, but the cattle ranchers appealed to the Court of Appeals. Eventually Oprah won the appeal as well. Since there are few who would have Oprah's resources to fight such a case, it had a very chilling effect on freedom of speech for those critical of the US food industry. No doubt the ranchers are very sensitive about their cattle being disparaged, and the courts decided that they were oversensitive since they failed in their libel case against Oprah. In any case, the point is that free speech is placed under a definite chill. It is no help at all that 13 states have food disparagement laws.[26]

The previously mentioned deadly pesticide Nemagon (Chapter 5), estimated to have affected 65,000 workers worldwide, arises again in this context. You will recall that the Nicaraguan court ordered Dole, Dow and Shell to pay those still alive (thousands have already died) a total of $489 million in damages, whereupon the corporations declared that they do not recognize the competence of the Nicaraguan court. In response to this, some progressive lawyers then launched a damages suit on behalf of 13 former banana workers against the corporations in a Los Angeles court. The jury awarded the workers $3.2 million, but the corporations intend to appeal. Further, one of the corporations countered with a $17 billion lawsuit against the impoverished Nicaraguan workers, under the Racketeer Influenced and Corrupt Organizations Act.[27]

CORPORATIONS AND SCIENCE

Capitalism has radically manipulated scientific research to serve its interest, and by so doing has undermined the credibility of science, whose integrity depends on making an effort to advance the disinterested search for truth. As is so clearly evidenced by the war on cancer, science has often been manipulated to advance profits and not human flourishing.[28] The big profits come from treating cancer and not preventing it. Similarly, in general profits are not to be made in public health measures that would prevent illness, but in treating illness. It is more profitable, and therefore logical, for capital to encourage a toxic food environment that helps generate obesity, and then let the dieting industry, fitness industry, pharmaceutical industry and medical industry rake in the profits by trying to cope with the consequences.

More often than not scientific research is not directed to areas that will advance human flourishing unless there is a strong prospect of profits. As we enter an age when human health and environmental health are tied more and more closely together, we can no longer afford such a misdirection of scientific research. We need an enormous amount of research directed towards "green solutions" and towards reorganizing our agricultural and food systems to promote healthy nutrition for all. In order for this to happen, we will need to shift wealth from the private to the public sector, since in order to succeed, this much-needed research should not be constrained by what is likely to be immediately profitable. It is increasingly clear that if there is one factor that is most fundamental to health, it is diet, and it is also clear that unsustainable agricultural practices and junk foods are undermining the possibilities for a healthy diet.[29]

And the problem is not limited to the misdirection of scientific research. Corporations have also paid scientists to use their authority to promote company interests. The most blatant case historically is of course the tobacco industry, but there are many other examples of scientists being compromised and corrupted by corporate money and power. For example, Wilhelm Hueper, a German emigré with profound knowledge of workplace carcinogens, was hired by DuPont in 1934 to study the relation between industrial dyes and bladder cancer after 23 dye workers developed cases of the cancer in one of its plants. When his research discovered a direct causal connection between exposure to dyes and cancer, "he was threatened with legal action if he tried to talk about or publish any of his findings regarding worker health dangers".[30] It was only in 1980 that "it became known that 364 cases of bladder cancer had occurred" in a single DuPont factory that produced industrial dyes.[31] Indeed, the evidence showed that 100 percent of "workers exposed to synthetic dyes for 20 or more years would develop bladder cancer".[32]

Another example comes from the tobacco industry. On 4 January 1954 the tobacco industry published a full-page statement entitled the "Frank Statement" which appeared in many papers across the United States. The gist of the statement was to reassure the public that not only were cigarettes not dangerous to human health, the tobacco industry was so concerned about this issue that it would form a Tobacco Industry Research Committee made up of distinguished scientists who will receive millions of dollars to carry out further research just to make sure. The full Frank Statement can be found in Davis,[33] but the following quotation indicates the extent to which the tobacco industry would go to appear to be totally socially responsible: "We accept an interest in people's health as a basic responsibility, paramount to every other consideration in our business." Robert Proctor, an historian of science at Stanford University, wrote of the Frank Statement:

> From a historian's point of view, the "Frank Statement" represents the beginning of one of the largest campaigns of deliberate distortion, distraction, and deception the world has ever known .... The industry became a gigantic engine of deceit, utilizing deceptive press releases, "decoy research," deceitful newsletters and pamphlets mailed to physicians, journalists, and stockholders, and many other strategies. Further strategies included misleading word-smithing, duplicitous scepticism (e.g., of research results), false reassurances to consumers, and (eventually) the hiring of historians to misrepresent history.[34]

Yet another example is the industry's reaction to the Environmental Protection Agency's (EPA's) declaration that tobacco smoke is a Class A human lung carcinogen, and that secondhand smoke causes as much as 20 percent of all lung cancer amongst non-smokers. In response, Philip Morris generated the following internal memo: "The growing perceptions about and animosity to EPA as an agency that is at least misguided and aggressive, at worst corrupt and controlled by environmental terrorists, offer one of the few avenues for inroads."[35] Philip Morris went on to organize a coalition of "sound science" in an effort to revise the standards of epidemiological proof to such a high level that no correlation between secondhand smoke and cancer could ever be proved.[36] Here we see an example of corporate power impacting on the epistemological and methodological norms of science itself in order to maximize short-term profits – totally in accord with capitalist rationality.

With the decline of the public sector, scientists have become more and more dependent upon the private sector for funding. This means that the short-term profit imperatives of corporations increasingly drive not only what is to be researched, but also what findings of that research are to be publicized and what findings are to be covered up. In the food sector this has meant that pesticides, food additives and transgenic seeds have been rushed into production without adequate testing. As mentioned above, tests that revealed some of the toxic properties of Nemagon were covered up, and subsequently it has been admitted that it never should have been approved.[37] But this only came to light after a high percentage of workers who produced the insecticide found themselves to be sterile. And for years after it was banned in the United States, it continued to be used in developing countries where tens of thousands of field workers who were exposed are now dying slow and excruciating deaths. All of this occurred after trusted scientists declared that Nemagon was safe to use.

The problem is that for the most part, regulatory bodies and the scientists who report to them tend to be heavily influenced by the very corporations they are supposed to regulate. If the cigarette were introduced as a new product today by a fledgling industry, and if we had the knowledge that we have of its deadly effects, there is no doubt that it would not be approved. And yet, given the knowledge that we have, it is surprising how widely and forcefully it is still marketed. Here we have a truly amazing example of corporate power overriding 50 years of efforts to combat this deadly commodity. Even today in North America where there are bans on marketing cigarettes to the young, we find tobacco companies marketing flavoured cigarillos and chewing tobacco to try to hook the youth on nicotine.

Regulatory bodies are under great pressure to quickly approve new products because time is money. Imagine the pressure when a giant company has invested huge amounts to develop a new transgenic seed. The company would be driven to insist on rapid approval because it cannot withstand a long period of testing before its huge investment begins to bring in profits. But this is very problematic in the case of transgenic seeds that may have enormous, dangerous and irreversible consequences. Can we really afford to have things like transgenic seeds be managed primarily by a private sector driven by the profit motive? In the case of GM seeds, they were approved by the US government based entirely on research funded by the corporations who wanted to market the seeds. There was no independent government testing.[38]

Recently newspaper articles have been appearing with titles such as "Whither the revered scientist?" (*Toronto Star*) or "A Hippocratic oath for science" (*Globe and Mail*), because much of the public no longer trusts scientists. Sir David King, chief science adviser to the UK government, has advocated a universal code of ethics for scientists much like the Hippocratic oath for doctors in order to rebuild trust between science and the public.[39] But such an oath is not likely to have much effect as long as research scientists are so dependent upon corporations for their funding. A survey of 3,000 American scientists in 2005 found that one-third had engaged in ethically questionable practices.[40] I attribute this primarily to the starvation for funds that exists within the public sector and the resulting influence that corporate money has over scientists.

The response of politicians to my urging of a strengthened public sector might be to claim that tax reductions are nearly universally popular, but in fact it is mainly the wealthy that benefit. The question is not simply tax increases or tax reductions, but where the tax burden falls. In the United States it would probably make sense for at least the lower 50 percent of income earners to pay no income taxes at all, and for there to be steeply progressive income taxes falling mainly on the top 20 percent of wealth, income and profit. Because of capitalism's propensities towards radical inequality, taxation should be used both to promote distributive justice and to fund vastly improved research, farming, education, health care, welfare, housing, transportation and cultural expression to serve the public interest.

In 1979 the WHO issued a report based on the research of top scientists in the field that stated "vinyl chloride is a human carcinogen ... there is no evidence that there is any exposure level below which no increased risk of cancer would occur in humans".[41] The chemical industry responded to this by hiring one of the world's most respected and prestigious epidemiologists, Sir Richard Doll of Oxford University, to carry out his own research on the safety of vinyl chloride. He concluded that the dangers of vinyl chloride to human health were grossly overestimated by previous research. Doll's conclusions no doubt made it difficult to get compensation awards for workers who developed tumours from working with vinyl chloride. After his death in 2005, it was discovered that Doll had received $1,500 a day as a consultant for Monsanto (a producer of vinyl chloride) since at least 1979.[42] More recently firms that carry out tests that are supposedly scientific on behalf of US chemical corporations trying to get products approved have come under scrutiny. Industrial Biotest Labs was found guilty of the "routine falsification of data", and Craven Labs, which carries out tests for 262 pesticide companies, was found guilty of "falsifying lab notebook entries" and of "manipulating scientific equipment in order to produce false results".[43] Monsanto was found guilty of false advertising with its claim that Roundup is perfectly safe.[44]

There is increasing evidence that if there is a primary determinant of human health it is good nutrition, yet research in the area of nutrition is grossly underfunded:

> The U.S. National Institutes of Health (NIH) is responsible for funding at least 80–90 percent of all biomedical and nutrition-related research that is published in the scientific literature.... Of the $28 billion NIH budget proposed for 2004, only about 3.6 percent is designated for projects that are related in some way to nutrition.[45]

Given the nature of corporate power this is understandable, but given the role of nutrition in human health it appears to be totally irrational.

The American Council on Science and Health (ACSH), founded in 1978, defines its purpose to be a "consumer education consortium concerned with issues related to food, nutrition, chemicals, pharmaceuticals, lifestyle, the environment and health".[46] The ACSH "claims to be an 'independent, nonprofit, tax-exempt organization', but they receive 76 percent of their funding from corporations and corporate donors".[47] In their reports that have claimed among other things "that cholesterol is not related to coronary heart disease ... endocrine disruptors are not a human health problem ... and implementation of fossil-fuel restrictions to control global warming should not be implemented".[48] There are too many examples where "coming to the 'wrong' conclusions from the point of view or corporations, even though first-rate science, can damage your career. Trying to disseminate these 'wrong' conclusions to the public, for the sake of public health, can destroy your career."[49]

A favourite ploy used by corporations, when governments try to interfere with their right to sell anything to anybody using any legal means, is to appeal to individual rights enshrined in the constitution. Philip Morris offered the following Bill of Rights for Smokers:

> As a smoker, I am entitled to certain inalienable rights, among them:
> The right to the pursuit of happiness;
> The right to choose to smoke;
> The right to be treated courteously;
> The right to accommodation in the workplace;
> The right to accommodation in public places;
> The right to unrestricted access to commercial information about products;
> The right to purchase products without excessive taxation;
> The right to freedom from unnecessary government intrusion.[50]

The Center for Consumer Freedom paid for a full page advertisement in a leading US news magazine which included the following:

> You are too stupid ... to make your own food choices. At least according to the food police and government bureaucrats who have proposed 'fat taxes' on foods they don't want you to eat .... We think they are going too far. It's your food. It's your drink. It's your freedom.[51]

Elsewhere the Center for Consumer Freedom offers this statement:

> Thanks to the relentless hounding by self-appointed "nannies" – those "food cops," health-care enforcers and vegetarian activists who "know what's best for us" – people are embarrassed to speak up in defense of adult beverages, high-calorie foods or their personal pleasure of smoking. Years of obscene and inflammatory rhetoric by the nanny culture have so demonized some products that the public is starting to equate any use with product abuse.[52]

These quotations are an indication of the very active role that corporations have begun to take in advancing their ideologies in the realm of public discourse. They are also an indication of the all too frequent lowering of the level of that discourse through the use of heavy-handed demonizing rhetoric. The aim of the rhetoric in this case is to appeal to those with very little power and who need to feel the power of personal choice even when that choice comes down to little more than clinging to unhealthy addictions. Technically, it can be described as right-wing populist rhetoric, a kind of misleading rhetoric that carries with it a lot of extremely destructive historical legacies.

CONCLUSIONS

Can we implement the basic human right to food advocated in various UN documents while remaining within our current capital-ist economy? I doubt it, because such a right could only be imple-mented in a world far more egalitarian than capitalism could generate or permit. For example, most of the labour in the produc-tion of coffee is carried out by farmers, their families and associated workers, but in return for all this work, they often get less than 5 percent of the final selling price of the commodity.

While there are numerous mobilizations going on to alter the capi-talist food regime, they continually run up against the power of giant food corporations and governments that support them. The current trend is for corporations to appear to be "socially responsible", and they are making some changes, but these cannot help but remain cosmetic as long as their core obligation is to generate profit. The fundamental responsibility of corporations is to maximize profits for stock holders, but this may conflict with being socially responsible.

This chapter has just touched the surface regarding the many ways that corporate power is increasingly undermining democracy. My emphasis has been on corporate power in the agricultural and food sectors, but it is a problem in all sectors where powerful corpo-rations hold sway. The larger issue really has to do with how our economic system is undermining the most progressive ideals of our political system. Instead of advancing democracy, our economic system is destroying it. Instead of enriching our ideals of democ-racy and finding new ways to advance towards those ideals, our economic system produces cynicism about even the possibility of progressive change.

PART IV

CONCLUSIONS

9 AGRICULTURE, FOOD AND THE FIGHT FOR DEMOCRACY, SOCIAL JUSTICE, HEALTH AND SUSTAINABILITY

Today, there is a mismatch between social and private returns. Unless they are more closely aligned, the market system cannot work well.[1]

Why must we put up with a global food system that ruins rural economies worldwide, drives family and peasant farmers off the land in droves, and into slums, ghettos and international migrant streams? ... That imposes a kind of agriculture that destroys the soil, contaminates ground water, eliminates trees from rural areas, creates pests that are resistant to pesticides, and puts the future productivity of agriculture in doubt? ... Food that is laden with sugar, salt, fat, starch, carcinogenic colours and preservatives, pesticide residues and genetically modified organisms, and that may well be driving global epidemics of obesity for some (and hunger for others), heart disease, diabetes and cancer? A food system that bloats the coffers of unaccountable corporations, corrupts governments and kills farmers and consumers while wrecking the environment?[2]

Even an entire society, a nation, or all simultaneously existing societies taken together, are not the owners of the earth. They are simply its possessors, its beneficiaries, and have to bequeath it in an improved state to succeeding generations.[3]

[200]

We live in a strangely unbalanced world. The flow of revolutionary inventions in communications technology seem so advanced and so amazing, yet we have not yet learned how to feed ourselves. And to the extent that we have turned our high-tech genius towards agriculture and food, we seem to have it all wrong. I have argued that the primary reason for this is that capitalism has tried to force high and quick profits from nature, when we probably need the kind of care towards nature that would enable us to study nature deeply, and to learn as much as we can before intervening with nature's patterns and rhythms. To put it a little differently, I have argued that the profit fixation of capital has led us deeply into a dangerously unsustainable system of food provision, a system that totally fails when it comes to distributive justice and to human and environmental health.

I always feel that as an individual, it is a little presumptuous to go very far in advocating changes that need to be worked out in detail by the democratic participation of all concerned. Further, in our highly complex societies things are so interconnected that if one advocates changing one thing, then it is always possible to raise hundreds of questions about other things that are connected to it and will be impacted by changing this one thing. For these reasons, this chapter will be short and will be limited to suggesting only a small number of quite general changes. Given the depth and breadth of the problems that we face, it is easy enough to say that we need a revolution, but in the current environment, the movements that could democratically and peacefully bring about the wide and deep changes that are needed are not in existence. Lacking a massive international movement, there are many smaller steps that can be taken, and these can be very worthwhile.

CAPITALISM'S FOOD FAILURES

Perhaps what most distinguishes this book from other critiques of our system of food provisioning is the emphasis on understanding this system as it is embedded within our capitalist economy. This is important, if, as I believe, capitalism plays the fundamental role in making this system what it is. For example, the most basic problem in terms of immediate human suffering is that over 25 percent of the people in the world do not have enough to eat, and this is largely a problem created by capitalism. While coffee corporations expand profits, Ethiopian coffee workers do not make enough money for an adequate diet. The price of chocolate corporation stocks go up in response to increased profits, while cocoa growers in Ivory Coast earn so little money for their crops that in desperation they enslave children to do work that waged workers could do if the cocoa farmers had the money to pay them.

In order to help the reader understand capitalism and its impact on our agriculture and food systems, I have utilized an approach to political economy that develops three levels of analysis. At the most abstract level, I have shown how even if we imagine capitalism to be working in accord with its most perfected forms of competition and market regulation, it cannot help but operate in irrational ways when it comes to agriculture and food provision. At the level of mid-range analysis, I have shown how the phase of capital accumulation that developed its most classic operating modes in the United States after World War II relied upon chemicalization and mechanization to subsume agriculture increasingly to capitalism, with results that we are now beginning to pay dearly for. At the level of historical analysis, I have argued that the resulting fossil-fuel-based industrial agriculture, which has spread to varying extents around the world, is an ecological nightmare. Further, it distributes food globally in ways that are radically unjust, and it is unhealthy and sometimes toxic to both producers and consumers of food.

I have argued that the sort of capitalism that now exists is very close to what economists refer to as a "command economy". Typically economists contrast a "free market economy", which is highly desirable, with a "command economy" which is highly undesirable. Presumably capitalism is a free-market economy and socialism is a command economy. I contend that in our current capitalist economy this distinction is breaking down, and that we are increasingly living in a capitalist command economy. Instead of the state being in command, giant corporations are. As a result, instead of fostering democracy through public debate and public participation in governing, more and more of public life is being manipulated and commanded by corporate elites. Given the size and importance of the agriculture/food sector both in the United States and globally, food corporations are often among the top commanders.

MOVEMENTS FOR CHANGE

Some readers may feel overwhelmed by my unrelenting focus on the failures of our system of food provision. To counter such a feeling, it is important to point out that there are organizations and movements in the thousands acting to alter every one of the failures that I have highlighted, and it is relatively easy to find their webpages on the Internet.[4] Further, it is here that our advanced communications technology has, at least in principle, the possibility of being an effective organizing and mobilizing tool. As the failures of our capitalist economy become ever more obvious to more people, chances are that the rivulets of transformation that exist now will flow together into powerful rivers of change and then into an international upsurge.

There are already some very large and significant movements for change based in the global South. Most important is Via Campesina, created in 1993 as an international coalition, and as of 2004 it included 149 organizations in 56 countries. The number of member organizations is likely to increase significantly at its fifth international conference to be held in Mozambique in 2008. It is already by far the largest popular movement in the world. The Landless Workers Movement (MST) of Brazil with over 1.5 million members has utilized the tactic of land occupations to settle over 350,000 families on the land, and has served as a model for similar movements that have arisen in other countries throughout the global South.[5]

These grassroots movements generally aim to create an agrarian environment in which family farmers can make a good living by growing nutritious food for local consumption. Such an environment, more common in the past, has been progressively undermined by policies that favour export-oriented, agro-industrial monocultures. As a result, developing countries become more dependent on food imports, further undermining small family farms and making the populace dangerously dependent on increasingly expensive food imports. Since the draconian structural adjustment policies increasingly imposed on developing countries from the 1980s, movements of self-protection against big capital's tendency to drive people from the land and to leave them hungry have been particularly important. Now they are even more necessary as food prices rise globally, and this is why Via Campesina and the Brazilian Landless Workers Movement have been so successful. Via Campesina's call for "food sovereignty" is essentially an effort to find ways of insulating the rural poor from the rapaciousness of global capitalism by rebuilding healthy rural communities that are, at least to some degree, self-sufficient. At the same time, given the violent and exploitative history of colonialism and imperialism, and the devastation that this history has caused throughout the global South, it is also necessary to think about longer-term means to significantly redistribute wealth on a global scale – a redistribution that will only become possible and effective to the extent that international cooperation is far more advanced than it is today.

The world generally rallies to feed hungry people who are victims of sudden and unpredictable natural disasters, but most people who are hungry do not earn this emergency entitlement. They lack entitlement because of their location within an economic system that is predominantly capitalist. They are hungry day in and day out because of the low incomes they receive for work that is often demanding and dangerous or because they can't find work. In order to deal with this problem, there is a need to provide land, other agricultural inputs and money to poor farmers around the world. Also we need to find ways to insure that the direct producers (family farmers and field workers) receive a much higher proportion of the final retail price of their commodity: say, at least 30 percent instead of the 3 percent that is now so common. "Fair trade" products may offer a start in this direction, although often the higher price of such products makes them unaffordable for working people. This could be changed, if they were subsidized, and in turn this implies states with the will and ability to do this.

TOWARD A MORE EFFECTIVE AND ACCOUNTABLE PUBLIC SECTOR

Many changes that are needed will require well-funded and more accountable public sectors at every level from the local to the global. The funds could come from two primary sources: first, by finding ways to stop the estimated $500 billion in global tax evasion each year, and second, by instituting steeply progressive taxes on the wealth, income and profits of those in the top 20 to 30 percent of each category globally.

Resurgent public sectors from the local to the global level could redirect social and financial resources towards socially just, healthful and sustainable alternatives in all sectors of economic life. As a long-term vision, we can imagine a world government that would collect steeply progressive taxes that could be utilized to provide everyone in the world with a guaranteed annual income well above existing poverty lines, and a minimum wage of at least twice this amount. While it is sometimes useful to consider distant goals as a way of directing overall efforts even if they seem rather utopian, in the shorter term and in the context of this book, we need to find ways to provide financial, material and social supports directly to family farmers and field workers throughout the world. Agriculture and food provision needs to become the very centre of our economic life as we begin to move away from a petroleum-based agriculture towards agriculture that is more organic. Eventually most agriculture will become organic, and will orient to local markets, and will become more sustainable if for no other reason than the rising costs of petro-chemical inputs and transportation costs, as well as the host of social costs associated with industrial agriculture.

At the same time that we try to find ways to make these positive changes, we need to also think about practices that we need to get rid of. One of these is state subsidies that enable rich countries to sell their agricultural surpluses at below costs of production, thus undermining agriculture in developing countries. Indeed, all "dumping" of agricultural products on international markets at below costs of production should become illegal.

Structural adjustment policies that promote export-oriented industrial agriculture for the purpose of debt repayment should also be cancelled along with the debts that they were designed to repay.

MORE ACCOUNTABLE CORPORATIONS

Since corporations appear to be more concerned about appearing to be "socially responsible" these days, perhaps it is worth pressuring them to act more in line with the dictates of social justice and ecological sustainability. But corporations will not voluntarily do things that will reduce their profits. Thus they will need incentives or new rules to help them carry out socially responsible changes that would likely reduce their profits: changes such as paying higher wages, creating more democratic workplaces, developing more ecological production processes or working cooperatively with other corporations to advance human welfare. The public sector would need to collect sufficient revenues to financially reward corporations for reducing social costs and maximizing social benefits, since more often than not this change of behaviour would otherwise decrease profits. In other words, a new system of profiting could work against the current trend to privatize profits and socialize costs. This is not such a radical idea, if we consider the extent to which corporations are already subsidized by the state. Indeed, it would be very interesting to have someone do a study that would show the extent to which corporate profits depend upon state subsidies. The problem is that these subsidies are not currently given to corporations in accord with their contribution to human and ecological flourishing. Instead they tend to be like bribes aimed at getting corporations to locate production facilities that will create jobs, by jurisdictions that are more or less desperate for more jobs, even if they are not very good jobs.

I have often referred to making corporations more democratically accountable. Some steps have been taken in this direction, but so far they are small steps. In most cases they are steps that place limits on corporate behaviour from the outside, through legislative regulations and regulative bodies that are not very effective. The effectiveness of such regulations depends on the independence and effectiveness of the regulating bodies in enforcing the regulations. We have seen how companies that are supposed to test pesticides for toxicity have sometimes been paid off by chemical companies to falsify results. Similarly, it is doubtful that environmental assessments are always made with sufficient objectivity when "big bucks" are at stake. Consider, for example, the Alberta oil sands.

Sometimes pressure from below can be asserted to get corporations to act with greater social responsibility. Boycotts and threats of boycotts have been used with success against some corporations in order to get them to act against particularly low wages and poor working conditions. Two examples are the anti-sweatshop campaign aimed against some clothing retailers, and threats to boycott fast food chains unless the pay of tomato pickers in Florida is increased.

A basic obstacle to creating a greater degree of accountability is that corporations, by law, are considered private "legal persons". As with other legal persons, that which happens inside the realm of their privacy is walled off from the purview of the public.

The privacy of corporations means that their inner workings are generally considered secret and not open to public view or debate. As a result, finding ways of making corporations more transparent is a prerequisite to taking large steps towards public accountability. For this to happen, corporations would need to become quasi-public institutions rewarded for advancing long-term human flourishing and not short-term profits. The transparency would also facilitate public input which could improve ecological practices, labour relations, and investment decisions just to mention a few areas of importance. Realistically these changes are unlikely to occur without very significant mass mobilizations to push them forward.

It has been estimated conservatively that corporations and individuals now escape their legal obligation to pay taxes globally to the amount of $500 billion a year through a variety of tax havens, tax loopholes and tax evasion schemes.[6] One way to strengthen the public sector and increase the transparency of corporations would be to find ways to reduce corporate tax evasion through increased corporate transparency. At minimum this would require the end of tax havens, numbered bank accounts and shell corporations, as well as exposing all financial transactions to public accountability. Admittedly, this would not be easy to achieve, for any effective control of corporate tax evasion would require a great deal more international cooperation than now exists.

Given the amount of power held by corporations and their consequent impact on present and future generations, it seems highly irrational that they are mainly accountable to wealthy stockholders who are interested in short-term profits and who are not accountable to society for the social costs that they create. The "mismatch between social and private returns" mentioned by Stiglitz is not just some economic imbalance that can be rebalanced by some skilful government tinkering.[7] It is fundamentally unacceptable, because it is, in effect, loading enormous social costs onto the backs of future generations, who will have shortened and more disease-ridden lives because of polluted environments, who will have unaffordable or poor-quality food, who will need to deal continually with extreme weather, who will lack sufficient fresh water, who will face serious shortages of non-renewable resources and who will face being deluged by rising oceans. Life for everyone and particularly the poor will become much, much harder.

MAKING MARKETS DEMOCRATICALLY ACCOUNTABLE

Besides making the public sector and corporate sector more democratically accountable, we should also consider ways to make markets more democratically accountable. This implies a different orientation towards markets. Instead of simply accepting market prices, we should alter them, when by doing so, social justice and human flourishing will be advanced. For example, surtaxes could be placed on commodities or services whose life cycles generate high social costs, and commodities or services that generate high social benefits could be subsidized. In this way social costs and benefits can be internalized into market prices instead of being treated as "externalities", and market prices could be made to reflect real social costs rather than the privatization of profits and the socialization of costs, as is currently the case.

This is already done to a small extent. Because education is seen to be a great social benefit it is publicly subsidized, while because smoking has great social costs attached to it, cigarettes have a surtax placed on them. Both of these could be increased. Starved of public funds, the quality of education has declined in recent years, and schools have had to scrounge to get money from parents and the private sector. Although cigarettes are taxed in the United States, the surtaxes do not come close to reflecting the actual social costs of smoking. It has been estimated that the medical costs alone of smoking one pack of cigarettes averages \$35.[8] The inclusion of "externalities" in market prices not only requires a radical rethinking of how things are priced, it also requires the development of effective measures for translating externalities that may have large qualitative components (such as education or health) into quantitative scales.

The carbon tax is one current effort to include some of the costs of global warming in market prices by placing a surtax on carbon emissions. Such a tax could in principle be effective, but only if it really cuts down on carbon emissions and only if it is combined with policies that redistribute wealth so that those with lower incomes do not have yet more difficulty "making ends meet" because of higher prices resulting from the surtax. For even if the surtax is placed upon corporations, typically they are in a position to pass on the extra costs to consumers. Furthermore, it is not enough to leave it to the private sector and the incentives of the "carbon tax" to find ways of reducing carbon emissions; we also need massive government spending on research that promotes environmental sustainability of all kinds, and we need government subsidies directed to important areas of strategic concern. There could be a programme aimed at helping farmers convert to organic farming, to help people start new organic farms, to help farmers decrease dependency on petrochemical inputs and to encourage the development of more local farmers' markets.

Placing a surtax on cars for everyone would be problematic, since lacking effective and affordable public transportation, most people depend on cars to get to work and carry out other responsibilities. Subsidizing cars with higher gas mileage and placing a surtax on cars with lower gas mileage makes more sense. Similarly, should the price of gasoline escalate yet higher, considerations of equity might suggest that people with incomes below a certain level should receive gasoline rebates from the government. At the same time, there are many other ways of discouraging the reliance on cars, from improved public transportation to systems that would encourage the use of bicycles and car-pooling.

Democratization of the labour market is particularly important because this is where our life energy and skills get priced. Distributive justice suggests that when work is particularly exhausting, mind-numbing, or dangerous, it should be paid more; but typically it is paid less. Capitalist labour markets tend to significantly over-reward management for their skills, whether they are very skilful or not. Thus the top management of the largest units of capital receive gigantic incomes which are totally unjustifiable. Yes, their work may be stressful, but it also comes with enormous wealth and privilege. Compare the income of the CEO of a large corporation with the income of a cocoa farmer in Ivory Coast. I cannot imagine any theory of distributive justice that would argue that the expenditure of one person's life energy is worth over 1,000 times that of another.

Further, given that there will always be unmet social needs, we need to design institutions that will track these needs and that will provide the training and personnel to meet them. Everyone who wants to work should be able to work, and where training is required, it should be offered. Where people work mainly doing unpaid care giving or domestic labour, we should find ways to pay this labour. One way would be a guaranteed annual income for everyone. Clearly, one of the worst aspects of capitalism is its terrible waste of human resources through unemployment or underemployment. And arguably it is this waste combined with poverty that is the major cause of crime and most other social maladies.

CONCLUSIONS

Our desires have been channelled and rechannelled by capital's protean abilities to contain and reabsorb resistance either through the promise of increased prosperity, through distractions and opiates, or through the use of force. A basic question posed by current history is, how much room for manoeuvre does capitalism still have? While I shall not offer any sort of definitive answer to this question, radical changes are certainly called for by the current state of the global economy, and most particularly our food system.

There are three basic problems with our food system:

- The global distribution of food is radically unjust.
- Much of the food produced and the means of producing it is not healthful for consumers or producers.
- Our food system is environmentally destructive primarily because it uses up non-renewable resources, pollutes the planet and promotes global warming.

While these are global problems, the means do not now exist to achieve truly effective global solutions. Yet efforts are being made by the United Nations, though often blocked or hindered by powerful corporations or lack of international cooperation. Efforts are also being made by many NGOs. As mobilizations grow on many fronts, as I believe they will in the near future, the sorts of changes needed will become more possible. In the meantime, even small changes are worth fighting for.

At the outset of this book I explained my focus on food – not only to demonstrate the way capitalism works, but also because food provides a crossroads for global/local, rural/urban, biological/cultural, ecological and economic interests. Faced with the global dangers of our era, we must open our minds to radical alternatives that bring economics and ethics into closer contact; that will place significant advances in democracy, sustainability and social justice on the agenda; and that advance international cooperation to deal effectively with truly global problems.

NOTES

Preface

1. FAO (2007b).
2. *Economist*, April 19, 2008.
3. Gardner and Halweil (2000, 6–7).
4. Typically it is asserted that we can feed the population of the world one and half times. According to Weis (2007: 165), this is the position of the FAO. Further, a recent study at the University of Michigan states that organic farming utilizing green manures (cover crops grown out of season and ploughed under) could yield up to three times as much food as conventional farming (Worldwatch, 2008: xxvii; University of Michigan, Ann Arbor, news release, July 10, 2007).
5. Gardner and Halweil (2000: 7–8).
6. *Globe and Mail* (4/15/08). Presumably some of the meat from the destroyed swine will end up in food banks as charity for the poor.
7. Mittelstaedt (2007b).
8. Paul Roberts loses his critical edge when he refers to the current food system as having such inertia that it is like trying to alter a fundamental force of nature. Further he claims that it is an economic system, that "like all economic systems, has its winners and losers" (Roberts, 2008: xii, xxi).

Chapter 1: Introduction

1. Annan (*Independent*, March 30, 2005).
2. Marx (1981: 754).
3. Patel (2007: 293).
4. The European Union and many countries have policies to increasingly substitute ethanol for petroleum, but I mention the United States because of the size and influence of its economy as dominant in the capitalist world economy. The United States produces over 50 percent of the world's ethanol, and nearly all of the ethanol from corn.
5. Gardner and Halweil (2000: 7–8). Under the category "malnutrition" they include the overfed and underfed, or over 3 billion people.
6. The FAO estimated 852 million undernourished people globally between

2000 and 2002, and my estimate takes into account the rate at which this number has been increasing plus the recent global increase of food prices. UNICEF's (2005) statistics show that of the world's 2.2 billion children, 1 billion live in poverty. A report released by the World Bank (August 26, 2008) stated that in 2005 the number of people living in poverty (incomes of $1.25/day or less) worldwide was almost 1.4 billion. (*Economist,* August 30, 2008: 70). If these statistics seem a little at odds, that has to do with different ways of counting the poor.

7. FAO (2006: 32).
8. See Chapter 7 for a fuller account of why people eat junk food.
9. Patel (2007: 3).
10. Patel (2007: 4).
11. Marx (1976: 381). Apparently this sentence was first expressed by Madame de Pompadour (1721–1764), the favourite consort of King Louis XV (1710–1774) of France (Knowles, 2001: 580).
12. Flannery (2006: 136).
13. Manning (2004: 8).
14. FAO (2007a: 14–15), Stern (2007: 196–7).
15. The yields of most tropical crops decrease 10 percent with every degree of increase in average temperature, and the basic grain crops – wheat, rice and corn – stop growing altogether at average daytime highs above 40 degrees celsius. (See Chapter 6.)
16. See "The real costs of agrofuels" (Smolker et al. 2008: 2–3).
17. "Human flourishing" is a concept used widely in ethical theory and it usually implies providing the material and the social conditions that will enable people to develop their capacities to the fullest in ways that are ecologically friendly. (See Albritton, 2007a: ch. 7; Nussbaum, 2006).
18. See WHO (2005); World Cancer Research Fund/American Institute for Cancer Research (2007).
19. In this book I do not analyse the alcoholic beverages industry because it has so many complexities of its own. Similarly I do not focus on various addictive drugs derived from agriculture, including heroin and cocaine.
20. See Chapter 5.
21. Following Marx, I understand capitalism to refer to production that depends fundamentally on wage labour as opposed to self-employed labour.
22. According to Tony Weis (2007: 172), "agriculture is the last major productive sector to have individual artisan producers fully 'proletarianized'".
23. 2.8 billion people or 40 percent of the world's population lives on less than $2 per day, while over 1.2 billion people live on less than $1 per day. (Weis, 2007: 12).
24. In 1980 the income of the average CEO in the United States was 40 times that of an average worker. By 2003 it was 400 times. Further there has been no real growth in incomes of the bottom 20 percent of income earners since the 1970s (*Economist,* September 6, 2003).
25. US tax policy, which was mildly redistributive in the 1950s and 1960s, is so

no longer. Arguably, anyone earning $50,000 or less a year in the United States should pay no income tax, while the percentage of income going to tax should rise steeply for incomes over $100,000.

26. Brandt (2007).
27. See Chapters 4, 5 and 8.
28. Brandt (2007: 450).
29. For example, Marx writes: "Human emancipation will only be complete when the real, individual man has absorbed into himself the abstract citizen; when as an individual man, in his everyday life, in his work, and in his relationships, he has become a *species-being*; and when he has recognized and organized his own powers (*forces propres*) as *social* powers so that he no longer separates this social power from himself as *political* power." (Tucker, 1978: 46).
30. See primarily the three volumes of *Capital* and the three volumes of *Theories of Surplus Value* and *Grundrisse*.
31. See Albritton (2007a) and Albritton (1991).
32. Marx (1976: 1014).
33. Albritton (2007a).
34. Marx (1981: 216).
35. Albritton (2007a).
36. See Polanyi (1944) for a focus on the difficulties in commodifying land, labour and money.
37. Commodification is complete when the economy is governed totally by markets without any human intervention by the state, or by organizations of capitalists or workers. For a fuller discussion of commodification see Chapter 2.
38. See Albritton (1991) for a fuller discussion.
39. Albritton (2008).
40. Stern (2007: xviii).

Chapter 2: The management of agriculture and food by capital's deep structures

1. Marx (1981: 216).
2. Marx (1981: 950).
3. Marx (1981: 751).
4. England is the only place where a quasi-capitalist agriculture developed early, and this development played an important role in capitalism developing first in England.
5. Without going deeply into the issue, a capitalist farm is one in which most labour is performed by wage labourers as opposed to self-employed labour or forced labour. Of course, in practice one type may fade into another without clear boundaries. Today many large "family farms" in the United States are so integrated into the circuits of capital through contract farming that they can be considered capitalist farms. Yet globally, according to Weis (2007:

25), "Small-farm households, after all, still constitute nearly *two-fifths of humanity*".

6. Gardner and Halweil (2000: 7–15).

7. Marx (1963: 158).

8. The enclosures of commons in Britain began as early as the thirteenth century, gained momentum in the 15th and 16th centuries, and continued until the mid-nineteenth century.

9. Strict settlement meant that the eldest son would inherit the entire estate (primogeniture), thus preventing the division of the estate amongst various heirs, but only if he agreed not to sell off parts of the estate or divide it in any way.

10. See Albritton (2007a) for a much fuller discussion of the importance of "commodification" to economic theory.

11. Marx (1976: chapters 26–33).

12. Marx (1976: 254).

13. At the time of writing this is all too real.

14. For example, until they faced strong international competition that forced them to change, the American auto industry was criticized for "planned obsolescence". The poor quality of some American cars was finally exposed by books like Nader's *Unsafe at Any Speed* (1965).

15. Marx (1976: 358).

16. Read any good history of trade union organizing for many examples.

17. Many of the welfare state gains and gains of trade unions in the 1950s and 1960s were later rolled back.

18. For an interesting discussion of temporality and capitalism see Postone (1996).

19. Marx (1976: Part V).

20. The average sleep time in the United States went down 20 percent in the twentieth century, while work time is increasing, with Americans now working on average 350 hours more per year than Europeans (Worldwatch 2004: 168).

21. Braverman (1998).

22. Sadler (1832).

23. Marx (1976: chapter 10).

24. Marx (1976: 353).

25. Marx (1976: 390).

26. This book is filled with examples of this, from slaughterhouse workers in the United States to sugar cane cutters in the Dominican Republic.

27. Norris (1901).

28. See Chapters 5 and 6. Tobacco crops are particularly depleting of soil fertility.

29. *Globe and Mail* (February 24, 2007). For more on the impact of global warming on agriculture see Stern (2007), the Consultative Group on International Agricultural Research (CGIAR), Earth Policy Institute and World Agroforestry Centre.

30. With the shrinking and weakening of trade unions in the United States and the shrinking of the welfare state, it would seem that between 1965 and 2007 there has been a significant recommodification of labour power.

31. Marx (1976: 548).

32. For an analysis of Marxian crisis theory see Albritton (2008).

33. Marx (1976: Chapter 25).

34. Marx (1976: Chapter 6).

35. See Albritton (2008) for an explication of crisis theory.

36. See Chapter 5.

37. Bales (1999, 2005) and Bowe (2007).

38. Roberts (2008: 44).

39. The South Sea Bubble involved the collapse in the value of the stock of a large monopolistic trading company, and as a result, legislation was passed limiting the corporate form to existing banks and trading companies.

40. Seeing the writing on the wall, US Sugar has agreed to sell its Everglades sugar plantations for $1.75 billion to the state of Florida, which will take possession in six years.

41. For a full treatment of monopoly see Baran and Sweezy (1966) or Foster (1986).

42. Historically capitalism was slow to recognize the legal personhood of women, including so basic a right as the right to own private property. See Albritton (1991: 212).

Chapter 3: The phase of consumerism and the US roots of the current agriculture and food regimes

1. Earl Butz, US Secretary of Agriculture, 1971–76 (cited in Patel, 2007: 91).

2. Patel (2007: 120).

3. The American "sub-prime" crisis was only one of many examples of what happens when present pleasure is promoted at the cost of future pain. In this case a giant credit bubble was created by encouraging people to buy houses that they could not afford.

4. May (1999: 301).

5. For a fuller discussion of this see Albritton in Albritton et al. (2001).

6. Brandon (2002: 296).

7. See Albritton (1991) for an extended development of mid-range theory or the theory of phases or stages of capitalist development. I argue for four stages: mercantilism, liberalism, imperialism and consumerism.

8. This position differs from that of Arrighi (1994) most fundamentally because of the importance that it places upon the centrality of the commodification of labour-power to capital accumulation.

9. Pollin (1996).

10. For example, England, France, Japan and Germany were decimated by the war.

11. Brandon (2002: 379); Hoogvelt (2001).

12. Kruse and Sugrue (2006).
13. See Putnam (2000) for an account of some of the depoliticizing aspects of television.
14. See Albritton (1991) for a fuller discussion of the phase of consumerism.
15. This is an enormous topic which I shall address at greater length in a future book.
16. Shah (2004: 21). According to Hoogvelt (2001: 46), between 1950 and 1970 the price of oil declined from $4 per barrel to $1.60. Eventually OPEC raised the price to over $12 per barrel.
17. President Johnson spent $120 billion on the Viet Nam war as opposed to only $15.5 billion on the "Great Society".
18. Shah (2004: 13).
19. "A survey of living with the car", *Economist* (1996: 5).
20. "A survey of living with the car", *Economist* (1996: 5).
21. In *State of the World 2004*, Worldwatch estimated that 1 million are killed annually in auto accidents globally, but more than this die each year from air pollution (Worldwatch 2004: 29).
22. "A survey of living with the car", *Economist* (1996: 8).
23. Pollan (2006: 42).
24. Pfeiffer (2006: 7).
25. See Pfeiffer (2006) and Manning (2004).
26. Weis (2007: 108).
27. Weis (2007: 56).
28. "A survey of America", *Economist* (1991: 4).
29. See the quotation by Butz at the beginning of the chapter.
30. It has been estimated that as much as one half of the extra food since 1950 is due to chemical fertilizers (Roberts, 2008: 21).
31. Drucker (cited in Serrin, 1974: 5).
32. The auto industry enhanced car-centred development by conspiring to undermine public transportation (Shah, 2004: 14).
33. "For years I thought what was good for our country was good for General Motors and vice versa. The difference did not exist. Our company is too big. It goes with the welfare of the country" (Charles Wilson, testimony to the Senate Armed Services Committee on his proposed nomination for Secretary of Defence, January 15, 1953, reported in *New York Times*, February 24, 1953).
34. Halberstam (1986: 324).
35. Flink (1988: 278).
36. Brandon (2002: 175).
37. Cross (2000: 87); Shah (2004: 18).
38. Sheehan (2001: 9).
39. Tobacco was the largest source of ad revenues for television in the 1950s and 1960s (Davis, 2007: 149, 169).
40. Davis (2007: 157).
41. Gardner and Halweil (2000: 6–7).

42. In a 1959 Moscow speech, President Nixon bragged that of 44 million American families, 31 million owned their own homes, and that Americans owned 50 million televisions and 56 million cars (May 1999: 298).

43. There is evidence that the pace of life speeded up after World War II because of increased work time, less sleep, and surveys where, for instance, 24 percent always felt rushed in 1965 and 38 percent in 1992 (Brennan 2003: 25).

44. Davis (2007: 9).

45. See Chapter 8 for examples.

46. Davis (2007: 9).

47. Davis (2007: 10).

48. Davis (2007: 427).

49. Pressinger (1997).

50. In the 1950s tobacco was the fourth largest cash crop in the US (Brandt, 2007: 97).

51. Brandt (2007: 14); WHO (2008).

52. Davis (2007: 173).

53. Cross (2000: 91).

54. Worldwatch (2004: 168), *New Internationalist* (2002 , no. 343: 19).

55. Brandon (2002: 340). It should also be noted that the production of concrete utilizes enormous amounts of energy usually provided by coal. It has been estimated that the production of concrete contributes 5 percent of greenhouse gases globally (*Toronto Star*, January 26, 2008).

56. Glickman (1999: 303), Mason (1982: 64).

57. Mason (1982: 61).

58. Cross (2000: 88).

59. Brandon (2002: 175).

60. Glickman (1999: 5).

61. Cross (2000: 50–70).

62. Spigel and Curtin (1997: 51).

63. By the early 21st century over half of all food consumption in the United States was outside the home (Lang and Heasman, 2004: 34).

64. See Chapter 5.

65. Davis (2007: 73, 81).

66. Davis (2007: 314).

67. Spigel and Curtin (1997: 51).

68. Gauntlett and Hill (1999: 33).

69. Spigel and Curtin (1997: 2).

70. Davis (2007: 149).

71. Cross (2000: 88). In the 1950s and 1960s US tobacco farmers grew 77 percent of total global tobacco.

72. See Chapter 7 for the recent shift to aim ads at children.

73. Ford and some other corporations were already big enough in Europe to collaborate with Hitler. "When the American Ambassador to Germany, William E. Dodd, referred in an interview to 'certain American industrialists [who] had a great deal to do with bringing fascist regimes into being in both

Germany and Italy', everyone knew that his was a coded reference to Ford" (cited in Brandon, 2002: 216). Other American corporations that aided the Nazi cause included Dupont, General Motors, Standard Oil and Ethyl Corporation. (Davis, 2007: 82–6).

74. In the 1972 federal election, David Lewis, leader of the Canadian New Democratic Party, coined the phrase "corporate welfare bums" to refer to the huge handouts of taxpayer's money received by corporations.
75. Keenan (2008: B5).
76. I do not focus specific attention on the military complex because it has been so frequently written about.
77. Califano (2007: 25).
78. Shah (2004: 39).
79. Brandon (2002: 240).
80. Edwards and Morgan (2004).
81. Patel (2007: 96).
82. Brandon (2002: 296).
83. Ndiaye (2007: 209).
84. Pawlick (2006: 163). By 1956 one half of US foreign aid was food aid (Patel, 2007: 91).

Chapter 4: The historical analysis of the US-centred global food regime

1. Gardner and Halweil (2000: 6–8).
2. Ziegler (2004) cited in Weis (2007: 11).
3. Marx (1976: 811).
4. Albritton (1991: chapter 5).
5. See Duncan (1996) for a full discussion of early quasi-capitalist agriculture in England.
6. Pollan (2006: 52); Pawlick (2006: 163).
7. Because the Soviet economy was more centralized some of its ecological failures were more spectacular, but if we add up all the more decentralized US failures, I suspect they would add up to roughly the same magnitude. For example, according to Davis there are 100 trillion pounds of hazardous waste in the American environment (Davis, 2007: 330).
8. Cited in Brandt (2007: 448).
9. Chopra and Darnton-Hill (2004: 1558–60).
10. Davis (2007: 19, 61).
11. Davis (2007: 64).
12. Brandt (2007: 153,160, 183, 215, 218).
13. Califano (2007: 143).
14. From the mid-1950s until the early 1990s Big Tobacco did not pay a cent as a result of 300 cases of litigation against them (Brandt, 2007: 6).
15. According to historian of science Robert Proctor, the 1954 "Frank Statement" published in the *New York Times* by the tobacco industry "represents the

beginning of one of the largest campaigns of deliberate distortion, distraction, and deception the world has ever known" (cited in Davis, 2007: 157).

16. Professor of epidemiology and author Devra Davis as quoted in the *Toronto Star*, November 1, 2002: F4.

17. Brandt (2007: 13).

18. Cited in Brandt (2007: 503).

19. Brandt (2007: 451). Most of these new smokers are young people in developing countries. The marketing is so aggressive that Marlboro may vie with Coca-Cola for brand name recognition in some parts of the world.

20. Brandt (2007: 487). One reason the US government encouraged the export of cigarettes is that it reduced the balance of payments deficit. A more aggressive approach to exporting cigarettes dates back to the Reagan presidency, when he tried to get rid of foreign tariffs on American cigarettes (Brandt, 2007: 459).

21. In 2003 the 192 member nations of WHO adopted the Framework Convention for Tobacco Control as an effort to reduce smoking globally. It is not clear how effective this will be. The US tobacco industry opposed this convention and the United States only ratified after 140 nations had already done so (Brandt, 2007: 486).

22. Etter (2007: A1). This has no doubt changed with increases in the price of corn due to ethanol production.

23. Nestle (2006: 9).

24. In the 1950s in the US tobacco was the fourth largest crop in terms of acreage (Brandt, 2007: 97).

25. Tobacco is the most labour-intensive of the major crops. Nicotine poisoning is common amongst tobacco workers and is called "green tobacco sickness". Also there is a heavy use of chemical fertilizers and dangerous pesticides in tobacco farming (Schmitt et al., 2007; Shore, 2007). Finally recent studies have found cigarette smoke to contain carcinogenic pesticide residues. (Siegel, 2006).

26. Geist (1997: 7–9).

27. Many governments get substantial revenues from cigarette taxes, but since in China for many years the production of cigarettes was a state monopoly, the state got the profits plus the taxes.

28. Tobacco corporations have successfully blocked raising taxes on cigarettes in many states even though this is one means of reducing smoking, particularly amongst the youth (Brandt, 2007: 428). And this is even the case in the face of the fact that by 1990 smoking-related diseases were killing 500,000 Americans and costing over $2 billion per year. It has been estimated that the medical cost of smoking a pack of cigarettes is $35, and while cigarettes are taxed, the taxes do not come close to covering the social costs of smoking (*Economist,* February 9, 2008).

29. "Tobacco regulation had crashed and burned in Congress, where the tobacco lobby had proven itself so powerful and effective, but public health would finally have its day in court" (Brandt, 2007: 353).

30. Postel (2005: 13).

31. Global warming is the most severe long-term problem that humanity faces. Never has humanity faced a looming crisis that could make the earth such a radically less habitable place.

32. "According to the FAO world food prices rose by almost 40 percent in 2007" (www.fao.org/newsroom/en/news/2008/1000808).

33. Coxe, quoted in Friesen and Gee (2008).

34. Pinstrup-Anderson and Cheng (2007).

35. Friesen and Gee (2008).

36. Friesen and Gee (2008).

37. Brownell (2004: 3).

38. Lang and Heasman (2004: 53).

39. Gardner and Halweil (2000: 13). The percentage is higher now given the impacts of the sub-prime crisis, higher oil prices and higher prices for food.

40. Nestle (2006: 10). According to Nestle, "soft drinks are prototypical".

41. Unless otherwise specified I use "sugar" loosely to refer to caloric sweeteners in general including, for example, high-fructose corn syrup (HFCS).

42. Wells (2005: L1).

43. In the United States half of all food consumption is outside the home (Lang and Heasman, 2004: 34).

44. Nestle (2006: 307). Of course some processing is required simply to preserve food.

45. Kraft guacamole was discovered to have less than 2 percent avocado (*Economist*, December 16, 2006).

46. Roberts (2008: 37).

47. *New Internationalist* (2001: 29).

48. Halweil (2007: 8).

49. Center for Science in the Public Interest (2008b: 1).

50. Center for Science in the Public Interest (2008b: 1).

51. According to Brownell (2004: 43), obesity is linked to at least 30 serious medical conditions. See also Lang and Heasman (2004: 69) for a partial list.

52. Belluck (2005: A19).

53. Califano (2007: 80).

54. Schor (2004: 35).

55. Popkin (2007: 94–5).

56. "A survey of food" (*Economist*, 2003: 6).

57. Popkin (2007: 91).

58. Pollan (2006: 102).

59. According to Brennan (2003: 35), cases of asthma in the United States increased 50 percent between 1985 and 1995.

60. Putnam (2000: 261, 331).

61. Gardner and Halweil (2000: 39).

62. There is not enough research yet to establish a strong connection between diet and depression, but the research that has been done indicates that there may be a connection of some significance in many cases.

63. Lang and Heasman (2004: 36).

64. Gardner and Halweil (2000: 6–7).
65. Brandt (2007: 487).
66. Worldwatch Institute (2007a: 120).
67. Lang and Heasman (2004: 53).
68. Lang and Heasman (2004: 70).
69. Also we need to remember that sugar was the cornerstone of the slave trade.
70. I use "quasi-addictive" because there is a range of definitions of "addiction", some emphasizing the psychological and some the biological aspects.
71. Lawrence (2007: 2).
72. Brownell (2004: 29).
73. Colantuoni et al. (2002).
74. Lawrence (2007).
75. "A survey of food" (*Economist*, 2003: 16).
76. Loefler (2005).
77. Chopra and Darnton-Hill (2004: 1558–60).
78. Shor (2004: 128).
79. Roberts (2008: 97).
80. Talago (2007: A 27).
81. Weis (2007: 13).
82. Lawrence (2007: 4).
83. Lawrence (2007: 4).
84. Lawrence (2007: 4).
85. Lawrence (2007: 4).
86. Dyer (2003).
87. Pollan (2006: 109).
88. Nestle (2006: 370–1).
89. Gardner and Halweil (2000: 15), Nestle (2002: 175).
90. Nestle (2002: 178).
91. Shor (2004: 35).
92. Schlosser (2001: 122).
93. *Economist* (July 16, 2005: 60).
94 *Economist* (August 27, 2005).
95. Pfeiffer (2006: 22).
96. Nestle (2006: 321, 327).
97. Veracity (2005).
98. Global Dump Soft Drinks Campaign (2007).
99. Chopra and Darnton-Hill (2004: 1558–60).
100. Gardner and Halwiel (2000: 15).
101. Worldwatch (2007a: 120).
102. Schlosser (2001: 53).
103. Brownell (2004: 12).
104. Worldwatch (2004: 146).
105. Worldwatch (2007a: 120).
106. Sibbald (2003).
107. *Economist* (February 17, 2007).

108. "A survey of food" (*Economist*, 2003: 5).

109. Critser (2003: 131).

110. Critser (2003: 131).

111. "A survey of food" (*Economist*, 2003: 5).

112. Popkin (2007: 93). Type-2 diabetes can no longer be accurately called "late onset", with more and more cases of it appearing at earlier and earlier ages.

113. Popkin (2003: 590).

114. *Economist* (2004).

115. Worldwatch (2007a: 110).

116. *Economist* (February 9, 2008: 66).

117. Manning (2004: 10); Worldwatch (2007a: 121).

118. Diabetes doubles the risk of heart disease and stroke (*Economist*, February 17, 2007). Further the rate of increase in diagnosed cases of diabetes in the past ten years is 50 percent, and it is predicted that in 2007, 3.8 million will die worldwide (*Toronto Star*, November 14, 2007).

119. Talago (2007: A27).

120. *Economist* (December 12, 1992: 6), *New Internationalist* (2003a, 17).

121. *New Internationalist* (2003c: 23–9).

122. McKenna (2005).

123. McKenna (2005).

124. *International Herald Tribune* (June 11, 2008).

125. *Wellness Newsletter* (August 2008); Talago (2007: A27).

126. Sopinka (2007: L4).

127. Weis (2007: 4).

128. Lawrence (2006a).

129. Lawrence (2006a).

130. Weis (2007: 18).

131. Critser (2003: 32), Pfeiffer (2006: 22).

132. Nestle (2007, 75).

133. Nestle (2006: 63), Brownell (2004: 5).

134. Starmer and Wise (2007: 1–3).

135. Nierenberg (2005: 5).

136. Lang and Heasman (2004: 144).

137. Nierenberg (2005: 6).

138. Nierenberg (2005: 24); Pawlick (2006: 94).

139. Weis (2007: 72).

140. Nierenberg (2005: 47).

141. Pawlick (2006: 129).

142. Pawlick (2006: 132).

143. Dove (2003).

144. *Toronto Star* (January 25, 2004).

145. "A survey of food" (*Economist*, 2003: 8).

146. *New Internationalist* (2003c: 10).

147. *Toronto Star* (September 1, 2008).

148. Popkin (2007: 92).
149. Chopra and Darnton-Hill (2004: 1558–60).
150. Eagle (2008: 1394–5).
151. Roberts (2008: 209–10).
152. Livestock are responsible for 18 percent of annual green house gas emissions (Steinfeld et al., 2006, cited in *Globe and Mail*, August 1, 2007).
153. *New Internationalist* (2003a: 20).
154. Cited in Weis (2007: 11).
155. Pinstrup-Andersen and Cheng (2007: 96–8).
156. Pinstrup-Andersen and Cheng (2007: 98–9), Lang and Heasman (2004: 51).
157. Lang and Heasman (2004: 61).
158. By the late 1990s, 3,000 children a day were dying of malaria (malaria affects 45 percent of the world's population) and 200 million people alive in 1998 will develop tuberculosis, and yet no major pharmaceutical firm had its own research programme to find drugs that would stem the tide of these infectious diseases, because these are the diseases of the poor. In contrast the profit margin for Viagra is 98 percent (*New Internationalist*, 2001: 24).
159. Pinstrup-Andersen and Cheng (2007: 101).
160. Pinstrup-Andersen and Cheng (2007: 101).
161. *New Internationalist* (2004a: 21).
162. Pinstrup-Andersen and Cheng (2007: 98).
163. Pinstrup-Andersen and Cheng (2007: 98).
164. Pinstrup-Andersen and Cheng (2007: 99).
165. Worldwatch (2004: 6).
166. Worldwatch (2004: 153).
167. Patel (2007: 127).
168. Campbell and Hendricks (2006).
169. Davis (2006: 17), Worldwatch (2007a: 114).
170. Brown (2007: 1).
171. Brown (2007: 1).
172. Hanson (2007).
173. Hanson (2007).
174. *Globe and Mail* (April 28, 2008); *Toronto Star* (April 4, 2008; April 1, 2008).
175. *Toronto Star* (April 23, 2008).
176. *Toronto Star* (April 23, 2008).
177. Nestle (2006: 366).
178. "A survey of food" (*Economist*, 2003: 9).
179. Nestle (2006: 365).
180. Nestle (2006: 367), *Toronto Star* (May 25, 2007).
181. Lawrence (2006a).
182. Weis (2007: 17).
183. Lawrence (2008: 283).
184. Townsend (2004).
185. "The Royal Society's report on Endocrine Disrupting Chemicals and Health" claims that soy estrogens in processed foods are "possible factors

in the growth in hormone-related diseases in the west" (cited in Lawrence, 2006b).

186. *New Internationalist* (20010: 10).
187. Pfeiffer (2006: 22).
188. Pawlick (2006: 108).
189. Pfeiffer (2006: 22–3).
190. Lang and Heasman (2004: 227).
191. *Macleans* (January 26, 2004: 29).
192. Yafa (2005: 293).
193. Yafa (2005: 293).
194. Pawlick (2006: 107).
195. For examples see Chapter 9.
196. Pfeiffer (2006: 23).
197. Cone (2005: A21).
198. *Environmental Defence* (2006) "Report on families" [online] <www.toxic nation.ca>.
199. *Toronto Environmental Defence* as cited in *Toronto Star* (June 2, 2006: D1).
200. *Toronto Star* (April 21, 2006: E5).
201. *Toronto Star* (April 21, 2006: E5).
202. Patel (2007: 298).
203. Lawrence (2004: 201).
204. Davis (2007: 417).
205. *Economist* (September 15, 2007: 98).
206. Davis (2007: 423).
207. *Economist* (July 12, 2008: 73).
208. Nestle (2003: 27).
209. Nestle (2003: 44).
210. Nestle (2003: 45).
211. Nestle (2006: 266).
212. *Economist* (September 23, 2006: 33).
213. The likely source turned out to be Jalapeno peppers.
214. Nestle (2003: 137).
215. Nestle (2003: 137).
216. Nierenberg (2005: 15).
217. Nierenberg (2005: 23).
218. Barndt (2002: 18).
219. Halweil (2007: 1).
220. Halweil (2007: 1).
221. Pawlick (2006: 6).
222. Halweil (2007: 9).
223. Halweil (2007: 10).
224. Halweil (2007: 1).
225. Schor (2004: 131).
226. Pollan (2006: 71). "Downers" are cattle too sick to stand up.
227. Jacobs and Steffen (2003).

228. Halweil (2007: 10).
229. Halweil (2007: 6).
230. Halweil (2007: 6).
231. Nierenberg (2005: 23).
232. Pollan (2006: 75).
233. Halweil (2007: 11).
234. Halweil (2007: 1).
235. Halweil (2007: 4).
236. Halweil (2007: 6).
237. Smith (2007).
238. Nestle (2003: 173).
239. Lawrence (2006a).
240. Cox (1998: 2).
241. Cox (1998: 1).
242. Cox (1998: 2).
243. Ashton (2007).
244. Cox (1998: 1).
245. Richard et. al. (2005).
246. Richard et. al. (2005, Part II: 6).
247. Richard et. al. (2005, Part II: 11–13).
248. Patel (2007: 139).
249. Pollan (2006: 19).
250. Roberts (2008: 243).
251. Nestle (2006: 15).
252. Pfeiffer (2006).
253. Cook (2004).
254. Nestle (2006: 336).
255. Weis (2007: 78).
256. Smith (2007).
257. Cook (2004).
258. "Toxic food environment" was the term used by Kelly Brownell, professor at Yale University, addressing the 2001 annual convention of the American Psychological Association.
259. *Economist* (August 27, 2005).
260. See their websites for the most recent statistics.
261. Critser (2003: 23).
262. Schlosser (2001: 117).
263. Martin (2007).
264. Starmer and Wise (2007).
265. Schlosser (2001: 102).
266. "A survey of food" (*Economist,* 2003: 10).
267. See the Universal Declaration of Human Rights, article five, and the International Covenant of Economic, Social and Cultural Rights, article eleven.

Chapter 5: The health of agriculture and food workers

1. Statement of Richard Estrada, Commissioner, US Commission on Immigration Reform before House Judiciary Subcommittee on Immigration, December 7, 1995. Available at: <www.utexas.edu/lbj/uscir/120795.html>.
2. *Economist* (December 8, 2007: 11).
3. Lien and Nerlick (2004: 201).
4. *New Internationalist* (2003a: 20).
5. *Economist* (September 6, 2003: 28), Lang and Heasman (2004: 90), Hacker (2004), *New Internationalist* (2004a).
6. Employment in manufacturing in the United States has decreased from 21.6 percent in 1979 to 9.86 percent in 2005 (Lardner, 2007).
7. Schlosser (2001: 4).
8. Hacker (2004: 38).
9. Schlosser (2001: 6).
10. According to legislation passed by Congress in 2007, the minimum wage is due to increase slightly (relative to its extremely low level) over the next several years.
11. *Business Week* (May 31, 2004: 50).
12. Hacker (2004: 39).
13. Read (2006: 1), *Economist* (October 21, 2006: 31).
14. *Economist* (September 10, 2005).
15. Ahn, Moore and Parker (2004: 2).
16. The poverty threshold for a single person under 65 in 2006 according to the US Census Bureau was an annual income of $10,488.
17. Ahn, Moore and Parker (2004: 2).
18. Ahn, Moore and Parker (2004: 2).
19. Herro (2007: 1).
20. Ahn, Moore and Parker (2004: 2–3).
21. Ahn, Moore and Parker (2004: 2–3).
22. Read (2006: 20).
23. Ahn, Moore and Parker (2004: 3).
24. *New Internationalist* (2003c: 23).
25. Bales defines slavery thus: "the state of control exercised over the slave based on violence or its threat, a lack of any payment beyond subsistence, and the theft of the labor or other qualities of the slave for economic gain" (Bales, 2005: 9).
26. McKenna (2005).
27. McKenna (2005).
28. All of this information about the sugar industry comes from McKenna (2005).
29. Rosset (2006: 49), Cook (2004).
30. *Economist* (September 9, 2006: 35).
31. *Economist* (September 9, 2006: 35).
32. *Economist* (March 26, 2005: 34).
33. *New Internationalist* (2007a, 12).

34. *New Internationalist* (2003a: 18).
35. *New Internationalist* (2003a: 19).
36. Yafa (2005: 306).
37. Rosset (2006: 42).
38. Yafa (2005: 305–6).
39. *Economist* (January 20, 2007: 34); *New Internationalist* (2007a: 13).
40. Since 1998, 150,000 Indian farmers have committed suicide (Fatah, *Star*, March 24, 2008).
41. Rosset (2006: 42).
42. Patel (2007: 37).
43. *New Internationalist* (2007a: 13).
44. Yafa (2005: 293).
45. Worldwatch (2004:163).
46. Weis (2007: 83).
47. *New Internationalist* (2003a: 10).
48. Schlosser (2002: 117).
49. *New Internationalist* (2003a: 10).
50. *Economist* (March 24, 2000: 16).
51. Ahn, Moore and Parker (2004: 3).
52. Ahn, Moore and Parker (2004: 3).
53. Striffler (2005: 8).
54. Parker (2006).
55. Striffler (2005: 115).
56. Cited in Striffler (2005: 129).
57. Schlosser (2002: 174).
58. Nierenberg (2005: 19).
59. Human Rights Watch (2008: 35).
60. Barndt (2002).
61. Schlosser (2002: 6).
62. Schlosser (2001: 68).
63. Schlosser (2002: 73).
64. Lardner (2007: 63).
65. Patel (2007: 37).
66. Schlosser (2002: 72).
67. Schlosser (2002: 72).
68. Schlosser (2002: 73).
69. Barndt (2002: 94).
70. *New Internationalist* (2003a: 12).
71. Worldwatch (2007a: 111).
72. *Economist* (March 24, 2000: 15); Weis (2007: 26).
73. Patel (2007: 37).
74. Robbins (2003: 13).
75. Robbins (2003: 3).
76. Robbins (2003: 15).
77. McKay and Miller (2005).

78. Patel (2007: 44).
79. Weis (2007: 69).
80. Davis (2006: 16).
81. Davis (2006: 23).
82. Rosset (2006: 62), Ahn, Moore and Parker (2004: 4).
83. Ahn, Moore and Parker (2004: 4).
84. Ahn, Moore and Parker (2004: 4).
85. Koeppel (2008: xiii).
86. Lang and Heasman (2004: 152).
87. Berube (2005: 2).
88. Berube (2005: 4).
89. Anitel (2007).
90. Berube (2005: 3).
91. Silva (2007: 2).
92. Berube (2005: 2).
93. Anitel (2007), Softpedia (2007), Wikipedia (2008), Silva (2007a, 2007b), Miller (2007), International Committee in Solidarity with the Victims of Nemagon (2008), Envio (2008), Berube (2005).
94. Anitel (2007).
95. Berube (2005: 5).
96. Berube (2005: 5).
97. Anitel (2007).
98. Human Rights Watch (2002).
99. *Toronto Star* (November 1, 2002).
100. Weis (2007: 31), Pawlick (2006: 126).
101. Yafa (2005: 293).
102. *New Internationalist* (2000: 23). According to Off, in 2002 "the cocoa companies agreed to accept a six-point program designed to eliminate child slave labour in the cocoa chain". In the wording, the companies substituted "the worst forms of child labour" for "child slave labour". The "worst forms of child labour" were to be eliminated by July 1, 2005. That date has now passed without the goal being reached. "Nowhere in the agreement does it suggest that the cocoa companies might simply undertake to make sure the farmers received a decent price for their beans. And yet almost every critic of the industry has identified the key problem: poverty among the primary producers" (Off, 2006: 144–6).
103. Off (2006: 146).
104. Off (2006: 140).
105. Mull and Kirkhorn (2005: 5).
106. Off (2006: 123–52).
107. Off (2006: 199).
108. BBC news (4/6/07).
109. *Human Rights Watch* (2004).
110. Etter (2007).
111. Etter (2007).

112. *New Internationalist* (2004b: 12).
113. *New Internationalist* (2004b: 12).
114. *New Internationalist* (2004b: 11).
115. *New Internationalist* (2004b: 11). Malawi is losing 3 percent of its forests per year. This is one of the fastest rates of deforestation in the world (Poitras, May 11, 1999).
116. *New Internationalist* (2004b: 18).
117. *New Internationalist* (2004b: 18).
118. Talbot (2004: 2).
119. OXFAM (2007).
120. Talbot (2004: 55).
121. Talbot (2004: 101, 115).
122. OXFAM (2003).
123. "Out of a $3 cappuccino that you might buy at a cafe, only 3 cents goes to the farmer who grew the beans" (World Vision, 2006).
124. *Guardian* (September 16, 2005).
125. Such low pay is common. For example, tea estates in Sri Lanka that employ 5 percent of all workers pay only $2 per day.
126. Talbot (2004: 103, 113).
127. Talbot (2004: 115).
128. Cohn (2005: A 13).
129. Smolker et al. (2008: 27).
130. Graham-Harrison (2007: B3).
131. Smolker et al. (2008: 29).

Chapter 6: Agriculture, food provisioning and the environment

1. Worldwatch (2008: 75).
2. Marx (1981: 948–9).
3. President Nixon, 1970 State of the Union Address (cited in Davis, 2007: 329).
4. Davis (2007: 9).
5. For example, President Reagan actually cut spending for testing chemicals. (Davis, 2007: 9).
6. Pfeiffer (2006: 19).
7. Manning (2004: 8).
8. Shah (2004: 149).
9. Woynillowicz (2007: 4).
10. Woynillowicz (2007: 5).
11. Worldwatch, (2004: 37); Pollan (2006: 83).
12. The percentage produced by the United States has lessened as it has been overtaken by China (Worldwatch, 2004: 11).
13. Manning (2004: 8).
14. Shah (2004: 144, 171).

15. Pfeiffer (2006: 7).
16. Cook (2004).
17. Pfeiffer (2006: 19).
18. Cook (2004).
19. *Toronto Star* (June 29, 2008).
20. Cook (2004).
21. Shah (2004: 45).
22. Roberts (2008: 223).
23. Pfeiffer (2006: 21).
24. Priesnitz (2007).
25. Nestle (2006: 139).
26. Nierenberg (2005: 27–9).
27. More in total because corn is such a large crop. Cotton uses more pesticides per acre.
28. Weis (2007: 33).
29. Weis (2007: 42).
30. Shah (2004: 168), Graham-Harrison (2007).
31. Monfort (2008: 1), Smolker et al. (2008: 15).
32. Smolker et al. (2008: 9).
33. Fifty percent of global ethanol production in 2006 was from corn. Corn farmers alone received $9.4 billion in federal subsidies in 2005. See Smolker et al. (2008: 15–16).
34. Roberts (2008: 216).
35. Roberts (2008: 48).
36. Roberts (2008: 17).
37. Smolker et al. (2008: 17).
38. Smolker et al. (2008: 57). The meaning of "biofuel" is a little wider in meaning than "agrofuel" because it could include any biological matter and not simply matter from agriculture.
39. Smolker et al. (2008: 20–5).
40. Smolker et al. (2008: 3).
41. Wilson (2007: C6).
42. Brown (2007).
43. Brown (2007).
44. Engdahl (2008); Hurst (2008); Chakrabortty (2008).
45. *Economist* (December 8, 2007: 11).
46. FAO (2007b).
47. Spencer (December 27, 2007).
48. This adds up to 35.1 million suffering frequent hunger (Patel, 2007: 3).
49. Spencer (December 22, 2007).
50. Pfeiffer (2006: 42).
51. Spencer (2007).
52. Shah (2004: 168).
53. Pollan (2006: 54).
54. Flannery (2006: 71).

55. Worldwatch (2008: xxiv).
56. *Economist* (June 2, 2007: 64).
57. Flannery (2006: 136).
58. *Globe and Mail* (September 2, 2007).
59. Hanson (2006: 13).
60. Flannery (2006: 136).
61. The latest study produced by the University of California and to be published in the *Journal of Environmental Economics and Management* estimates that China passed the United States in total greenhouse gas emissions in 2006 (Hanson, 2006: 16; *Economist*, January 27, 2007: 24).
62. Smolker et al. (2008: 4).
63. Smolker et al. (2008: 27).
64. *Globe and Mail* (September 1, 2007, January 5, 2008, October 12, 2007).
65. Preisnitz (2007).
66. Presnitz (2007).
67. Not only is nitrous oxide a long-lasting greenhouse gas, nitrates that get in the drinking water are also a risk factor for premature births.
68. Mittelstaedt (2007c: A8).
69. Lang and Heasman (2004: 231).
70. Roberts (2008: 147).
71. Flannery (2006: 130).
72. Mittelstaedt (2007b).
73. Mittelstaedt (2007b).
74. Pfeiffer (2006: 13).
75. Davis (2007: 330).
76. "A survey of agriculture and technology" (*Economist*, 2000), *Economist* (July 19, 2003).
77. Pfeiffer (2006: 16).
78. Pfeiffer (2006: 12).
79. Leahy (2007: 1).
80. *Independent* (May 14, 2007).
81. Cited in *Independent* (May 14, 2007).
82. Shah (2004: 128).
83. Worldwatch (2007a: 103).
84. Smolker et al. (2008: 50).
85. Smolker et al. (2008: 50).
86. Weis (2007: 33).
87. Worldwatch (2008: 109).
88. Weis (2007: 42, 64).
89. Weis (2007: 42).
90. *Economist* (July 12, 2008: 94).
91. Flannery (2006: 113).
92. Flannery (2006: 114).
93. Weis (2007: 32).
94. Roberts (2008: 229).

95. *Economist* (December 8, 2007: 41).
96. *Economist* (December 8, 2007: 41).
97. Nestle (2006: 405).
98. Weis (2007: 33).
99. Worldwatch (2008: xxvi), Indiana School of Medicine (2007).
100. *Nature* (7 November 2006).
101. Worldwatch (2007a: 92).
102. Flannery (2006: 99).
103. Weis (2007: 31).
104. Worldwatch (2008: xxiv).
105. Nestle (2006: 206).
106. Worldwatch (2008: 67).
107. *Science* (November 3, 2006).
108. *New Internationalist* (2003b: 7)
109. Worldwatch (2008: 61).
110. Worldwatch (2007a: 26).
111. Worldwatch (2008: 68).
112. Preisnitz (2007).
113. Flannery (2006: 110).
114. *New Internationalist* (2002: 19).
115. *New Internationalist* (2000: 10).
116. Koeppel (2008).
117. Roberts (2008: 219).
118. Patel (2007: 138).
119. "In India in 2005, the Indian state of Andhra Pradesh (population 75 million) banned Monsanto from licensing its genetically modified cotton seed on the grounds that they had been ineffective. Yields were lower, and more prone to disease, than non-genetically modified crops" (Patel, 2007: 138).
120. Roberts (2008: 262).
121. Worldwatch (2008: xxvii).
122. Patel (2007: 140).
123. *Toronto Star* (February 9, 2008).
124. Chakrabarti (2007: 1).
125. Nieremberg (2005: 5).
126. Lang and Heasman (2004: 144).

Chapter 7: Food, marketing and choice in the United States

1. Schor (2004: 190).
2. Linn (2004: 1).
3. Linn (2004: 6).
4. Brandt (2007: 79–80).
5. Brandt (2007: 79–80).
6. Davis (2007: 4).
7. Davis (2007: xiii).

8. Smoking cigarettes is the second leading cause of death in the world (Epstein, 2007: 38).
9. Brandt (2007: 153).
10. Epstein (2007: 38).
11. Brandt (2007: 167).
12. Brandt (2007: 394).
13. Califano (2006: 143).
14. Brandt (2007: 227).
15. Brandt (2007: 249).
16. Brandt (2007: 249).
17. Brandt (2007: 459).
18. Brandt (2007: 7–9).
19. Brandt (2007: 10).
20. Nestle (2006: 64). "Food is an area where influence marketing and the decline of parental control has been most pronounced" (Schor, 2004: 24).
21. Schor (2004: 121), Gardner and Halweil (2000: 29), Nestle (2006: 64).
22. Schor (2004: 128).
23. Putnam (2000: 222, 240).
24. Schor (2004: 33).
25. Linn (2004: 6).
26. Schor (2004: 11).
27. Patel (2007: 271).
28. *Economist* (December 2, 2006: 66).
29. Linn (2004: 1).
30. Schor (2004: 203).
31. Schor (2004: 13).
32. Linn (2004: 49).
33. Schor (2004: 20).
34. Schor (2004: 23).
35. Schor (2004: 21).
36. Schor (2004: 12).
37. Schor (2004: 23).
38. Schor (2004: 120).
39. *Toronto Star* (June 11, 2006); US Census Bureau (2006b; 2007: 709).
40. Schor (2004: 128).
41. Schor (2004: 126).
42. Schor (2004: 34).
43. Center for Science in the Public Interest (2008b: 1).
44. Schor (2004: 134).
45. Worldwatch (2004: 14).
46. Schor (2004: 35).
47. Brownell (2004: 112).
48. Moyer (2005: 169–79); Weeks (2008).
49. Schlosser and Wilson (2006: 58–62).
50. Linn (2004: 89).

51. Roberts (2008: 105).
52. Schor (2004: 88).
53. Schor (2004: 121).
54. Critser (2003: 47).
55. Center for Science in the Public Interest (2008a: 1). "Consumer organizations in 20 countries today urged the Coca-Cola company and PepsiCo to limit soft drink marketing and help stem the global tide of childhood obesity. The letters are the latest salvo in the Global Dump Soft Drinks Campaign launched last fall."
56. Schor (2004: 94).
57. Schor (2004: 93).
58. Schor (2004: 93).
59. Schor (2004: 86).
60. Linn (2004: 97).
61. Linn (2004: 103).
62. Patel (2007: 280).
63. Schor (2004: 35, 167).
64. *New Internationalist* (2004: 6).
65. Brownell (2004: 13), Patel (2007: 271).
66. Schor (2004: 24).
67. Davis (2007: 9).
68. Schor (2004: 203).

Chapter 8: Corporate power, food and liberal democracy

1. Brandt (2007: 51).
2. Brandt (2007: 53).
3. Patel (2007: 258).
4. For example, right-wing Nicaraguan Contras in their war against the Revolutionary Sandanista government (1981–90) were funded in part by a cocaine trade which the CIA secretly facilitated and which resulted in a very significant increase of cocaine use in the United States. At the same time as the CIA was turning a blind eye to the importation of cocaine into the United States, the US government was supposedly carrying out a "war on drugs" which resulted in huge numbers of inner city blacks being incarcerated (Scott and Marshall, 1998).
5. Nestle (2003: 14), Cox (1998: 12).
6. The Center for Science in the Public Interest has launched a campaign against food disparagement laws, which now exist in 13 states. See <www.cspinet.org/foodspeak/laws/existlaw.htm>.
7. Brandt (2007: 380–4).
8. Brandt (2007: 167).
9. A good example of this is the recent effort by industry to get Congress to subsidize ethanol production.
10. Lang and Heasman (2004: 147).

11. Lang and Heasman (2004: 150).

12. Nestle (2006: 9–10).

13. Jacobs and Dube (2004: 1), Wright (2005), Good Jobs First (2008). According to Wright (2005), "investigators documented 244 Wal-Mart subsidy deals with a total value over $1 billion".

14. Brandt (2007: 469).

15. Brandt (2007: 484).

16. When Brandt was writing his book in 2006, the United States had not yet ratified the FCTC, which by then had been ratified by 140 countries (Brandt, 2007: 486).

17. The Report of the Joint WHO/FAO Expert Consultation on Diet, Nutrition, and the Prevention of Chronic Diseases was launched in Rome on April 23, 2003.

18. Schor (2004: 129).

19. Lawrence (2008: 143), International Baby Food Action Network (2006).

20. New York Times (September 1, 2004).

21. Schor (2004: 129).

22. The Center for Science in the Public Interest has worked hard without success to get the food industry to put the total of added sugars on labels.

23. Nestle (2003).

24. Schor (2004: 131); Greenpeace (August 8, 2008) recently announced that as a result of consumer pressure Monsanto has decided to stop producing bovine growth hormone rBST.

25. Smolker et al. (2008: 16).

26. Schor (2004: 130).

27. Berube (2005: 6).

28. Davis (2007).

29. Campbell and Campbell (2006: 3).

30. Davis (2007: 77).

31. Davis (2007: 96).

32. Davis (2007: 105).

33. Davis (2004: 154–6).

34. Cited in Davis (2006: 157). Robert Proctor "Tobacco and Health," expert witness report filed on behalf of plaintiffs in the USA, Plaintiff v. Philip Morris, reprinted in Journal of Philosophy, Science, and Law, No.4 (March 2004).

35. Brandt (2007: 306).

36. Brandt (2007: 306–7).

37. Berube (2005: 4).

38. Patel (2008: 139).

39. McIlroy, Globe and Mail (December 15, 2007).

40. McIlroy, Globe and Mail (December 15, 2007).

41. Davis (2007: 377).

42. Davis (2007: 378).

43. Cox (1998: 11).

44. Cox (1998: 12).
45. Campbell and Campbell (2006: 314–15).
46. Campbell and Campbell (2006: 260).
47. Campbell and Campbell (2006: 260).
48. Campbell and Campbell (2006: 260).
49. Campbell and Campbell (2006: 265).
50. Brandt (2007: 299–300).
51. Brownell (2004: 274).
52. Brownell (2004: 274).

Chapter 9: Agriculture, food and the fight for democracy, social justice, health and sustainability

1. Stiglitz (2008).
2. Rosset (2006: 79).
3. Marx (1981: 911).
4. For example, I have referred to the Center for Science in the Public Interest, Worldwatch, Baby Milk Action, the Organic Center, Bread for the World Institute, Earth Policy Institute, the Canadian Centre for Policy Alternatives, Commercial Alert, Human Rights Watch, Earthscan, Reclaim Democracy, Envio, Environmental Defense, Global Dump Soft Drinks Campaign, International Committee in Solidarity with Victims of Nemagon, Commercialization in Education Research Unit, OXFAM, Grist, Global Forest Coalition, World Vision, Pesticide Action Network, Greenpeace, Corporate Watch and Good Jobs First.
5. See Patel (2007) for an extended discussion of these organizations and others.
6. Gillespie (*Economist,* April 28, 2008).
7. See note 1.
8. *Economist* (February 9, 2008: 65).

BIBLIOGRAPHY

Ahn, C, Moore, M. and Parker, N. (2004) "Migrant farmworkers: America's new plantation workers", *Backgrounder*, Food First, Spring, Vol. 10, No. 2 [online] <www.foodfirst.org/pubs/backgrdrs/2004/sp04v10n2.html>.

Albritton, R. (1991) *A Japanese Approach to Stages of Capitalist Development*, London: Macmillan.

Albritton, R. (1993) "Did agrarian capitalism exist?" *Journal of Peasant Studies*, Vol. 20, No. 3, April.

Albritton, R. (1995a) "Theorising the realm of consumption in Marxian political economy", in R. Albritton and T. Sekine (eds), *A Japanese Approach to Political Economy, Unoist Variations*, Basingstoke, Hampshire: Macmillan.

Albritton, R. (1995b) "Regulation theory, a critique", in R. Albritton and T. Sekine (eds), *A Japanese Approach to Political Economy, Unoist Variations*, Basingstoke, Hampshire: Macmillan.

Albritton, R. (2003b) "Marx's value theory and subjectivity", in R. Westra and A. Zuege (eds), *Value and the World Economy Today*, Basingstoke: Palgrave.

Albritton, R. (2004a) "Socialism and individual freedom", in R. Albritton et al. (eds), *New Socialisms, Futures Beyond Globalisation*, London: Routledge.

Albritton, R. (2007a) *Economics Transformed: Discovering the Brilliance of Marx*, London: Pluto.

Albritton, R. (2007b) "Objectivity and Marxian political economy", in J. Frauley and F. Pearce (eds), *Critical Realism and the Social Sciences: Heterodox Elaborations*, Toronto: University of Toronto Press.

Albritton, R. (2007c) "Eating the future: capitalism out of joint", in R. Albritton, R. Jessop and R. Westra (eds), *Political Economy and Global Capitalism: The 21ˢᵗ Century, Present and Future*. London: Anthem.

Albritton, R. (2008) "Marxian crisis theory and causality", in R. Groff (ed.), *Revitalizing Causality: Realism about Causality in Philosophy and Social Science*, London: Routledge.

Albritton, R., Itoh, M., Westra, R. and Zuege, A. (eds) (2001) *Phases of Capitalist Development*, Basingstoke, Hampshire: Palgrave.

Albritton, R. and Simoulidis, J. (eds) (2003) *New Dialectics and Political Economy*, Basingstoke, Hampshire: Palgrave.

Albritton, R., Bell, S., Bell, J. and Westra, R. (eds) (2004) *New Socialisms, Futures Beyond Globalization*, London: Routledge.

Albritton, R., Jessop, R. and Westra, R. (eds) (2007) *Political Economy and Global Capitalism: The 21ˢᵗ Century, Present and Future*, London: Anthem.

Anderson, M. (2006) "Why cancer pandemic", *Toronto Star*, October 30.

Anelauskas, V. (1999) *Discovering America As It Is*, Atlanta, Ga.: Clarity Press.

Anitel, S. (2007) "Nemagon, the pesticide that kills people: a history of infamy", *Softpedia*, May 15.

Arrighi, G. (1994) *The Long Twentieth Century: Money, Power, and the Origins of Our Times*, London: Verso.

Ashton, G. (2007) "Multiple studies show Roundup is toxic", *Cape Times*, March 16.

Baby Milk Action (2008) "Tackling obesity—watch out for undue corporate influence", Baby Milk Action [online] <www.babymilkaction.org>.

Baker, J. (1987) *Arguing for Equality*, London: Verso.

Bales, K. (1999) *Disposable People*, Berkeley: University of California Press.

Bales, K. (2005) *Understanding Global Slavery*, Berkeley: University of California Press.

Baran, P. and Sweezy, P. (1966) *Monopoly Capital*, New York: Monthly Review.

Barndt, D. (ed.) (1999) *Women Working the NAFTA Food Chain*, Toronto: Second Story Press.

Barndt, D. (2002) *Tangled Routes: Women, Work, and Globalization on the Tomato Trail*, Aurora, Ontario: Garamond Press.

Bartlett, D. L. and Steele, J. B. (2008) "Monsanto's Harvest of Fear", *Vanity Fair*, May.

Battacharya, S. (2003) "Cut sugar to battle obesity," New Scientist, March 3 [online] <www.newscientist.com/article.ns?id=dn3453>.

BBC news (2007) "Slavery behind Easter chocolate," BBC Newsvote, April 6 [online] <http://newsvote.bbc.co.uk?mpapps/pagetools/print/news.bbc.co.uk/1/hi/uk/6533405.stm>.

Belluck, P. (2005) "Obesity could shrink average life span, study says", *Globe and Mail*, March 17.

Benbrook, C. et al. (2008) "New evidence confirms the nutritional superiority of plant-based organic foods", Organic Center [online] <www.organic-center.org>.

Bergson, H. (2007) *Creative Evolution*, Basingstoke: Palgrave.

Berube, N. (2005) "Chiquita's children", *In These Times*, May.

Bowe, J. (2007) *Nobodies: Modern American Slave Labor and the Dark Side of the New Global Economy*, New York: Random House.

Brandon, R. (2002) *Automobile: How the Car Changed Life*, London: Macmillan.

Brandt, A. (2007) *The Cigarette Century*, New York: Basic Books.

Brass, T. (2000) *Peasants, Populism, and Postmodernism*, London: Frank Cass.

Braverman, H. (1998) *Labor and Monopoly Capital*, New York: Monthly Review.

Bread For the World Institute (2003) *Agriculture in the Global Economy*, Washington D.C.

Brennan, T. (2003) *Globalization and Its Terrors*, London: Routledge.

Brown, E. and Jacobson, M. (2005) "Cruel oil", Center for Science in the Public Interest, May.

Brown, L. (2004) *Outgrowing the Earth*, New York: W. W. Norton.

Brown, L. (2007) "World may be facing highest grain prices in history", Earth Policy Institute, January 5.

Brownell, K. (2004) *Food Fight: The Inside Story of the Food Industry, America's Obesity Crisis and What We Can Do About It*, New York: McGraw-Hill.

Business Week (2004) May 31, pp. 50–5.

Buttel, F. H. and McMichael, P. (2005) *New Directions in the Sociology of Global Development*, Oxford: Elsevier.

Calamai, P. (2007) "Whither the revered scientist?" *Toronto Star*, November 4, 2007.

Califano, J. A. (2007) *High Society: How Substance Abuse Ravages America and What to do About It*, New York: Public Affairs.

Campbell, C. and Campbell, T. (2006) *The China Study*, Dallas, Texas: Benbella Books.

Campbell, M. and Hendricks, T. (2006) "Mexico corn farmers see their livelihoods wither," *San Francisco Chronicle*, July 31.

Canby, P. (2005) "The specter haunting Alaska", *New York Review of Books*, November 17.

Carson, R. (1962) *Silent Spring*, Boston: Houghton Mifflin.

Center for Science in the Public Interest (CSPI) (2008a) "Consumer groups in 20 countries urge Coke, Pepsi to limit soft drink marketing to children", January 3.

Center for Science in the Public Interest (CSPI) (2008b) "Obesity on the kids' menus at top chains", August 4.

Chakrabarti, M. (2007) "And how would you like that cooked?....Green", Wbur.org [online] <www.wbur.org/news/local/dininggreen/story.asp>.

Chakrabortty, A. (2008) "Secret report: biofuel caused food crisis," *Guardian,* July 4.

Chopra, M. and Darnton-Hill, I. (2004) "Tobacco and obesity epidemics: not so different after all," *British Medical Journal*, No. 328, June 26, pp. 1558–60.

Clarke, T. (2007) *Inside the Bottle: Exposing the Bottled Water Industry*, Ottawa: Canadian Centre for Policy Alternatives.

Cohn, M. R. (2005) "Finally a chance to escape plantation," *Toronto Star*, October 23, p. A 13.

Colantuoni, C. et al. (2002) "Evidence that intermittent, excessive sugar intake causes endogenous opioid dependence," *Obesity Research* No. 10, pp. 478–88.

Commercial Alert (2005) "American Diabetic Society bought off", 16 May [online] <www.commercialalert.org>.

Cone, M. (2005) "Dozens of chemicals found in most Americans' bodies", *Los Angeles Times*, July 22, p. A21.

Cook, C. (2004) "Thanksgiving's hidden costs", Alternet, November 23 [online] <http://www.alternet.org/story/20556>.

Cox, C. (1998) "Glyposate factsheet", *Journal of Pesticide Reform*, Vol. 108, No. 3, Fall [online] <www.mindfully.org/Pesticide/Roundup>.

Critser, G. (2003) *Fat Land: How Americans Became the Fattest People in the World*, New York: Houghton Mifflin.

Cross, G. (1993) *Time and Money: The Making of Consumer Culture*, London: Routledge.

Cross, G. (2000) *All-Consuming Century*, New York: Columbia.

Crouzet, F. (1982) *Capital Formation in the Industrial Revolution*, London: Methuen.

Darrah, C. N., Freeman, J. M. and English-Lueck, J. A. (2007) *Busier Than Ever: Why American Families Can't Slow Down*, Stanford, Calif.: Stanford University Press.

Davis, D. (2007) *Secret History: War on Cancer*, New York: Basic Books.

Davis, K. (1996) *Poisoned Chickens Poisoned Eggs*, Summertown, Tennessee: Book Publishing.

Davis, M. (2006) *Planet of Slums*, London: Verso.

De La Perriere, R. A .B. and Seuret, F. (2000) *Brave New Seeds: The Threat of GM Crops to Farmers*, Halifax, NS: Fernwood.

de Villiers, M. (1999) *Water*, Toronto: Stoddart.

Dolphijn, R. (2004) *Foodscapes: Towards a Deleuzian Ethics of Consumption*, Delft, Holland: Eburon.

Dove, R. (2003) "The American meat factory", in A. M. Ervin, C. Holtslander, D. Qualman and R. Sawa (eds), *Beyond Factory Farming: Corporate Hog Barns and the Threat to Public Health, the Environment, and Rural Communities*, Saskatoon: Canadian Center for Policy Alternatives.

Dow, K. and Downing, T. E. (2006) *The Atlas of Climate Change*, London: Earthscan.

Duncan, C. A. M. (1996) *The Centrality of Agriculture,* Montreal: McGill-Queen's University Press.

Dyer, G. (2003) "Sugar lobby copies big tobacco", *Toronto Star*, April 29.

Eagle, K. (2008) "Coronary artery disease in India: challenges and opportunities", *The Lancet*, Vol. 371, No. 9622, April 26, pp. 1394–5.

Economist (1991) "A survey of America", October 26.

Economist (1993) "A survey of the food industry", December 4.

Economist (1994) "A survey of television", February 12.

Economist (1996) "A survey of living with the car", June 22.

Economist (2000) "A survey of agriculture and technology", March 25.

Economist (2003) "A survey of food", December 13.

Edwards, J. and Morgan, M. (2004) "Abolish corporate personhood", [online] <www.reclaimdemocracy.org/personhood/edwards_morgan_corporate.html>.

Eisenitz, G. (1997) *Slaughterhouse*, New York: Prometheus.

Ellis, H. (2007) *Planet Chicken*, London: Sceptre.

Ellwood, W. (2001) *The No-Nonsense Guide to Globalization*, Toronto: New Internationalist Publications.

Engdahl, F. W. (2008) "World Bank Secret Report Confirms Biofuel Cause of World Food Crisis", *Global Research*, July 10 [online] <www.global esearch.ca/index.php?context=va&aid=9547>.

Engler, M. (2003) "Cattail country", *New Internationalist,* No. 363.

Envio (2008) "Victims of Nemagon hit the road", Envio [online] <www.envio. org.ni/articulo/2972>.

Environmental Defence (2005) *Toxic Nation* [online] <www.toxicnation.ca>.

Environmental Defence (2006) *Toxic Families* [online] <www.toxicnation.ca>.

Epstein, H. (2007) "Getting away with murder", *New York Review of Books*, July 19, pp. 38–40.

Etter, L. (2007) "Nicotine buzz: U.S. farmers rediscover the allure of tobacco", *Wall Street Journal*, September 18.

UN Food and Agriculture Organization (FAO) (2006) *The State of Food Insecurity in the World*, Rome.

FAO (2007a) *The State of Food and Agriculture: Paying Farmers for Environmental Services*, Rome.

FAO (2007b) "FAO calls for urgent steps to protect the poor from soaring food prices", December 17 [online] <www.fao.org/newsroom/en/news/ 2007/1000733/index.html>.

FAO (2008a) "Countries in crisis requiring external assistance", *Crop Prospects and Food Situation*, No. 1, February.

FAO (2008b) "Biodiversity is vital for human survival and livelihoods", February 18 [online] <www.fao.org/newsroom/en/news/2008/1000788>.

FAO (2008c) "EBRD and FAO call for bold steps to contain soaring food prices" [online] <www.fao.org/newsroom/en/news/2008/1000808>.

Fine, B. (2002) *The World of Consumption*, London: Routledge.

Flannery, T. (2006) *We are the Weather Makers*, Toronto: Harper Collins.

Flink, J. (1988). *The Automobile Age*, Cambridge, Mass.: MIT.

Foster, J. B. (1986) *The Theory of Monopoly Capitalism*, New York: Monthly Review Press.

Fox, N. (1997) *Spoiled: The Dangerous Truth About a Food Chain Gone Haywire*, New York: Basic Books.

Friedman, M. (1982) *Capitalism and Freedom*, Chicago: University of Chicago Press.

Friedmann, H. (1999) "Remaking 'traditions': how we eat, what we eat and the changing political economy of food", in D. Barndt (ed.), *Women Working the NAFTA Food Chain*, Toronto: Second Storey Press.

Friedmann, H. (2004) "Feeding the empire: the pathologies of globalized agriculture", in L. Panitch and C. Leys (eds), *Socialist Register 2005*, London: Merlin.

Friesen, J. and Gee, M. (2008) "The world's hottest commodities are in your cereal bowl," *Globe and Mail*, February 16.

Gardner, G. and Halweil, B. (2000) "Overfed and underfed, the global epidemic of malnutrition", Worldwatch Institute, Paper No. 150, March.

Garner, L. (2003) "How Americans became the fattest people in the world", *Sunday Mail*, 2 March [online] <www.ourcivilization.com/diet/fastfood.htm>.

Gauntlett, D. and Hill, A. (1999) *TV Living: Television, Culture, and Everyday Life*, London: Routledge.

Geist, H. (1997) "How tobacco farming contributes to tropical deforestation" [online] <www.psychologie.uni-freiburg.de/um welt-spp/proj2/geist.html>.

Gillespie, P. (2008) "Rich prosper, society suffers", *Toronto Star*, April 28.

Giroux, H. (2004) *The Terrors of Neoliberalism*, Aurora, Ontario: Garamond Press.

Glickman, L. (1999) *Consumer Society in American History, A Reader*, Ithaca: Cornell University Press.

Global Dump Soft Drinks Campaign (2007) [online] <www.dumpsoda.org/>.

Goldman, R. and Papson, S. (2000) "Advertising in the age of accelerated meaning", in J. Schor and D. Holt (eds), *The Consumer Society Reader*, New York: New Press.

Good Jobs First (2008) "Subsidizing the world's largest corporation", [online] <www.goodjobsfirst.org/corporate_subsidy/walmart.cfm>.

Graham-Harrison, E. (2007) "*Green* fuel worsens global warming", *Toronto Star,* January 27.

Greenpeace (2008) "Good news of Canadian consumers: Monsanto is dropping a genetically engineered hormone in milk", August 8 [online] <www.green-peace.org/canada/en/recent/monsanto>.

Griffiths, S. and Wallace, J. (eds) (1998) *Consuming Passions: Food in the Age of Anxiety*, Manchester, UK: Mandolin Press.

Grossberg, L. (2005) *Caught in the Crossfire: Kids, Politics, and America's Future*, Boulder, Colo.: Paradigm.

Guardian (2005) "Free trade leaves world food in grip of global giants", June 27.

Hacker, A. (2004) "The underworld of work", *New York Review of Books*, February 12.

Halberstam, C. (1986) *The Reckoning*, New York: Avon.

Halweil, B. (2004) *Eat Here: Reclaiming Homegrown Pleasures in a Global Supermarket*, New York: W. W. Norton.

Halweil, B. (2006) *Catch of the Day*, Worldwatch Paper No. 172.

Halweil, B (2007) "Still no free lunch", *Organic Center*, September [online] <www.organic-center.org>.

Hanson, J. (2006) "The threat to the planet", *New York Review of Books*, July 6.

Heintzman, A. and Solomon, E. (2004) *Feeding the Future: From Fat to Famine How to Solve the World's Food Crises*, Toronto: Ananzi.

Herro, A. (2007) "Pesticides pose risk in rural and urban communities alike", World Watch Institute, September 19.

Holmes, R. (1994) *Additive Alert!*, Toronto: McClelland & Stewart.

Hoogvelt, A. (2001) *Globalization and the Postcolonial World*, Baltimore: Johns Hopkins University Press.

Horowitz, R. (2006) *Putting Meat on the American Table*, Baltimore: Johns Hopkins Press.

Hough, P. (1998) *The Global Politics of Pesticides*, London: Earthscan Press.

Human Rights Watch (2002) "Tainted harvest: child labor and obstacles to organizing on Ecuador's banana plantations" [online] <www.hrw.org>.

Human Rights Watch (2004) "El Salvador: turning a blind eye", Vol. 16, No. 2.

Human Rights Watch (2008) "On the margins of profit: rights at risk in the global economy", Vol. 20, No. 3.

Hurst, L. (2008) "Hungry for answers", *Toronto Star,* June 28.

Independent (2007) "Deforestation: the hidden cause of global warming", May 14.

Indiana University School of Medicine (2007) "Premature births may be linked to seasonal levels of pesticides and nitrates in surface water", press release, May 7, Bloomington, Indiana.

International Committee in Solidarity with the Victims of Nemagon (2008) [online] <www.opticalrealities.org/Nicaragua/NemagonAction.html>.

International Baby Food Action Network (2006) "EU and US block Thailand's proposal to reduce sugar in baby foods", November 3.

Jacobs, D. and Steffen, L. (2003) "Nutrients, foods, and dietary patterns as exposures in research: a framework for food synergy", *American Journal of Clinical Nutrition,* September, Vol. 78, No. 3.

Jacobs, K. and Dube, A (2004) "Hidden costs of Wal-Mart jobs", UC Berkeley Labor Center, August 2.

Keenan, G (2008) "Record VW aid changed the auto game," *Globe and Mail*, September 12.

Kimbrell, A. (ed.) (2002) *The Fatal Harvest Reader*, London: Island Press.

Knowles, E. (2001) *The Oxford Dictionary of Quotations*, Oxford: Oxford University Press.

Koeppel, D. (2008) *Banana: The Fate of the Fruit that Changed the World,* New York: Hudson Street Press.

Kruse, K. and Sugrue, T. (eds) (2006) *The New Suburban History*, Chicago: University of Chicago Press.

Lang, T. (2003) "Food industrialisation and food power, implications for food governance", *Development Policy Review,* Vol. 21, No. 5–6.

Lang, T. and Heasman, M. (2004) *Food Wars: The Global Battle for Mouths, Minds, and Markets,* London: Earthscan.

Lardner, J. (2007) "The specter haunting your office", *New York Review of Books,* June 14.

Lawrence, F. (2004) *Not on the Label,* London: Penguin.

Lawrence, F. (2006a) "Should we worry about soya in our food?" *Guardian,* July 25.

Lawrence, F. (2006b) "A bean too far?" *Guardian,* July 27.

Lawrence, F. (2007) "Sugar rush", *Guardian,* February 15 [online] <http://www.guardian.co.uk/lifeandstyle/2007/feb/15/foodanddrink.ethical-food>.

Lawrence, F. (2008) *Eat Your Heart Out: Why the Food Business is bad for the Planet and your Health,* London: Penguin.

Lawes, C., Vander Hoorn, S. and Rodgers, A. (2008) "Global burden of blood-pressure-related disease, 2001", *Lancet,* No. 371, pp. 1513–18.

Leahy, S (2007) "Dirt isn't so cheap after all", IPS News [online] <http://ipsnews.net/print.asp?idnews=39083>.

Lien, M. E. and Nerlich, B. (eds) (2004) *The Politics of Food,* Oxford: Berg.

Linn, S. (2004) *Consuming Kids: Protecting Our Children from the Onslaught of Marketing and Advertising,* New York: New Press.

Loefler, I. (2005) "No sweet surrender," *British Medical Journal,* No. 328, April 9.

Los Angeles Times (2005) "CDC – largest study", July 1, A21.

Ludwig, D., Bak, K. and Sears, B. "Our research", Allergy Kids [online] <www.allergykids.com/index.php?id=4&page=Our_Research>.

Macleans magazine (2004) January 26, Toronto.

Manning, R. (2004) "The oil we eat", *Harpers,* February, v308.

Magdoff, F., Foster, J. B. and Buttel, F. (eds) (2000) *Hungary For Profit,* New York: Monthly Review.

Marx, K (1963) *Theories of Surplus Value,* Vol. I, Moscow: Progress.

Marx, K. (1968) *Theories of Surplus Value,* Vol. II. Moscow: Progress.

Marx, K. (1976) *Capital,* Vol. I, New York: Penguin.

Marx, K. (1978) *Capital,* Vol. II, New York: Penguin.

Marx, K. (1981) *Capital,* Vol. III, New York: Penguin.

Martin, A. (2007) "Will diners swallow this?" *New York Times,* March 25.

Mason, J. B. (1982) *History of Housing in the U.S. 1930–1980,* Houston: Gulf Publishing.

May, E. (1999) "The commodity gap, consumerism and the modern home", in L. B. Glickman (ed.), *Consumer Society in American History, A Reader,* Ithaca: Cornell University Press.

McCann, D. et al. (2007) "Food additives and hyperactive behaviour", *The Lancet,* June 9 [online] <www.thelancet.com>.

McGinn A.P. (2000) *Why Poison Ourselves? A Precautionary Approach to Synthetic Chemicals,* Worldwatch Paper No. 153.

McGinnis, J. M., Gootman, J. and Kraak, V. (eds) (2006) *Food Marketing to Children and Youth,* Institute of Medicine, Washington D.C.: National Academies Press.

McKay, K. and Miller R. (2005) "Nicaragua: Nemagon workers are dying", *Zmag*, March 30 [online] <www.zmag.org/content/print_article.cfm?itemID=7553>.

McIlroy, A. (2007), "A Hippocratic oath for science", *Globe and Mail*, December 15.

McKenna, B. (2005) *Big Sugar*, Montreal: Galafilm.

McMurtry, J. (1999) *The Cancer Stage of Capitalism*, London: Pluto.

Menzies, H. (2005) *No Time, Stress and the Crisis of Modern Life*, Vancouver: Douglas and McIntyre.

Miller, T. (2007) "Plantation workers look for justice in the north," *Los Angeles Times*, May 27.

Mintz, S. (1986) *Sweetness and Power*, New York: Penguin.

Mittelstaedt, M. (2007a) "Poor diet ratchets up cancer risk", *Globe and Mail*, November 1.

Mittelstaedt, M. (2007b) "Decade to avert climate catastrophe, experts say", *Globe and Mail*, December 6 [online[<www.climate.unsw.edu.au/bali/>.

Mittelsteadt, M. (2007c) "How global warming goes against the grain," *Globe and Mail*, February 24.

Molnar, A. and Boninger, F. (2007) "Adrift: schools in a total marketing environment: the tenth annual report on schoolhouse commercialism trends: 2006–2007", Commercialism in Education Research Unit, Arizona State University [online] <http://epsl.asu.edu/ceru/CERU_2007_Annual_Report.htm>.

Monfort, J. (2008) "Despite obstacles, biofuels continue surge", Worldwatch [online] <www.worldwatch.org/node/5450>.

Mull, D. and Kirkhorn, S. (2005) "Child Labor in Ghana Cocoa Production", *Public Health Report* Vol. 120, No. 6 [online] <www.pubmedcentral.nih.gov/anticlererder.fcgi?artid=1497785>.

Murray, B. (2001) "Fast-food culture serves up super-size Americans" *Monitor On Psychology*, Vol. 32, No. 11, December [online] <www.apa.org/monitor/dec01/fastfood.html>.

Nader, R. (1965) *Unsafe at Any Speed*, New York: Grossman.

Nature (2006) "Climate change reducing the productivity of phytoplankton", November 7.

Ndiaye, P. A. (2007) *Nylon and Bombs: Dupont and the March of Modern America*, Baltimore, Md.: Johns Hopkins Press.

Nestle, M. (2002) *Food Politics*, Berkeley: University of California Press.

Nestle, M. (2003) *Safe Food*, Berkeley: University of California Press.

Nestle, M. (2006) *What to Eat*, New York: North Point Press.

New Internationalist (1998) August, No. 304.

New Internationalist (2000) May, No. 323.

New Internationalist (2001) Jan./Feb, No. 331.

New Internationalist (2002) March, No. 343.

New Internationalist (2003a) Jan./Feb, No. 353.

New Internationalist (2003b) July, No. 358.

New Internationalist (2003c) December, No. 363.

New Internationalist (2004a) Jan–Feb, No. 364.

New Internationalist (2004b) July, No. 369.

New Internationalist (2007a) April, No. 399.

New Internationalist (2007b) December, No. 407.

New York Times (2004) "The food pyramid scheme", September 1.

New York Times (2006) "Selling junk food to toddlers," February 23.

Nierenberg, D. (2005) *Happier Meals: Rethinking the Global Meat Industry*, Worldwatch Paper No. 171.

Nolen, S. (2006) "When coffee fuels a nation", *Globe and Mail*, May 29.

Norris, F. (1901) *The Octopus*, New York: Doubleday, Page.

Nussbaum, M. (2006) *The Frontiers of Justice*, Cambridge, Mass.: Harvard University Press.

Off, C. (2006) *Bitter Chocolate*, Toronto: Random House Canada.

Orford, J. (2001) *Excessive Appetites: A Psychological View of Addictions*, Toronto: John Wiley.

OXFAM (2003) "Coffee companies doing little to help struggling farmers" [online] <www.oxfam.ca/news-and-publications/news/squeezed-to-the-last-drop>.

OXFAM (2007) "Seeking common grounds: analysis of the Draft Proposals for the International Coffee Agreement", January.

Parker, S. (2006) "Finger-lickin bad," Grist, February 21 [online] <www.grist.org/news/maindish/2006/02/21/parker/>.

Patel, R. (2007) *Stuffed and Starved: Markets, Power and the Hidden Battle for the World Food System*, Toronto: HarperCollins.

Pawlick, T. (2006) *The End of Food*, Toronto: Greystone.

Pfeiffer, D. A. (2006) *Eating Fossil Fuels*, Gabriola Island, BC: New Society Publishers.

Picard, A. (2008) "Smoking deaths an epidemic in India," *Globe and Mail*, February 14.

Pingali, P., Stamoulis, K. and Stringer, R. (2006) "Eradicating extreme poverty and hunger: towards a coherent policy agenda", ESA Working Paper No. 06-01 [online] <www.fao.org/es/esa>.

Pinstrup-Andersen, P. and Cheng, F. (2007) "Still hungry", *Scientific American*, September.

Pollan, M. (2006) *The Omnivore's Dilemma*, New York: Penguin Press.

Pollin, R. (1996) "Contemporary economic stagnation in world historical perspective", *New Left Review*, No. 219.

Polanyi, K. (1944) *The Great Transformation*, Boston: Beacon Press.

Popkin, B. (2003) "The nutrition tranisition in the developing world", *Development Policy Review*, Vol. 21, No. 5–6.

Popkin, B. (2007) "The world is fat", *Scientific American*, September.

Postel, S. (1996) *Dividing the Waters,* Worldwatch Paper No. 132.

Postel, S. (2005) *Liquid Assets*, Worldwatch Paper No.170.

Postone, M. (1996) *Time, Labor, and Social Domination*, Cambridge: Cambridge University Press.

Pressinger, R. (1997) "Chemical food additive exposure during pregnancy: links to learning disabilities, ADD and behaviour disorders" [online] <www.chemtox.com/pregnancy/artificial.htm>.

Priesnitz, W. (2007) "Ask natural life: how green is my diet?" [online] <http://forum.stlc.com>.

Putnam, R. D. (2000) *Bowling Alone*, New York: Touchstone.

Read, A. (2006) "Protecting worker rights in the context of immigration reform", *Journal of Law and Social Change*.

Reardon, T., Timner, P. and Berdoque, J. (2004) "The rapid rise of supermarkets in developing countries: induced organizational, institutional, and technological change in agrifood systems", *Journal of Agricultural and Development Economics*, Vol. 1, No. 2.

Rees, A. (2006) *Genetically Modified Food*, London: Pluto Press.

Richard, S., Moselmi, S., Benachour, N. and Seralini, G. E. (2005) "Differential effects of glyposate and Roundup on human placental cells", *Environmental Health Perspectives*, Vol. 113, No. 6.

Riggins, T. (2007) "Is a world wide famine in the works?" Countercurrents, December 21 [online] <www.countercurrents.org>.

Robbins, P. (2003) *Stolen Fruit*, Halifax: Fernwood Books.

Roberts, P. (2008) *The End of Food*, New York: Houghton Mifflin.

Roberts, W. (2008) *The No-Nonsense Guide to World Food*, Toronto: New Internationalist Publications.

Rocha, J. (1994) "Child sugar cane cutters exploited in Brazil", *British Medical Journal*, No. 308, April 16.

Rosset, P. (2006) *Food Is Different: Why We Must Get the WTO out of Agriculture*, Halifax: Fernwood.

Rudd Center for Food Policy and Obesity (2008) "Advertising to children" [online] <www.yaleruddcenter.org/what/advertising/index.html>.

Runge, C. F., Senauer, B., Pardy, P. G. and Rosegrant, M. W. (2003) *Ending Hunger in Our Lifetime*, Baltimore, Md.: Johns Hopkins University Press.

Sadler, M. (1832) House of Commons interview [online] <http://www.spartacus.schoolnet.co.uk/IRhebergam.htm>.

Schor, J. and Holt, D. (2000) *The Consumer Society Reader*, New York: New Press.

Schor, J. (2004) *Born to Buy*, New York: Scribner.

Schlosser, E. (2001) *Fast Food Nation*. New York: Harper Collins.

Schlosser, E. (2002) *Fast Food Nation*. New York: Harper Collins.

Schlosser, E. and Wilson, C. (2006) *Chew On This: Everything You Don't Know About Fast Food*, Boston, Mass.: Houghton Mifflin.

Schmitt, N. M., Schmitt, J., Kouimintzis, D.J. and Kirch, W. (2007) "Health risks in tobacco farm workers: a review of the literature", *Journal of Public Health*, Vol. 15, pp. 255–64.

Scott, D. and Marshall, J. (1998) *Cocaine Politics: Drugs, Armies, and the CIA in Central America*, Berkeley, Calf.: University of California Press.

Seabrook, J. (2002) *The No-nonsense Guide to Class, Caste, and Hierarchies*, Toronto: New Internationalist Publications.

Sekine, T. (1997) *An Outline of The Dialectic of Capital*, 2 vols, London: Macmillan.

Serrin, W. (1974) *The Company and the Union*, New York: Vintage.

Shah, Sonia (2004) *Crude: The Story of Oil*, Toronto: Seven Stories Press.

Sheehan, M. O. (2001) *City Limits: Putting the Brakes on Sprawl*, Worldwatch Paper No. 156.

Shelley, T. (2005) *Oil: Politics, Poverty, and the Planet*, Halifax: Fernwood Books.

Shiva, V. (1992) *The Violence of the Green Revolution: Third World Agriculture, Ecology and Politics*, London: Zed.

Shore, K. J. (2007) *Cutting Down Tobacco* [online] <http://www.idrc.ca/en/ev-109250-201-1-DO_TOPIC.html>.

Sibbald, Barbara (2003) "Sugar industry sour on WHO report", *Canadian Medical Association Journal*, June 10, Vol. 168, No. 12.

Siegel, J. (2006) "Pesticides discovered in tobacco smoke", *Jerusalem Post*, April 27 [online] <www.jpost.com/servlet/Satellite?cid=1145961235065&page...>.

Silva, J. (2007a) "'Invisible' victims of pesticide protest government neglect" [online] <http://ipsnews.net/news.asp?idnews_38968>.

Silva, J. (2007b) "Nemagon is still alive and kicking" [online] <www.reluita.org/agricultura/agrotoxicos/nemagon/nemagon_sigue_vivo-eng.htm>.

Singer, P. and Mason, J. (2006) *The Way We Eat: Why Our Food Choices Matter*, Rodale Press.

Smith, J. M. (2003) *Seeds of Deception*, Fairfield, Iowa: Yes Books.

Smith, J. M. (2007) "Genetically modified foods unsafe? Evidence that links GM foods to allergic responses mounts", *Global Research*, November 8 [online] <www.globalresearch.ca/index.php?context=va&aid=7277>.

Smolker, R., Tokar, B., Peterman, A., Hernandex, E. and Thomas, J. (2008) "The real cost of agrofuels: impacts on food, forests, people, and climate", Global Forest Coalition [online] <www.globalforestcoalition.org>.

Softpedia (2007) "Nemagon, the pesticide that kills people" [online] < www.softpedia.com>,

Sopinka, H (2007) "To go green, eat your greens – and meat, too", *Globe and Mail*, October 12, p. L4.

Specter, M. (2008) "Big foot", *New Yorker*, February 25.

Spencer, N. (2007) "Severe food shortages, price spikes threaten world population", WSWS, December 22 [online] <www.wsws.org>.

Spigel, L. and Curtin, M. (1997). *The Revolution Wasn't Televised: Sixties Television and Social Conflict*, New York: Routledge.

Squires, S. (2007) "TV ads make kids fat," *Toronto Star*, March 20.

Starmer, E. and Wise, T. (2007) "Feeding at the trough: industrial livestock firms saved $35 billion from low feed prices", Global Development and Environmental Institute, Tufts University, Policy Brief No. 07–03, December.

Steed, J. (2002) "What you can't see can kill you," *Toronto Star*, November 1.

Steinfeld, H., Gerber, P., Wassenaar, T., Castel, V., Rosales, M. and de Haan, C. (2006) "Livestock's long shadow", FAO, Rome.

Stern, N. (2007) *The Economics of Climate Change*, Cambridge: Cambridge University Press.

Stiglitz, J. E. (2008) "A global lesson in market failure", *Globe and Mail*, July 8.

Strasser, S. (1999) *Waste and Want*, New York: Henry Holt.

Striffler, S. (2005) *Chicken, The Dangerous Transformation of America's Favorite Food*, New Haven, Conn.: Yale University Press.

Talago, T. (2007) "Too poor to avert diabetes", *Toronto Star,* December 27.

Talbot, J. M. (2004) *Grounds for Agreement*, New York: Rowman & Littlefield.

Taylor, B. and Tilford, D. (2000) "Why consumption matters", in J. Schor and D. Holt (eds), *The Consumer Society Reader*, New York: New Press.

Townsend, M. (2004) "Boys will be girls – eventually", *Observer,* July 18.

Tucker, R. (1978) *The Marx-Engels Reader*, New York: Norton.

Tullis, F. L. and Hollist, W. L. (1986) *Food, the State, and International Political Economy*, Lincoln: University of Nebraska Press.

UNICEF (2005) *The State of the World's Children 2005: Executive Summary*.

UNICEF (2008) *The State of the World's Children 2008: Executive Summary.*

Uno, K. (1980) *Principles of Political Economy*, Sussex: Harvester Press.

US Census Bureau (2006a) "Poverty thresholds" [online] <www.census.gov/hhes/www/poverty/threshld/thresh06.html>.

US Census Bureau (2006b) "Nearly half of our lives spent with TV, radio, internet, newspapers, according to Census Bureau", news release, December 15.

US Census Bureau (2007), *Statistical Abstract of the United States: 2007.*

Veracity, D. (2005) "The politics of sugar: why your government lies to you about this disease-promoting ingredient", Natural New, July 21 [online] <www.naturalnew.com>.

Watson, J. I. and Caldwell, M. I. (eds) (2005) *The Cultural Politics of Food and Eating: A Reader*, Oxford: Blackwell.

Weis, T. (2007) *The Global Food Economy: The Battle for the Future of Farming*, Halifax, NS: Ferwood.

Wellness Newsletter (2004) University of California, Berkeley. February, Vol. 20, No. 5.

Wellness Newsletter (2008) University of California, Berkeley. August.

Wells, J. (2005) "Chewing the fat about what's really in fast food," *Toronto Star*, January 29, p. L1.

Westra, R. and Zuege, A. (eds) (2003) *Value and The World Economy Today*, Basingstoke: Palgrave.

Wikipedia (2008) "Nemagon" [online] <http://en.widipedia.org/wiki/1,2-Dibromo-3-chloropropane>.

Wilson, B. (2008) "The last bite", *New Yorker*, May 19.

Wilson, J. (2007) "Food, land prices rise ..." *Toronto Star*, February 22, p. C6.

World Bank (2007) *The World Development Report 2008: Agriculture for Development.* Washington D.C.

World Bank (2008) Press release no. 2009/065/DEC.

World Cancer Research Fund/American Institute for Cancer Research (2007) *Food, Nutrition, Physical Activity, and the Prevention of Cancer*, Washington D.C.

World Health Organization (2002) *Report of the Joint Expert Consultation on Diet, Nutrition, and the Prevention of Chronic Diseases* [online] <Whqlibdoc.who.int/trs/WHO_TRS_916.pdf>.

World Health Organization (2005) *Preventing Chronic Diseases: A Vital Investment*, Geneva.

World Health Organization (2008) *WHO Report on the Global Tobacco Epidemic.*

World Vision (2006) "Slave to coffee and chocolate" [online] <http://www.worldvision.com.au/wvconnect/print.asp?topicID=97>.

Worldwatch Institute (2003) *Vital Signs*, New York: W. W. Norton.

Worldwatch Institute (2004) *State of the World*, New York: W. W. Norton.

Worldwatch Institute (2007a) *Vital Signs 2006–2007*, New York: W. W. Norton.

Worldwatch Institute (2007b) *Biofuels for Transport*, London: Earthscan.

Worldwatch Institute (2007c) *State of the World: Our Urban Future*, New York: W. W. Norton.

Worldwatch Institute (2008) *State of the World: Innovations for a Sustainable Economy*, New York: W. W. Norton.

Woynillowicz, D. (2007) "Worldwatch", September 17 [online] <www.alternet.org/story/62325>.

Wright, J. (2005) "Wal-Mart welfare: how taxpayers subsidize the world's largest retailer", *Dollars and Sense*, January/February.

Yafa, S. (2005) *Big Cotton*, New York: Viking.

Yates, Michael (2003) *Naming the System, Inequality and Work in the Global Economy*, New York: Monthly Review.

York, G. and Mick, H. (2008) "A clockwork orange", *Globe and Mail*, July 12.

Index

DISCARD